Preventing Violence and Crime
in America's Schools

Preventing Violence and Crime in America's Schools

From Put-Downs to Lock-Downs

William L. Lassiter and Danya C. Perry

PRAEGER
An Imprint of ABC-CLIO, LLC

A B C 🟰 C L I O

Santa Barbara, California • Denver, Colorado • Oxford, England

Library of Congress Cataloging-in-Publication Data
Lassiter, William L.
   Preventing violence and crime in America's schools: from put-downs to lock-downs / William L. Lassiter and Danya C. Perry.
       p. cm.
   Includes bibliographical references and index.
   ISBN 978-0-313-35396-3 (hard copy : alk. paper) — ISBN 978-0-313-35397-0 (ebook)
   1. School violence—United States—Prevention. 2. Schools—United States—Safety measures. I. Perry, Danya C. II. Title.
   LB3013.3.L375   2009
   371.7'820973—dc22
                          2009011849

13   12   11   10   9   1   2   3   4   5

This book is also available on the World Wide Web as an eBook.
Visit www.abc-clio.com for details.

ABC-CLIO, LLC
130 Cremona Drive, P.O. Box 1911
Santa Barbara, California 93116-1911

This book is printed on acid-free paper ∞

Manufactured in the United States of America

The authors dedicate this book to their children, Chloe, Katie, and Donovan in the sincere hope that schools will become safer places for them to attend because of the efforts put forth by writing this book.

Contents

Acknowledgments

I thank my wife, Stacey, and my two daughters, Chloe and Katie, who so willingly sacrificed to make this book possible. I also thank my mom, dad, grandmother, and sister-in-law. You have all served as educators in our public schools and have inspired me to dedicate much of my life to making schools safer places for kids to learn and teachers to teach.

William L. Lassiter

I thank my wife, Jacqueline, and my son, Donovan, for their eternal love and support as we reached out to help youth. Without you I would not have been able to make it. To my parents—thanks for being my "first" teachers in life. Without those lessons, I am nothing. To my brother and sisters—you have made life enjoyable. Each of you has special places in my heart. To my mentees (eleven boys and one girl)— you have all made us proud. Just know that education is a lifelong process and we are always students. To my mentees (five boys) who have ascended to heaven—please know that I keep you close to my heart and that your stories will be told with the promise of saving lives. I love you all.

Danya C. Perry

The authors also acknowledge the tremendous contribution of Megan Q. Howell in making this book possible. We are deeply indebted to Megan for serving as our content editor. In this role she provided the authors with a reality check of what would be the most interesting content for the reader. Thanks, Megan, for your tireless efforts.

Introduction: Our Motivation

William L. Lassiter

April 23, 1993. The rumors of a fight have spread around campus all day today. The word is that students are going to gather after school to decide a dispute that started over the weekend. At the end of the school day some 250 students gather behind the school to witness a fight. Of course, the school administrators have also heard about it, so they are here to try to prevent the fight from occurring. After school staff members repeatedly ask students to move on, the crowd slowly starts to make its way to the city park, which is right next door to the school. The school administrators figure it is no longer their responsibility, so the crowd is let go and no further steps are made to intervene.

Within minutes, the long-awaited fight breaks out and students begin cheering. The crowd is massive, and a 20-year-old nonstudent gets involved to try to help one of his friends. He is quickly taken to the ground, at which time he reaches for a gun in his pocket. It is a semiautomatic pistol, and a few seconds later six rounds are fired and the crowd scurries to escape the mayhem. At least three students have been hit, and the gunman flees the scene. Almost immediately law enforcement and emergency responders arrive to find my friend Bryan Stewart Greene shot to death and two other wounded students lying on the ground.

The next day the local newspaper led with the story: "One of the shots struck Millbrook junior Bryan Stewart Greene in the chest, killing him. Jamie Robert Vivian, a 17-year-old junior, and senior Jason Scott Kellam, 18, were wounded.

"Jason said he began running when he heard gunfire and almost made it to his car before he was shot. 'When it hit me, I couldn't walk anymore,' said Jason, who was struck in the back. 'I got dizzy. I kind of leaned up against my car. It burned real bad. It was pretty much the worst pain I've ever felt.' A 20-year-old man from Wendell, who is not a Millbrook student, was charged late Monday in the shooting."[1]

I was one of the few students who chose not to stay and watch the fight that afternoon, but within minutes the news started to spread like wildfire. I got a call from one of my friends, who informed me that Bryan had been shot in the heart, and although Bryan and I were not best friends, I remember my heart breaking too. The incident had a profound effect on the whole school and surrounding community. The paper wrote about the incident: "Millbrook High School students and staff, buttressed by psychologists, ministers and city leaders, endured their longest day on Tuesday."[2] Our hearts were broken, but more than that, our innocence had been lost. Sixteen-year-olds are not supposed to die, and they are especially not supposed to be shot at school. Bryan was not even involved in the fight; he just went to see what all the commotion was about.

Bryan's funeral was overrun by students seeking to say their final goodbyes. The local newspaper described it this way:

RALEIGH—Bryan Stewart Greene had so many friends and classmates that they overflowed the church at his funeral Thursday, forcing many to watch the service on television in an adjacent building.

More than 450 people attended the funeral for the popular Millbrook High School student who was killed Monday when gunfire broke out during an after-school brawl. Greene, 16, was one of hundreds of students who had gathered to watch the fight. Many also picked up green bumper stickers that read "Bryan Greene We Love You" as they entered the church.

By the time Greene's drama teacher, Cheryle Prater, had finished remembering her former student, few in the congregation were not sobbing or hugging each other for support. Prater cited an English paper Bryan wrote this year. In it, he listed his main fears as "staying home Friday night and boring people. I love parties, I love drama, and, boy, do I love to sleep."

She remembered how Bryan, who wanted to become an architect, liked nothing better than to design props for theater productions at the school. "He'd be backstage in the shadows, changing props," Prater said. "He was a free spirit and a lover of plays."

Prater said she met Bryan three years ago when he came to her and asked if he could work in school drama productions. "I said, 'If you give me your heart and soul.'

"Little did I know he'd end up taking my heart and soul," Prater said. "He had a smile that would light up the room."

During the service, the Rev. James C. Lee said their confusion was understandable. "Life is sometimes uncertain, and at midafternoon Monday, all hell broke loose," Lee said. "Life also is unfair. Inequity and injustice too often dwell among us, and 16-year-old men fall prey to an assailant's bullet. When the senseless comes, we are baffled. Bryan

Greene was not only interested in architecture and design. He built a life of love and laughter that will never be obliterated, and in Bryan Greene's living, we have been blessed."[3]

In the moments after the shooting, I did not know how this single event would help to determine much of my future, but looking back on the incident that occurred some 15 years ago, I see now that it shaped me as a person. This book is dedicated to the memory of Bryan Stewart Greene and all the other students who have lost their lives too soon to youth violence.

This shooting at Millbrook High School prompted then Governor James B. Hunt of North Carolina to call together a task force to address school violence. Out of that task force one of the top recommendations was that there needed to be a primary point of contact for information on school violence and school violence prevention. To meet that recommendation an executive order by the governor created the Center for the Prevention of School Violence (Center). I, of course, was still in high school when these events were transpiring, so I was oblivious to these goings-on, but as I continued through my school career I remained haunted by the violence of that day in 1993. As it turns out, when I was moving in as a college student at North Carolina State, the center was also moving into the university. The Center, which up until 1995 was housed with the Governor's Crime Commission, was moved under the School of Education and Psychology at North Carolina State University. One day while I was taking a research methodology class, a researcher came into our class to offer an internship at the Center, which I, of course, jumped at. I remember thinking that day that this feels like something I am destined to do.

Danya C. Perry

"Did you hear what happened?" Those were the first words that my best friend asked me when I sat down beside him on the school bus. "Naw," I replied. "What happened?"

"Ninja was shot! He's dead!"

Some remember what they were doing during defining moments of their life: the day when Dr. Martin Luther King, Jr., was assassinated; the moment when we landed on the moon; or the activity that you were engaging in when you heard of the *Challenger* spaceship tragedy. My defining moment was not a national headline and did not receive top billing on the local news media. But it certainly changed how I viewed life and my ultimate purpose.

Rashad Williams, also known as Ninja, was known by most people in my neighborhood. His death in the housing projects down the street from my house opened my eyes to what had been seemingly the norm in my school and community. Rashad's death was not the first time that I knew of someone being affected by violence in the school and community. Interestingly enough, I always saw violence as a necessity: if you could not protect yourself or assert appropriate aggression, then you could easily fall into the category of victim. What was "appropriate" in my community may not be "appropriate" in the schools, yet that did not make any difference in it being manifested in the school building.

My moment of clarity came approximately a few weeks after Rashad's passing as I questioned whether this was really normal. Why was the violence so easy to accept for many around me? Why did some of my friends believe that they would not reach the ripe old age of 21? Why did another person have to die for something that had no rational explanation? Why was fighting the first strategy in dealing with conflict?

I had no answers and certainly did not know the trajectory of my own life. After I began attending North Carolina State University (NCSU), I realized that my school and community experiences were completely different from those of some of my classmates. There were obvious social injustices, family dysfunction, negative peer influence, and other contributors to the lack of success for many of our youth— all which I considered normal.

While at NCSU I started to become involved in the community as a mentor. As a mentor, I tried my best to serve as a role model for these young impressionable minds. At one time, I mentored seven boys, and I would invite them to attend classes with me so that they could get the college experience. All of them knew that they could call on me if they needed help. These boys were into drugs and gangs and were short-sighted about their future. Most of them had been suspended or expelled and saw no need for school. With these youth, I saw too many times where their stories were similar to what I saw in my neighborhood. This led to the next defining moment in my life. That same week, I decided to start writing my first book, about these boys. The book had no title and no real focus; I simply wanted to put together a piece that described my feelings toward the state of youth at the time and what I could do as an individual to change their trajectory. I rambled on and on about my opinions regarding how our youth could be successful and shared ideas on what adults needed to do to ensure that another young person would not have to feel the pain that Ninja and his family had to endure. That book was never completed, but it is being manifested in my newfound trajectory: advocating for positive youth development and youth violence prevention.

A CULMINATION OF EVENTS

On April 16, 2006, the unthinkable happened . . . again. A student opened fire on his classmates at Virginia Tech University, where 32 were killed.

This incident again set off the alarm clock, and we cannot afford to hit the snooze button anymore. Like many Americans, we were deeply saddened by the incident at Virginia Tech. However, it is time to wake up. We know what works when it comes to preventing school and youth violence, and although this incident occurred in a university setting, previous lessons learned from primary and secondary schools are applicable. We know the lessons, but we are not applying them.

One of the most important lessons learned from past shootings is to make sure we recognize early warning signs. These signs include social withdrawal, excessive feelings of isolation and being alone, and being a victim of violence, depression, feelings of rejection, and bullying. In fact, in a study completed by the U.S. Secret Service, it was discovered that 81 percent of school shooters told someone they were going to commit the act, and almost three-quarters of them stated they were victims of bullying and abusive behavior. Why did they not speak up? Did we not listen, or were we asleep?

According to the federal government, during the 2005 school year there were 48 school-associated deaths in elementary and secondary schools in the United States.[4] But this statistic only captures the most extreme forms of school violence. The reality is that most schools in the United States are facing some form of disorder. In fact, incidents of crime are reported at 96 percent of high schools, 94 percent of middle schools, and 74 percent of primary schools.[5] Although it is major incidents like Columbine or Virginia Tech that grab the headlines, the reality is that everyday occurrences of bullying, harassment, and physical intimidation are what are driving our kids out of public schools. For example, "six percent of students had not gone to school on one or more of the 30 days preceding the survey because they felt they would be unsafe at school or on their way to or from school."[6] These incidents are destroying the public's faith in the public education system in this country.

School violence today is one of the most pressing challenges that directly impacts the entire community. This book will provide educators, parents, law enforcement, and other youth-serving professionals with a unique perspective on the topic of school violence. The chapters will examine the specifics relating to the problem of school violence; opportunities to prevent and intervene; and the importance of planning and being prepared for a crisis. In our nation's attempt to address this problem, we must collectively take a step back to determine the root causes for such violent incidents. Understanding the problem is crucial to developing effective strategies. This book will take a closer look at analyzing the problem and demonstrating the need to employ effective practitioner-based solutions. It presents research on the topic and also gives real-life examples of how youth violence can be prevented in schools. The authors' experiences from the field of school violence prevention are as diverse as the writing styles, but the message is the same: it is time for all of us to wake up.

PART I

Understanding School and Community Violence

Chapter 1

What Is School Violence?

William L. Lassiter

To understand school violence, one must start from the beginning by defining what school violence is. In this chapter and throughout this book, one will see that school violence starts long before those things happen that are typically reported on the evening news. School violence starts with trash talk, bullying, insults, harassment, and threats, and when these behaviors go unchecked, they become those incidents that we read about in the paper the next day. This book will make the case for early prevention and intervention; but before we can prevent anything, we must start by defining what "it" is.

John Dewey, who is often credited with being the founder of the philosophy of pragmatism, the father of functional psychology, and a leader in the progressive movement in U.S. schooling during the first half of the 20th century, once stated, "A problem well defined is a problem half-solved."[1] He, of course, could not be more correct, which leads us to ask, "What is school violence?" This may seem like a question that can be answered in a sentence, not a chapter, but of course it is not that simple; after all, defining school violence is half the problem.

DEFINITIONS OF SCHOOL VIOLENCE

The North Carolina Department of Juvenile Justice and Delinquency Prevention–Center for the Prevention of School Violence (NC DJJDP–Center) defines school violence as "any behavior that violates a school's educational mission or climate of respect or jeopardizes the intent of the school to be free of aggression against persons or property, drugs, weapons, disruptions, and disorder."[2] Other definitions focus on certain aspects of student behavior. Emphasizing a psychological perspective, *Early Warning, Timely Response: A Guide to Safe Schools* defined school-related violence as a "broad range of troubling behaviors and emotions shown by students—including serious aggression, physical attacks, suicide, dangerous use of drugs, and other dangerous interpersonal behaviors."[3] The California Commission of Teacher Credentialing (CCTC) provided a more comprehensive definition of school-related violence. According to the CCTC's Recommendations for Reducing Violence in California Schools, "Violence is a public health and safety condition that often results from individual, social, economic, political and institutional disregard for basic human needs. Violence includes physical and nonphysical harm which causes damage, pain, injury or fear. Violence disrupts the school environment and results in the debilitation of personal development which may lead to hopelessness and helplessness."[4] Although this is a very comprehensive definition, it may be over the heads of some students and families. The National Youth Violence Prevention Center defines school violence in their "School Violence Fact Sheet" by stating, "While the media has focused on school shootings, school violence includes a range of activities, including assaults with or without weapons, physical fights, threats or destructive acts other than physical fights, bullying, hostile or threatening remarks between groups of students, and gang violence."[5] This definition touches on a few components of what I call the "youth violence continuum" (see Figure 1.1). We started working with this continuum years ago after seeing a similar concept created by Jim Bryngelson of CARE (Courtesy and Respect Empower), but we saw its true potential after completing a seminar in which a teacher operationalized it in her classroom.

Many years ago, when Danya and I were starting our careers working for the NC DJJDP–Center, we presented a weeklong seminar at the North Carolina Center for the Advancement of Teaching (NCCAT). This was among the first major seminars we were asked to do, and we were very much still "wet behind the ears." Thirty participants from across the state were invited to attend, including teachers, counselors, assistant principals, and principals. The purpose of the seminar was to give these individuals an opportunity to start to develop their school's safe school plan.

On the first day of the seminar we conducted a small get-to-know-you activity. During the activity we asked the participants to do three things for us: (1) tell us their name; (2) tell us why they came to this seminar; and (3) tell us one thing they hoped to learn this week. We made it almost halfway around the room when we encountered our "troubled student." She started out by stating her name, which I won't repeat here. Next, she added, "I have been teaching for 29 years and this is my 30th year coming, and at the end of this year I am retiring!"

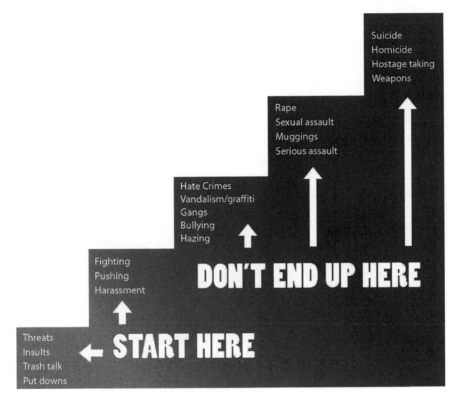

Figure 1.1. The Youth Violence Continuum

She went on to add that she was the "teacher of the year" at her school. Being picked teacher of the year allowed her to attend one seminar of her choice. She stated, "I needed a weeklong vacation from my family and school so I came on up here." After concluding with this remark she sat down.

Danya and I had been feverishly taking notes as the teachers told us what they wanted to learn that week so that we would make sure to cover all of their concerns. But this teacher sat down before telling us what she wanted to learn, so I asked her to tell us. Since I was quite "wet behind the ears," I did not realize that she really did not want to be bothered and that she simply had come to this seminar for a vacation. To the teacher's credit, she did try to tell us that.

After standing back up, she looked me straight in the eyes and said, "Well Billy, I will be honest with you. I really do not expect to learn anything from you, YOU LITTLE YOUNG PUNK!"

I kid you not; she actually used the word "punk." I stood there in amazement for a moment, thinking, "I can't believe she just said that to me." But after a few seconds I came to my senses and realized that if I did not take control of this situation right now we were at risk of losing the group's respect on day one of a weeklong seminar. So I looked back at her and said, "Well, I think you're joking, but just in case you're not, let's move on to the next person." This comment garnered a couple of chuckles from the crowd and broke the tension.

By the end of the week Danya and I had won that teacher over, and when it came to evaluating the seminar she had some really positive things to say about it, such as this: "When I walked into the seminar the first day, I thought to myself, what in the world, they have sent two college brats up here to teach veteran teachers. What do these boys think they can teach me about school safety? But, I tell you what; you two really impressed me and yes even shocked me a little bit with your knowledge."

In fact, at the end of the seminar she came up to me and said, "Mr. Lassiter [simply addressing me in such a professional manner was a good sign], I think I did learn something from you this week. That continuum that you put up on the board; I think you have got something there. Fifteen years ago when a child put down another child in my classroom or threatened another child in my classroom or bullied another child in my classroom, there was going to be a consequence for that behavior; that child was going to know that that behavior was unacceptable."

"Today," she stated, "if a child in my classroom does those exact same behaviors, I most likely do not say anything about it. If I were to say something about it, that child would probably look at me like I was crazy. They would say to me, what are you talking about, we were just playing around, or no, that is just how we do it."

She continued, "In the past I have accepted those excuses, but this year I am going to go back to my classroom using your continuum and crack down on those behaviors at the bottom of it."

She did, and at the end of the year she gave me a call. The call started with her explaining who she was, as if I could have forgotten her. She started out by exclaiming, "Mr. Lassiter, I wanted to let you know that I have retired! But I also wanted to let you know that this was the best year I had in teaching in I do not know how long. On the first day of class I showed my students your continuum. I pointed to it and said, 'Children, this is the school violence continuum, and if I see one of these behaviors on the continuum in my class I am going to let you know about it.'"

She said that students immediately responded to the continuum by asking questions about it. They asked what this word means and what do you mean by that. Inspired, she decided that she was going to have her class create their own continuum. She told the kids to get into groups and come up with a list of behaviors that would be unacceptable in the classroom. She gave the kids markers and flip chart paper to write all those behaviors down that the students found to be unacceptable. Once all the groups had presented, they discovered that they had a list of over 120 unacceptable behaviors.

She told the class that there were way too many behaviors on the list and that no one could be expected to remember this many things. The next step was for the class to strike out all those words that meant the same thing and then vote on all the remaining behaviors. She instructed the class that there must be a unanimous vote for a behavior to make the final list. She told me that this process took most of the morning on the first day of class. After the students selected the behaviors that they thought were unacceptable, she got them to rank them from the worst behaviors to the least worst. By the end of this activity they had created their own continuum. That afternoon she took that continuum down to the office and had it laminated.

When class started the next day, she pointed to the continuum and told the class, "Here is our continuum. If I see one of those behaviors on the continuum in our class, I am going to point at the continuum to let you know that I see an unacceptable behavior taking place."

She said the first time she saw such a behavior and pointed to the continuum her students looked at her as if she was crazy. The second time she pointed to the continuum, one of her young men said, "What? I am not doing anything."

She stated, "I was not pointing at you. I was pointing at the continuum."

He replied, "Oh, I just wanted to let you know I was not doing anything."

She said, "Well I just want to let you know I did not come up with this list of unacceptable behaviors. You did."

To this the young man could not respond. She said to me, "What was he going to say? What could he say? He did vote for all the behaviors on the list." She added, "That was the last time all year anyone argued with me about that." At this point I was already quite impressed with her success, but she wanted to continue, full speed, about her year.

She said, "Mr. Lassiter, you want to know the best part? I only had 2 incidents in my classroom this year that I had to send kids down to the office for. That was a vast improvement over the year before, when I had to send 52 kids down to the office."

I said, "Fifty-two!" and I thought to myself, "She had 52 incidents in her classroom and was teacher of the year. My goodness, they must have given that award to her for simply surviving the year. Like a Purple Heart or something."

She said, "You heard me right, Mr. Lassiter; I said 52. I went from 52 down to 2 this year. Amazing, right?"

I said, "Extraordinary!"

She said, "I just wanted to thank you because it was your continuum that made the whole thing possible."

But it was really her class's continuum that made the whole thing possible. Her class defined what school violence was in their classroom, and by designing their own continuum together they created buy-in.

I often tell this story to people during presentations. Many principals respond by saying, "Mr. Lassiter, I agree with what you're saying, but I have guns in my school, I have gangs in my schools, I have drugs in my school; I do not have time to deal with put-downs, trash talk, and bullying." To this I always respond, "You do not have the time because you did not take the time in the beginning." Many schools honestly believe they are too busy to deal with the small issues, but really all they are doing is ignoring the small things that grow into big challenges down the road.

CULTURAL MILIEU OF SCHOOLS

Adolescents and young children are limit testers: they like to find out at what point adults will draw the line on unacceptable behavior. Some adults are much more tolerant of unacceptable behavior than others. For example, you may go to a restaurant and see a family that allow their kids to talk loudly, jump around on the seats, roll around on the floor, and throw food across the table at their brothers and sisters, while at another table you have a family who make their children sit perfectly still and the children do not speak unless they are spoken to. These are obviously extreme ends of the parenting spectrum, but classrooms and schools often operate in the same fashion. Within the same school you can find classroom teachers who allow a great deal of freedom in student behavior and those who are strict disciplinarians. This is why it is important for schools as a whole to define what school violence is. In order to create a safe and conducive learning environment, schools must establish what the boundaries will be and enforce those boundaries consistently.

How should your school develop its definition of what school violence is? Could you use one from this book? Of course you could, but often the most important part of making a decision is the process that the group has to go through to arrive at that decision. For example, let's look back at the story just presented. What made the discipline policy in the teacher of the year's classroom so strong? Was it how the code of conduct was developed in that classroom? The fact that the students were involved in the process created buy-in. Adults are no different from students in this respect; we all like to know that our voice has been heard on a topic. So when a school goes about creating a definition for what school violence is, it should invite the whole school community in on the process, including students, parents, teachers, administrators, and all other staff members. People are much more likely to support an idea if they believe they were part of the process that made the rules. Will involving the whole school be more time consuming and more frustrating? Of course it will be at first, but in the long run it will pay great dividends. Going back to the example given at the beginning of the chapter, would it have been easier for that teacher to come in and read out a list of rules to the students instead of spending the whole day establishing them as a class? Certainly it would have been quicker and easier, but I am sure that same teacher would tell anyone that the time she spent on the first day of school was well worth it in the long run. As Ross Perot once said, "Democracy is not pretty; it is kind of like making sausage." Creating the rules for a school is not pretty either, but if we do not involve people in the process, it will be much uglier.

ZERO TOLERANCE: HOW MUCH SENSE?

Now this may sound like a call for zero tolerance. The term "zero tolerance" was created by people who wanted to take all the flexibility and decision making out of the hands of those who work with children every day. Zero tolerance usually leads to people making decisions with zero common sense. We will discuss zero tolerance in greater detail in later chapters, but for now it is important to note that it is possible to have high expectations for children and not punish them all in the same way. We have principals, assistant principals, counselors, social workers, and psychologists working at schools so they can do what is in the best interest of the child and the school. If we take all the decision-making authority away from these individuals, why have them in the first place? When some principals advocate for zero tolerance, they do so mainly because they are not in favor of making controversial decisions. When deciding whether or not to suspend a child for the long term, it is easy to say to a parent, "Well I have no choice; that is what the policy requires me to do." Zero tolerance takes the responsibility of making hard decisions away from educators and puts it into the hands of people who do not interact with the child or have never met the child before in their lives. That just does not make good sense.

SCHOOL SAFETY, FEDERAL REQUIREMENTS

One cannot discount the role that the "No Child Left Behind Act" plays in this equation. Most do not know that the "No Child Left Behind Act" included something on school safety, but it did. Although the legislation was well over a thousand pages long and only included one paragraph on school safety, it was included. Basically, the legislation stated that a student should be allowed to transfer out of a school that is considered to be persistently dangerous or if the student has been the victim of a violent crime.

Well, what is a persistently dangerous school? That was left up to each of the State Boards of Education to determine, and the definitions were as different as the states that came up with them. Some included purely incident-based definitions, whereas others included survey data and suspension data. An analysis of 43 adopted or proposed policies conducted by the Education Commission of the States found a variety of factors that would identify a school as persistently dangerous.

The first characteristic by which states differed greatly was the length of time required to be labeled a "persistently dangerous school." The Education Commission of the States found that lengths of time ranged from three years to two years, with some states using a combination of lengths of time. Of course, most states adopted the three-year standard, which allowed students to stay in an identified school for three years before affording them the opportunity to move to a safer school. Although many would argue that having a child attend a school that is dangerous for one year is one year too long, states tried to push the time horizon out as far as possible so as to not necessitate too many schools appearing on the list.

The second characteristic that varied greatly was how the states calculated the offenses that would determine whether a school was dangerous or not. The Education Commission of the States found that states used a combination of specific numbers of incidents (such as no more than 10 incidents in one school year) and incident rates that were based on school population. The states that used rate calculations varied in the level of acceptable incidents from half an incident per 100 students all the way up to 5 incidents per 100 students.

Finally, a variety of different types of offenses were considered as those that might make a school "dangerous." According to the Education Commission of the States, "states' definitions of offenses/incidents vary from considering only weapon possession to considering as many as ten different types of incidents."[6]

One of the problems the U.S. Department of Education had when it sent out guidelines on how states should be defining a persistently dangerous school was that less than half of the states were requiring schools to collect specific data on incidents beyond what was required in the Federal Gun-Free School Act. The other problem was that different states had different definitions for the same types of crime. For example, one state might define an assault as an event in which a person must get seriously injured, whereas in another state an assault may be defined as any type of unwanted touching. So, if the federal government stated that any school with a certain amount of assaults should be deemed persistently dangerous, there would still be an inconsistent standard across the country.

Often people ask: Why not allow the federal government to create standard definitions for certain offenses and force schools to uses those definitions to determine whether they are dangerous or not? Many believe that this would be overly burdensome on the schools, to which I would agree. And it would also take away the right of the school to determine what is violent and what is not violent. Putting that decision into the hands of a lawmaker 3,000 miles away from a school really does not make sense.

The overwhelming problem with the "No Child Left Behind Act" and specifically its provision on persistently dangerous schools is that it ultimately discourages schools from reporting data. Schools and the people that work in them do not want their schools to be labeled unsafe or dangerous because it makes them look bad. Interestingly enough, communities do not really like it either, because the quality of a school often directly correlates with the value of property in a community. Who would want to move to a community where one's child would be attending a persistently dangerous school?

In Schonfeld's chapter on school violence, he found many of the same obstacles in the way of gathering accurate data on school violence:

> At the school level, officially recorded crime statistics often undercount crimes because of a lack of candor on the part of administrators doing the counting. Political pressures, the avoidance of embarrassment, and the administrator's desire to avoid jeopardizing his or her career motivate the lack of candor. Moreover, crime-related surveillance at the school level is rarely audited by external agents and the states' annual reporting of the numbers of students expelled for carrying firearms to school provides misleadingly low estimates of school-related firearms violations.[7]

CONCLUDING THOUGHT

One can see that defining school violence is not an easy process for any school or community, but it is one that these groups should be pursuing. After all, how are we going to solve the problem if we do not know what the problem is?

Chapter 2

Separating Myth from Reality

William L. Lassiter

Before we get too far along, I think it is important that we pause and dispel some of the common myths that people have about school violence and school violence prevention. These myths, often held as common knowledge, truly distort and frequently make it hard to move forward in a productive manner. The goal of this chapter is to present convincing evidence that these myths are just that—myths—and should no longer be used to back up people's arguments on what works to prevent school violence.

MYTH: SCHOOL VIOLENCE IS AN EPIDEMIC

Merriam-Webster Online defines an epidemic as "1: affecting or tending to affect a disproportionately large number of individuals within a population, community, or region at the same time. 2 a: excessively prevalent b: contagious."[1] When most people think of an epidemic, they think of a virus that is spreading across the country uncontrollably. Today, many are saying that because youth violence and school violence are public health issues, we should view them in public health terms. There are many good reasons to see youth and school violence in these terms, but should they be labeled as an epidemic?

Figure 2.1 shows the trend line for the number of school-associated violent deaths that have occurred since 1993. One can see from the chart that, if anything, there have actually been fewer school-associated violent deaths over the past few years. This statistic alone does not give us enough information to make many inferences beyond the fact that we know that it is pretty rare that a student is killed on school

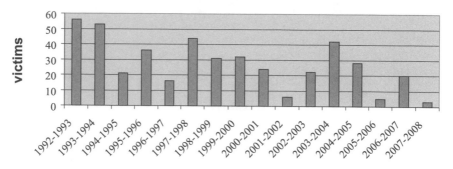

Figure 2.1. School-Associated Violent Deaths

property through violence. According to the U.S. Department of Education, during the 2005–2006 school year an estimated 54.8 million students were enrolled in prekindergarten through 12th grade,[2] and according to the National School Safety Center, only 5 students died from school-associated violence.[3] That means that during the 2005–2006 school year a student had a 1 in 10 million chance of falling victim to a school shooting.

Nowhere in the definition of an epidemic does it say that people have to be dying before we can consider it an epidemic, so let's consider some of the other facts. In order for school violence to be an epidemic, one would think that it would have to be on the rise across the country. However, it is hard to know whether that is the case because no truly standardized national statistics exist on school violence. We do have data from the national victimization study that is reported annually in the *Indicators of School Crime and Safety.* According to the U.S. Department of Education, "the percentage of students who were threatened or injured with a weapon fluctuated between 7 to 9 percent in all survey years from 1993 through 2005."[4] If school violence were an epidemic, one would expect these numbers to be constantly increasing, but the reality is that they seem to be holding constant or decreasing. Over the last few years we have seen that more schools are experiencing school violence: "The percentage of public schools experiencing one or more violent incidents increased between the 1999–2000 and 2003–04 school years, from 71 to 81 percent."[5] However, this statistic can be misleading because the overall number of incidents does not seem to be on the rise: "Between 1992 and 2005, the total crime victimization rates for students age 12 to 18 generally declined both at school and away from school; this pattern held for the total crime rate as well as for thefts, violent crimes, and serious violent crimes."[6] Although it may be true that more schools are experiencing school violence, this does not translate into school violence being an epidemic. One would expect that if school violence were an epidemic, not only would it be spreading to more schools, but it would also be occurring to more students.

Actually, the increase in the number of schools reporting crimes is more likely a symptom of better awareness and reporting than of a wildly spreading epidemic. Anyone who studies public health and social science can tell you that when awareness begins to be raised about a problem, reporting will automatically increase. There is no doubt about it; incidents such as Columbine, 1999, and Virginia Tech, 2006, have raised the awareness level of schools to the issue of school violence. Once you start looking for something, you are much more likely to find it than if you were not looking for it at all. Most schools are looking for school violence today, whereas they may not have been looking 10 years ago.

Lastly, when I think about an epidemic, I always think about those movies in which whole towns are being taken out by a virus that we cannot stop by any other means other than blowing up the town. There always seems to be a lack of control associated with an epidemic, and although some believe there is no way to stop school violence, I am not one of those people. School violence is controllable and preventable—not in every case, but it is certainly something we as a society can control if we put the resources and manpower in to do it. Research has shown that there are hundreds of effective programs and strategies out there that have reduced or almost eliminated violence from school environments. You will learn more about these options throughout the book. Remember, when people start throwing out words such as "epidemic," their motives may not be pure. They may be the character in that movie saying we need to blow up the town before the disease spreads. In the case of school violence, many see the town as the public education system, and they are trying to convince you that we need to blow it up rather than fix it. All too often the media are willing accessories to the crime because they believe that printing or saying words like "epidemic" will help them sell papers or get ratings.

Having grown up in a family of public educators, my worldview is definitely painted by that experience, so I believe there are very few government functions more important than providing education. Any rational person can see that there are solutions to the challenge of school violence and that those solutions do not have to involve throwing out the whole public education system. Part of the solution has to be that people in the public education system be willing to face the challenge head-on and not deny its existence, which brings us to our next myth.

MYTH: IT CAN'T HAPPEN HERE

After a major event such as Columbine or a tornado hitting a school or community, we hear people say, "I never thought it could happen here." My question is, Why not? What makes your school or community immune to a crisis event?

Before we go further, we must first think back on what "it" is when schools say it cannot happen here, "it" being school violence. School violence, as you may recall from Chapter 1, is any behavior that disrupts the mission of the school, or any of those behaviors that can be found in the violence continuum.

Sometimes I have been called to work at a school at the request of the superintendent or the school board, rather than the principal. These are never good situations because the principals always believe that I am out to get them. These principals say, "We have good kids here; nothing ever happens here." To this I often reply, "Nothing, Wow! How do you do it?"

The reality is that there is no such place as a violence-free school. That can be the vision, but I am yet to actually walk in the door of that school. It goes back to what we were saying in the last chapter when we described violence as a continuum of acts, not just major incidents. Schools should be willing to discuss the level of violence they are experiencing, and parents should see a school that is willing to talk about its flaws as a good sign.

In fact, in findings from the School Survey on Crime and Safety: 2003–2004 generated by the National Center for Education Statistics, "incidents of crime were reported at 96 percent of high schools, 94 percent of middle schools, and 74 percent of primary schools."[7] This was a survey done of school principals, who willingly admitted on the survey that, yes, they do have crime and disorder in their schools.

MYTH: SCHOOLS ARE UNSAFE PLACES

Although any level of school violence should been seen as unacceptable, are schools inherently more dangerous than most other places our kids go? The answer is no; schools tend to be as safe or unsafe as the communities in which they exist. According to statistics reported in the *Indicators of School Crime and Safety: 2006*, a report published by the U.S. Departments of Education and Justice,

> In 2005, four percent of students ages 12–18 reported being victimized at school during the past six months. Approximately three percent reported theft, one percent reported violent victimization, and less than half of a percent reported serious violent victimization.
>
> From 1992 to 1997, the victimization rates for violent crime were generally lower at school than away from school; however, there were no measurable differences in these rates in the years between 1998 and 2005, except in 2000, when victimization rates at school were lower. The rates for serious violent crime were lower at school than away from school in each survey year from 1992 to 2005. In 2005, students age 12 to 18 were

victims of 5 serious violent crimes per 1,000 students at school, compared to 10 serious violent crimes per 1,000 students away from school.[8]

These statistics point out that students are slightly less likely to be victims of a violent crime at school than to be victims of a nonviolent crime such as theft at school. So just what can these statistics tell us about whether a school is safe or not? I submit that they tell us very little about an individual school, but they do show us that, in general, schools are some of the safest places that our kids go. Could we do better? Absolutely, our society could do better at limiting violence and crime in our schools and in our communities.

MYTH: THE SOLUTION TO SCHOOL VIOLENCE IS GUN CONTROL

If you are passionate about gun control, your answer to this question may be clouded by your position on the issue. Although it is true that gun violence is a problem in the United States, it remains a relatively small problem for schools. Contrary to what you see on the news, most school violence has nothing to do with guns. In fact, less than 1 percent of the violence that occurs on school campuses has anything to do with a gun. Each local education agency is required to report to the U.S. Department of Education the number of students who carried a gun to school in the last year. Although the U.S. Department of Education would be the first to admit that their data are flawed, these are the only true incident data that are collected nationwide on firearm possession in schools. In the 2007 report, which reports on the 2003–2004 school year, "states reported that they expelled a total of 2,165 students from school for bringing a firearm to school or possessing a firearm at school."[9] On the Youth Risk Behavior Surveillance, students were asked if they had carried a weapon such as a gun, knife, or club in the past 30 days on school grounds: "Between 1993 and 1999, the percentage of students who reported carrying a weapon at school declined from 12 to 7 percent. However, there was no measurable change in the percentage of students who carried a weapon at school between 1999 and 2005."[10] An estimated 54.8 million students were enrolled in prekindergarten through grade 12 in the United States during the 2004–2005 school year, and according to the Youth Risk Behavior Surveillance, 7 percent of those students carried a weapon to school in the last 30 days. That would mean that on average 3.86 million students carried a weapon onto school property sometime in the last 30 days. Almost 4 million weapons is extremely far from from the 2,165 reported guns found on school campuses in the previously mentioned report on guns in schools. It is important to note that the Youth Risk Behavior Surveillance includes all weapons, not just guns, whereas the Gun-Free Schools Report only looks at firearms. That being said, one would still think those two numbers would be closer together.

Does that mean that guns are not a problem? No, access to weapons by young people who have no understanding of the incredible responsibility that goes along with guns is a problem. Even if we got rid of all the guns in the world, there would still be school violence. So exactly how many guns are being carried onto school campuses each day in America? Frankly, no one knows, and I am not convinced that it really matters because one gun is too many.

If we really want to look at getting rid of guns from our school campuses, we should look at why students bring guns to school in the first place. In most localities in our country, bringing a gun to school is a very serious offense, yet students bring them anyway. Why? Students overwhelming state that they carry a gun to school for protection. Although some kids bring guns to school to show them off, the vast majority bring a gun to school to protect themselves. So naturally the next question is, Who are they trying to protect themselves from? It could be a bully, a gang member, or a drug dealer. Regardless, those students believe that the danger is so great that they are willing to risk a felony charge, a long-term suspension, and their educational future to bring that gun to school. I would contend that if we really want to get serious about guns coming onto our school campuses, we must first start by dealing with the reasons kids bring guns to school. We have to create environments where bullying, gangs, and drugs are not acceptable. More detailed discussions about each of these negative symptoms are to come in future chapters.

MYTH: THE CAUSE OF SCHOOL VIOLENCE IS THE MEDIA

Many want to blame the media for turning our kids into violent killers, and although these people may be partially correct, there is no way we can completely blame the media. There has been plenty of research done that shows the effect that video games and violent movies have on an adolescent brain. In an analysis of the research currently available, the authors of "The Influence of Media Violence on Youth" found the following: "Research on violent television and films, video games, and music reveals unequivocal evidence that media violence increases the likelihood of aggressive and violent behavior in both immediate and long-term contexts. The effects appear larger for milder than for more severe forms of aggression, but the effects on severe forms of violence are also substantial ($r = .13$ to $.32$) when compared with effects of other violence risk factors or medical effects deemed important by the medical community (e.g., effect of aspirin on heart attacks). The research base is large; diverse in methods, samples, and media genres; and consistent in overall findings. The evidence is clearest within the most extensively researched domain, television and film violence. The growing body of video-game research yields essentially the same conclusions."[11]

Anderson and Bushman stated the same even more emphatically in their study, "Effects of Violent Video Games on Aggressive Behavior, Aggressive Cognition, Aggressive Affect, Physiological Arousal, and Prosocial Behavior: A Meta-Analytic Review of the Scientific Literature." They stated, "The size of the media-violence effect is equal to or larger than the size of many medical effects that our society deems large, such as the effect of condom use on sexually transmitted HIV, the effect of passive smoking on lung cancer at work, and the effect of calcium intake on bone mass."[12]

Since the research appears to be so clear, why do parents allow their children to be exposed to violent media material? The media industry would claim it is not their fault if a child is exposed to their materials, that it is the job of the parents to protect their children from things they do not think are healthy. Although this is true, the industry does not make it easy for parents. Often violent material is targeted at younger audiences. The video game industry is probably the most obvious example of using trickery to deceive parents about their products. Most video games allow the users to enter secret codes that will make the content of the game more profane, more obscene, and more violent. Parents may purchase a game for their child and even play the game with their child and think that it is not that bad. Little do parents know that many times their child has surfed the Internet and found a secret code to make that game more graphic, thus making a game that was acceptable to most parents into something that is completely unacceptable.

With all of this being said, the research is pretty clear that a child's exposure to media violence is a variable that explains only about 4 percent of why a child becomes violent. This fact does not diminish the effect of media violence, since social scientists have been able to find few other variables that are greater contributors, but it does mean that we cannot blame it all on the media.

MYTH: ZERO TOLERANCE IS THE SOLUTION

What is zero tolerance? Zero tolerance means that a school looks at every situation as being the same and chooses the exact same punishment in every circumstance. Most schools adopted zero tolerance policies after Columbine, which led them down some pretty slippery slopes. For example, you may remember the child who was suspended for threatening another student with a chicken finger that happened to look like a gun. Many have said you cannot have zero tolerance with zero common sense.

Zero tolerance policies got their start at the national level with the passage of the Gun-Free Schools Act (GFSA), which is part of the Elementary and Secondary Education Act of 1965 (ESEA) as amended by the No Child Left Behind Act of 2001 (NCLB; Public Law 107–110). "GFSA requires that each state or outlying area receiving federal funds under the ESEA have a law that requires all local education agencies (LEAs) in these states and outlying areas to expel from school for at least one year any student found bringing a firearm to school or possessing a firearm at school. State laws also must authorize the LEA chief administering officer to modify, in writing, any such expulsion on a case-by-case basis. In addition, the GFSA states that the law must be construed so as to be consistent with the Individuals with Disabilities Education Act (IDEA)."[13]

The discipline technique most often associated with zero tolerance is suspension or expulsion. Reliance on these methods to remove students from school has reached alarming levels. Across the United States in 2000, there were over 3 million school suspensions and over 97,000 expulsions. In some states, the number of suspensions exceeded 10 percent of the number of students enrolled in school.[14] This kind of wholesale exclusion from the educational process reduces the likelihood of teaching children positive behavior. "Moreover, taking children out of school for even a few days disrupts their education and often escalates poor behavior by removing them from a structured environment and giving them increased time and opportunity to get into trouble. Studies have shown that a child who has been suspended is more likely to be retained in grade, to drop out, to commit a crime, and/or to end up incarcerated as an adult."[15]

The reality is that removing a child from the school environment often does not create the desired effect that administrators or teachers are looking for. One would want to believe that the purpose for suspending children would be to change their behavior by sentencing them to a harsh consequence. Although I could never imagine getting suspended from school as a child, mainly because of the embarrassment it would have brought to my parents, many of the children being suspended today almost see it as a reward for being bad. In fact, while studying suspensions in the state of North Carolina, I discovered a sizable proportion of suspensions being issued to students for truancy. So let me get this right: a child violates school policy by deciding not to come to school and what does the school do but suspend the same child right back to the streets. Now that makes a lot of sense.

Suspension can weaken school connectedness and bonding of students to the school and undermines healthy social development. School connectedness has been shown to be one of the most highly correlated variables to school success, and there is no doubt that removing students from the school environment breaks that connection. Research has taught us that, second only to family, school is the most important stabilizing force in the lives of young people.[16] Connectedness to school has been shown to protect against violence, risky sexual behavior, drug use, and dropping out of school. Moreover, youth at school who feel good, perceive meaningful attachment to adults, and possess a sense of belonging are also more likely to feel engaged, to work harder, and to be involved with positive activities in and outside of school time.[17] In fact, other studies have shown that "connectedness to others in conjunction with group norms are the two most important factors in explaining and addressing risk behavior in adolescence."[18]

On the basis of this research, one can conclude that by suspending a child educators actually do more to harm the child than help. So why do schools still use suspension and zero tolerance policies to address bad behavior? They do so mainly because they have few other options. Principals often state that they are caught between a rock and a hard place when it comes to disciplining a child. They can either suspend the child or send the child back to class with no consequence. Neither of these options is good to pursue. If the principal sends the child back to class with no punishment, the child believes he or she has gotten away with the behavior, and teachers feel that the administration is not supporting them. If the principal suspends the child, well, you have just read about the dire consequences that may result.

So what should school districts be doing to address this issue? First, schools should consider the behaviors that are causing children to be suspended and develop programming to address those behaviors. We will discuss how schools can go about doing this later in this book. Second, schools should consider alternatives to suspensions, including after-school detention, Saturday school, in-school suspension, and alternative placement. All of these options keep the student engaged in school and create a consequence most children would rather avoid.

MYTH: IT IS ALL THE PARENTS' FAULT

As parents are quick to point the finger at schools, schools are in turn quick to point the finger at parents when it comes to discipline problems. Well, who is right? Is it the parents' fault, or should we be blaming the school? The answer is that we all can accept some of the blame, and we all must accept some of the responsibility. Furthermore, we all need to work together to address the issues leading to violence in schools.

The Centers for Disease Control found that "family experiences play a critical role in causing, promoting, or reinforcing violent behavior by children and adolescents," but they also found that "parents are not the only adults who shape the beliefs and behavior of young people.

Individuals such as teachers, coaches, child care providers, and neighbors often influence how a child or adolescent feels about violence."[19] A comprehensive review of the literature on parental involvement done by the Northwest Regional Educational Laboratory found that "parents often begin their participation doubting that their involvement can make much difference, and they are generally very gratified to discover what an important contribution they are able to make. In this connection, it is important for school people and parents to be aware that parent involvement supports students' learning, behavior, and attitudes regardless of factors such as parents' income, educational level, and whether or not parents are employed."[20] As one can see, acquiring parental involvement can be something of a challenge because most parents do not believe their involvement will make a difference, but the benefits are well worth the effort. We have devoted a whole chapter to how schools can foster and maintain parental involvement, so we do not go into great detail on that subject here.

MYTH: THERE IS A SINGLE SOLUTION OR PROGRAM THAT WILL WORK FOR ALL KIDS

I included this myth because I hear it all the time from vendors of programs. They often say, "I have a program that will work in any school in America, with any type of violence problems a school may be having." The truth is there is no such thing. There is no magic formula to erase all possibility of violence in schools. Kids are different, schools are different, communities are different all across this country, and there is no single solution to school violence. Addressing this challenge must take into account a comprehensive plan. This is not to say that schools should not look at best-practice models and at what research has shown to be effective. In fact, I am saying the exact opposite: schools should look at what programs are available, but they will discover from the research that whole-school programs can address the problems of only about 80 to 85 percent of the students on that school campus. For the remainder of the students, it will take intensive interventions, including wrap-around services, to address their needs. These interventions will depend completely on the needs of the child if they are to be effective in changing behavior.

To address school violence in an effective way, schools should start with an assessment process that will help determine the challenges the school needs to work on to create a safer school environment. They should assess everything from the physical plant to the social culture climate of the school. The assessment will help the school determine the next steps that are needed to address the challenges students are facing.

MYTH: BY GETTING TOUGHER WITH JUVENILES AND WAIVING THEM TO ADULT COURT, WE REDUCE THE LIKELIHOOD OF THOSE JUVENILES RECIDIVATING

The practice of waiving (or transferring) juveniles to adult court has become more common across the United States as legislators and judges want to appear to be tougher on crime. The reality is that by getting tougher on crime they may actually be making the problem worse. There are four methods for waiving a juvenile to adult court: legislative exclusions, prosecutorial transfer, judicial waiver, and blended sentencing.[21] As expected, the definitions are directly related to the terminology. The most common form, or at least the most closely tracked method of transfer, is judicial waiver. Legislative exclusions, which are evident in the majority of states, allow for transfer of juveniles only when they are a certain age (generally 13 or 14) and are charged with committing a serious and/or violent offense (such as rape, murder, manslaughter, or robbery). For youth who have committed serious and/or violent offenses that do not meet the statutory requirements, prosecutors have the authority in many states to waive the juvenile's case to adult court for a judge to decide which jurisdiction should hear and determine the juvenile's sanction. Lastly, in blended sentencing a judge can determine the best punishment or treatment from an array of options. Convicted juveniles may have a sentence that requires a juvenile *and* adult sentence; a juvenile *or* adult sentence; or an option to sentence the juvenile to remain in the juvenile system until a certain age, at which time the court reassesses whether adult prison time is justified.

Judicial waiver is the most common form of transfer; it occurs when a juvenile court judge transfers a case from juvenile to adult court in order to deny the juvenile the protections that juvenile jurisdictions provide. All states except Nebraska, New York, and New Mexico, currently provide for judicial waiver and have set a variety of lower age limits. In most states, the youngest offender who can be waived to adult court is a 17 or 18-year-old, although in some states, this age is as low as 13 or 14. Usually, the offense allegedly committed must be particularly egregious in order for the case to be waived judicially, or there must be a long history of offenses.

The move toward judicial waiver began in the 1960s after many in our country had decided the juvenile justice system was ineffective at rehabilitating juvenile offenders. The juvenile justice system was declared to be a threat to public safety. "The increasing data that rehabilitative juvenile programs were not effective coupled with the perception of a rising rate of serious juvenile violence in the 1980s and 1990s prompted a push for using the waiver process to transfer youthful offenders to adult criminal court."[22]

The impact of recent legislation providing for enhanced transfer is unclear. Less than 2 percent of all formal juvenile delinquency cases were judicially waived each year from 1988 to 1992. In 1988, only 1.2 percent of all cases were waived to adult criminal court, or 7,005 of 569,596 cases. The number of judicially waived cases steadily climbed to 11,748 of 743,673 cases in 1992, to comprise 1.6 percent of all cases.

According to the federal Office of Juvenile Justice and Delinquency Prevention, "studies have found that youth incarcerated in adult institutions are five times more likely to be sexually assaulted, twice as likely to be beaten by staff, and 50 percent more likely to be attacked with a weapon than their counterparts in a juvenile facility.[23] Juveniles waived to criminal court are more likely to recidivate and commit more serious offenses, and they have a shorter survival rate than youth who are prosecuted through the juvenile court system.[24]

MYTH: THERE IS NOTHING SCHOOLS AND COMMUNITIES CAN DO TO REDUCE SCHOOL VIOLENCE

Of course this is false, or else there would be no need to write a book about the topic. A number of prevention and intervention programs that meet very high scientific standards of effectiveness have been identified. Throughout this book you will learn more about how schools and communities can address school violence, and you will be exposed to models that have been effective in reducing or in some cases almost eliminating violence from schools.

Chapter 3

Root Causes of School Violence

Danya C. Perry

In an effort to curb thefts at a school in the northeastern part of the country, I was asked to assist in evaluating and developing strategies aimed at changing the school climate. I had an opportunity to work with educators and law enforcement to understand the dynamics of theft that was occurring, as well as an opportunity to speak directly with youth. In any student assembly format, I try to limit my talks to 30 or 45 minutes, because of short attention spans, and to be as interactive as possible. I walked into this situation pretty excited about the opportunity to impart some knowledge on the youth and get their perspective. As the students filed in, I started looking over my notes and was startled by a kid shouting "WEST-SIDE!" I looked up and saw a group of kids way in the back twisting their fingers into the shape of a "W." I understood that this could be either a gang-related hand sign or just youth mimicking. As soon as I started to dismiss the idea of this being actually gang related, another youth near the front of the auditorium yelled "EAST-SIDE!" OK, now this was a potential problem in trying to maintain the session's purpose without any escalation of aggression. What could I do to ensure that words did not manifest into action? I immediately grabbed the microphone and with the most robust voice that I could muster, I yelled "Good morning!" Not profound, I know, but I just wanted to get their attention and buy myself some time as I decided to turn this into an opportunity to talk about destructive decisions. I started to talk about how our words can lead to aggressive acts, thus making the school an unsafe environment. I asked students to give me examples of how something small, like an insult, escalated to a fight. Most students had pretty good answers, but I will never forget the last young man that I called on to share his answer. He stood up quickly, and his friends around him started to laugh. He looked at them and said, "What are ya'll laughing at?" They began to laugh even louder, which made the entire auditorium erupt in laughter. As I began to see this young man's disposition change right before my eyes, I asked him to reveal his answer. He yelled out, "I ain't saying nothing 'cause THEY ain't respecting me!"

I then asked him, "How does this make you feel?" (thinking that this would be a great teachable moment).

He then said, "Mr. Perry, I am pumped like the plump Pillsbury doughboy!" This was the first time that I ever lost my composure and laughed uncontrollably. A big grin came across his face, and I began to dissect what had just occurred. We talked about how a simple insult or "laugh" could have created an opportunity for aggression. He had the ability to deescalate the situation and resolve the potential conflict with humor. In this example, school violence has many derivatives: individual put-downs, feelings of being disrespected, and possible lowered self-esteem. Knowing various catalysts and causes of violence can lead to the development of strategies that are effective. OK—now I'm pumped!

It is critical to understand the root causes of school violence to develop sound and effective prevention and intervention strategies. A thorough problem assessment analyzes all possible reasons for an action or occurrence. A problem that is as complex as violence in schools requires the study of many factors. School violence today cannot be attributed to one or two factors. Nor can any factor be said to absolutely predict violence at the school-building level. The factors that lead to violence are random and change from case to case. What is important is to recognize that these root causes and factors, including actions as commonplace as bullying, can lead to a violent incident.

DOMAINS OF DEVELOPMENT

The root causes of school violence come from five domains: individual, family, peers, community or neighborhood, and school. Each of these domains can be viewed as a potential asset or liability to a student's success. As an asset, each entity has a role in positive youth development and the creation of success. As a liability, each entity can seriously hamper youth success. It is important to note that the domains are more influential at different points in the developmental process. For example, the family, or lack thereof, is more influential than the school and peer group in the early years of a child's life.

Another important facet to consider is the developed assets of some youth. Resiliency is the ability to bounce back from a challenge or obstacle. Some youth are resilient enough not to be affected by the factors in these domains that may lead to violent and aggressive behavior. An introduction and connection to a caring and competent adult at school or through a youth program could offset negativity from the family or community. Yet in many instances the majority of domains are positive and the introduction of a single negative peer influence still offsets any of the positive attributes attained. The bottom line is that determining the exact root cause of school violence is not an exact science.

PRECURSORS TO SERIOUS, VIOLENT BEHAVIOR: THE INDIVIDUAL

Why would an individual student be compelled to bully others or engage in a violent school act such as a school shooting? Addressing the issue of school violence from the individual's perspective is the backdrop to understanding the entire problem. After each school shooting, you often hear the question "What set off this particular youth?" The nation struggles with trying to understand something so irrational as a school shooting. Now, when the question is asked in regard to an incident of bullying, the answer seems to be more visible. Important factors worth discussing include self-esteem, high impulsivity, self-destructive behaviors, and being a past victim of violence.[1]

Many people believe that aggressive youth are naturally tough and have high levels of confidence. This may be the fact for some, but it surely is not always the rule. Esteem has a huge role in aggression. There are multiple categories of bullying behavior. Some who engage in bullying activities tend to be confident and have high self-esteem. This group is physically aggressive and has a pro-violence attitude. The second group tends to exhibit early aggressive behaviors to hide feelings of insecurity and self-loathing. "Bullying" others makes them feel better about themselves. Either way, youth with low or high self-esteem who exhibit aggressive behaviors tend to have a strong need to dominate others and do not show any empathy toward victims of violence. Youth who are more aggressive in this manner have a tendency to be more disconnected from the school environment. This disconnection often fuels the dissatisfaction and aggressiveness and starts a cycle of continuous violence or increased levels of aggression if left unchecked.

Youth impulsivity is the next quality to discuss that leads to aggressive behaviors. Being impulsive often means one is quick to make a decision, typically with little thought. Mental health professionals classify impulsiveness into two categories: behavioral and cognitive.[2] Behavioral impulsivity refers to actions, or the way youth act. Cognitive impulsivity refers to how impulsive youth think. Ultimately, this means that some youth do not take the time to stop, think, and then act; they just act. Both categories explain youth who do not have the skills to "stop and think first" or "make rash decisions" that are not based on good judgment. Problem-solving skills for impulsive youth are often lacking. Usually the ability to stop and think is a function of adolescent brain development and guided practice from the home, school, or examples in the community. Youth who do not have an opportunity to practice effective problem-solving skills will continue to act without thought, which leads to ineffective ways to deal with conflict. Impulsive youth often do the following:

- Act without thinking first
- Cut in line
- Cannot wait their turn in line or in a game
- Blurt out answers in class
- Speak when they're supposed to be quiet
- May show aggressive behaviors
- Are often a little too loud
- Sometimes fight
- Often have poor social skills
- Say the wrong thing at the wrong time

Engaging in self-destructive behaviors is the next individual characteristic that could lead to an aggressive mindset. The act of self-destruction can be viewed as either intentional or unintentional and often is a reflection of all of the domains of violence development. The terms "intentional" and "unintentional" explain the perceived outcomes of the individual who engages in a particular activity. "Did Jamal understand the consequences of his actions?" Youth engage in these types of activities with or without knowledge of their potential negative impact or consequence. Mental health professionals agree that intentional self-destructive behaviors serve the purpose of escaping a problematic situation or occur as a result of a great deal of stress. Both intentional and unintentional types of behavior can exacerbate youth's limited capacity to think clearly and further pile on factors that cause aggression and impulsivity.

Many youth have a mentality of "indestructibility" or think that their risky actions will not cause them harm. Unintentional self-destructive activities are seen as normal risky behaviors that youth engage in as part of growing up and experiencing the world around them. Youth who engage in these activities do not perceive their behaviors as destructive. Alcohol and drug abuse is a great example of a self-destructive behavior that some youth do not see as a potential threat to their success or as having some negative outcome. The reasons for engaging in such activities range from peer pressure to ineffective personal coping skills. Other risky behaviors include negligent behavior such as driving fast, inappropriate weapon use or possession, sexual misconduct, and crime. Regardless of what youth might perceive as outcomes, self-destructive behaviors can lead to utilizing violence to solve problems. Even if violence is not evident, concerns should arise once the behaviors have become repetitive actions without remorse and have increased in intensity and severity.

The last discussion in the individual domain is a young person's past violent victimization or abuse. Being a victim of violence is an incredibly traumatic experience. The damage can have a long-lasting mental effect on youth. Why does being a victim cause potential violent outbursts? Research indicates that kids who are a victim of violence tend to provoke future episodes of violence.[3] Youth who have experienced violence or abuse tend to be more withdrawn from social situations. They may even develop the mentality that the world is out to get them, depending on the severity of their abuse. This type of withdrawal can lead to a "lashing out" that can make them become bullies themselves or, in extreme cases, murderers in a school shooting.

Victims of violence have a higher likelihood of developing a mental disorder. Antisocial personality disorder is common among youth who are abused. This conduct disorder can manifest itself in taking advantage of weaker individuals to gain power.[4] Exhibiting cruelty to defenseless animals is a sign of such a disorder developing. These diagnoses are not confined to youth who are victimized, as other contributing factors can lead to later violent outbursts.

FAMILY FACTORS

The next domain to analyze is the family and/or parents. The family is another important root cause of school violence. It is important to note that dysfunctional families do not all look the same. Some families that exhibit dysfunction have both parents, whereas others have only a single parent in the home. Some families have a higher socioeconomic status, whereas others are below the poverty line. The same can be said in regards to ethnicity and culture. Regardless of these factors, the common denominator is the disconnectedness of youth from their family. Youth who come from homes where parents are withdrawn or provide little to no emotional support generally have a hard time adjusting to the school environment. These students may engage in bad behavior, such as bullying, to draw attention to themselves because of the lack of attention in the home.

Another family factor is the discipline style of the parents. An extremely permissive or excessively harsh approach to discipline can increase youth aggression.[5] Youth with parents who were exposed to an authoritarian childrearing attitude can inadvertently model that behavior by interacting with peers in an unacceptable manner. Families that have loose or inconsistent disciplinary patterns can weaken the relationships between youth and school authority figures such as principals and teachers, thereby further extending the inability to behave as expected in the school setting.

There are many examples of parents who fail to monitor youth activities or lack involvement in their lives. Often parents toward whom these allegations are targeted explain away the problem by citing factors that limit the amount of face-to-face time with their child(ren). Some examples include work schedules, health disabilities, or that their current parental style is similar to how "they" were raised. Regardless of the explanations, this is still a priority concern for most educators: how to involve parents.

Another factor that leads to family disconnection and poor behavior in school is low parental commitment to education. Some believe that parents who may have received little to no formal education will more than likely not emphasize the importance of education to their children. This is not necessarily the case. Parents who may have had little to no formal education usually see the value of an education. Education "commitment" is the key. Families, regardless of their economic or social situation, must be committed and express the importance of academic proficiency. Parents who do not see the value of education will not be as involved in activities related to school. Usually parents who are involved in the school setting are rearing the youth who have the least number of issues.

Another factor that prohibits parental involvement is the parents' "personal" experiences while attending school. If parents had a poor educational experience, they will be more hesitant to even walk into the school, let alone be highly involved in their child's school experience. Administrators across the nation have noted that some parents are uncomfortable when simply attending parent-teacher meetings. These meetings are sometimes intimidating to parents, especially those who feel they are ill equipped to help their child to do better. A perceived feeling of inferiority is another barrier to parental involvement at school. This feeling of inferiority does not always result from interaction with an administrator and/or teacher. Regardless of its origin, the fact remains that this discomfort does exist.

The last family factor regards parental substance abuse or criminality. Parents who have a substance abuse problem put their children at greater risk of having an addiction. For obvious reasons, parents who are not stable because of alcohol or drugs certainly will have problems in creating academic stability in the lives of their children. Well-intentioned parents still fall short of the mark. The same goes for parents involved in crime. Youth who are exposed to these factors on a daily basis are more likely to be involved in crime themselves. There are many instances in which single-parent homes are created because of the incarceration of a parent. This type of instability can also create resentment toward the family or parent. Feelings of embarrassment and inferiority are other burdens for youth with a parent(s) in prison. When these youth compare their own families to their peers' families, often their relationships can become strained and they may resort to expressing their feelings aggressively or engage in violent acts that may start as incidents of bullying. They may feel that "life isn't fair" and create an aggressive "me against the world" attitude.

PEER FACTORS

A student's peer group can also perpetuate aggressiveness and violence. Association with delinquent peers is the most potent factor in helping youth to become disenfranchised from the school community. Negative peer groups can greatly influence students' attitudes and behavior. Because of the all-important desire to be seen as "cool," these associations are socially important to many youth. Peer pressure can coerce some youth to make poor decisions. To avoid any chance of social rejection, youth will commit to negative associations and problem behavior. If no intervention is available, this consistent peer pressure can cause long-term effects on a student's perception of school and academics.

Youth who share a pro-violence attitude and problem behaviors (drinking, smoking, fighting, etc.) are just as popular as youth who are "A" students and on an athletic team. The shared experience of engaging in antisocial and self-destructive behaviors allows youth to bond and justify actions. This negative group dynamic helps in understanding the formation of gangs. By definition, gangs are groups of individuals who are associated on the basis of geography, ethnicity, and/or sociopolitical beliefs. Negative peer group associations are the precursors of gangs. Youth convening is not the problem; the negative behaviors associated with a group dynamic are the issue.

Peer-backing is a violent notion that only perpetuates the behavior and flawed thought process. One of the most infamous cases in which a school shooting was the result of negative peer influence was at Columbine High School in Littleton, Colorado. The two offenders, Eric Harris and Dylan Klebold, were part of a negative peer association named "The Trenchcoat Mafia." Both Klebold and Harris were identified by educators and peers as isolated from the rest of their classmates, a situation that led to feelings of insecurity, helplessness, and a strong need for attention. Being bullied was a strong motivating factor for both offenders, and being victims made them more susceptible to influences from negative peer groups. The two now had a common bond and could share in thoughts of retaliation and revenge similar to the notions of "The Trenchcoat Mafia."

When examining the Columbine case, experts identify the fact that the actions of two young boys were the result of a group encouragement. Without such a negative influence and support from each other that a school shooting was justifiable, the incident may have not occurred. This, of course, is not to neglect the many contributing factors to the actions of Klebold and Harris, but it is stated to shed light on the powerful influence and role of peers in school violence.

COMMUNITY FACTORS

It is important to make the statement that the school is a microcosm of the community. Whatever is going on in the community will be a school problem as well. It would be naïve to think that all youth grow up in communities that support their success and provide them with a plethora of positive role models and examples of success. The reality is that there are far too many communities that have deteriorated so much that it is now a challenge for youth to function, and often their goal is to escape. Community risk factors include availability of drugs, availability of firearms, inappropriate community norms, media violence, low neighborhood attachment and community disorganization, and extreme poverty.

The more available drugs are in a community, the more likely it is that youth will abuse drugs. It is also safe to assume that if the neighborhood is drug infested, then more than likely drugs are sold at school. Research also indicates that the perceived availability of drugs is associated with increased risk of use.[6] Students who perceive that a drug is more available have a higher rate of drug use.

The same goes for the availability of firearms. Since the 1950s, firearm homicides have increased tremendously. Research states that if a gun is present in the house, it is much more likely to be used against a friend or relative than against an intruder or stranger.[7] Although studies report no association between firearm availability and violence, they do show a positive correlation. Simply stated, when a firearm is present, the likelihood of conflict escalating into homicide increases.

It is important to also mention community norms toward destructive behaviors. When communities are accepting of drugs, guns, and violence, this attitude can deeply affect how youth view the world. The result is a clash between neighborhood norms and the school environment. Each entity has a set of guidelines and rules that govern people's actions. For instance, school educators say that if someone is being bullied, you must report it. But in some neighborhoods, the same action of informing an authority figure is regarded as "snitching." Usually youth will rely on the neighborhood rules and will be punished at school because the rules are not congruent. This navigation of "two worlds" is difficult to understand, but youth are faced with these types of decisions daily. Whereas in school fighting is not tolerated, in the streets it is accepted as a strength. It becomes even more confusing for students if they are not taught why these behaviors are unacceptable at the school and community levels.

Community disorganization and deterioration provide absolutely no support for positive youth development. Increased rates of drug problems, violence, and juvenile delinquency provide further detachment from the community. Deteriorated communities have high rates of vandalism and little to no surveillance, and this situation can be found in both poor and wealthy neighborhoods. These communities also have no role models for education and positive conflict management. Youth measure themselves not only against their peer group, but also against accessible adults that they could possibly aspire to emulate. Teachers, preachers, law enforcement personnel, and doctors are all professionals within the community that youth may rely on as a measure for success. And there are also drug dealers, gang members, and other negative adult influences that are competing for the attention of our youth. The absence of educated professionals or legitimate entrepreneurs provides youth with few known options in their career path. An old African proverb, "It takes a village to raise a child," speaks to the interdependency of its members. In addition, some communities have no conventional activities to engage youth. In America's poorest communities, access to activities and programs is limited and sometimes nonexistent. Especially absent are activities that promote academic excellence. Stakeholders, both public and private, attempt to develop strategies to address the growing needs within some of the most desolate communities. No matter how many individuals outside the community provide assistance, the real issue affecting community attachment is whether residents feel that they can make a difference in the lives of youth.

Youth who live in communities that have extreme economic deprivation are more likely to develop problems associated with delinquency, teen pregnancy, school dropout, and especially violence. It is no shock that youth bring into the classroom what they have learned within the community. The community (including parents) is the first and foremost teachers of youth. Youth receive lessons on appropriate behaviors and conflict management on a daily basis. Even if these lessons are not being facilitated by the most capable individuals, youth are taking cues.

SCHOOLS

Lastly, root causes of school violence include educator-to-student relationships. A caring and competent staff is critical to the academic and social success of youth. Often these relationships are not what they should be and are a combination of the educator's inexperience, intolerance, and belief structure. Some teachers are prepared, while others lack the skills to manage a classroom or school environment. Research states that the national retention rate of teachers is three to five years.[8] This statistic indicates that teachers are leaving the profession early, but for what reason? The same study states that the top reason for teachers leaving the classroom is student behavior or inexperience in managing conflict. Universities and colleges are responsible for teacher preparation. Curricula of the past did little to address the growing trends of school violence and the prevention measures that could be taken to effectively deal with simple classroom disruptions. At the collegiate level, there has been a movement toward a more stringent focus on effective classroom management skills. The recognition that teachers are not prepared to handle student behavior causes serious concern across the nation. Schools are also formulating professional development trainings on the subject for current educators in the classroom. Ineffective management can affect not only the student, but also the entire classroom. Youth are always watching and taking note of how a teacher handles a situation. Improper classroom management will allow for students to take advantage of educators and become dismissive of their authority.

The same can be said about an experienced and veteran teacher. Often the sentiments are that they teach the way they were taught. Today there is a different type of child, and the generational gap is more obvious than ever. Old-school ways of dealing with aggression are not as effective for today's youth. This is not to say that discipline should be thrown out the window. But there needs to be a better understanding that youth today are reared differently, that values and morals have changed, and that a new definition of respect has emerged. The threat of informing a parent of inappropriate behavior is not as powerful a deterrent as it has been in the past. Suspensions and expulsions are at an all-time high, simply because of ineffectiveness in dealing with the root problem. Youth are increasingly being released every day into unsupervised care. This occurrence is a reflection of, once again, the inability to connect.

A teacher's intolerance to others' differences can also perpetuate student aggression. Teachers' sensitivity to a student's ethnicity, learning style, and stage-setting rituals is critical to the rapport building needed to foster student success. If an educator is discriminative because of the ethnicity of a student, then this is an obvious problem that can detract from a positive learning environment. In cases such as this, educators who bring a negative belief in the classroom will cause harm. Other attitudes are less deliberate and conscious. Often educators are unaware of their inconsistencies while working with students. But students are astute in observing these inconsistencies and will react in various ways, from withdrawal to aggression. Jacqueline gets more attention than Donovan, with the result that Donovan's self-esteem and perception of schools in general are affected.

Acceptance of students' learning styles is also important. Students learn differently across the board. This is not news to any educator. There are visual learners, audio learners, and haptic learners. The teacher has a challenge to present the curriculum to reach each one of these different learners. If a child does not "get it," then it may or may not be the fault of the educator's style of teaching. Regardless, in some cases students have been misidentified as exceptional children simply because of the teaching pedagogy. This inability to assess a student's learning style and play to his or her strengths can lead to student disconnection from the learning environment.

Other reasons for a teacher's inability to cater to all styles are the pressure to increase test scores and the ever-changing curriculum rigor. These can easily make educators less tolerant to learners who cannot keep up. It is certainly easy to classify a child as an exceptional student; it is harder to make that child exceptional. There is also a theory among educators that one child could potentially slow the entire classroom academic progress. Whether this is true or not, there should be assistance in the form of after-school tutoring or learning labs that can assist the teacher. Yet the reality is that teachers are asked to do more with less. Classroom size has been an issue for the last decade and does not appear to be losing its importance. The classroom dynamics that are not in the control of the teacher will indeed have a negative impact on achievement. Developing a pro-social environment should not be an "add-on" to academics, but rather a *part* of the academic process.

It is also understood that there is some culpability on the students' part. Students' relationships with their teachers can also be a function of how they were reared to respect authority and also their level of commitment toward academic proficiency. Youth who take on adult roles at home will find it difficult to take orders from educators or any other form of authority. Parents who do not convey respect for authority or the importance of education are setting their children up for failure, and this failure reflects poorly on the effectiveness of the school system. Teachers are frustrated daily with student performance and are sincere in their attempt to change lives. The notion that teachers do not give 100 percent in the classroom is inaccurate. Yet the results are undeniable. Either way, this relationship is a two-way street. Putting the blame squarely on the teacher's shoulders is not our intention. Realistically, educators do have a responsibility to connect with youth and to eliminate some of their personal and professional barriers, but it is important to recognize the student's as well as the teacher's role in perpetuating potential aggression.

There are other issues related to the school's role in perpetuating violence that demand recognition. Other culprits include ineffective and inconsistent school policies. Codes of conduct and discipline policies that are not communicated to students and staff, and are not enforced, can lead to potential problems. With little to no enforcement, students may have an opportunity to manipulate rules or even show little respect for the rules. This disrespect can also be facilitated by dilapidated and deteriorated buildings. When schools do not take care of their facilities, then students will follow suit. Some schools may be old and "outdated," but that does not mean they have to be left unattended. Finally, unsupervised time while at the school can lead to undesirable behaviors. Notorious places for nonsurveillance include the bathrooms, under stairwells, behind tall shrubbery, and other secluded areas. Schools that do not create strategies for supervision are inviting potential violence.

CONCLUDING THOUGHT

The domains discussed all contribute to the existence of school violence. The root cause of school violence is hard to categorize under any one domain, and predicting the propensity for incidents of student violence is an inexact science. However, there is a correlation between increased dysfunction in these domains and the potential threat of violence. Understanding these causes is the beginning of a process to develop strategies to prevent and intervene. Because these root causes are interdependent, strategies should be comprehensive as well. Not understanding these causes will not only create ineffective strategy development but will also make violent incidents at the school commonplace.

Chapter 4

Early Warning Signs of Aggressive Behavior

Danya C. Perry

Lamar is a 16-year-old junior at High School High in the metropolis of Everytown, USA. Lamar is a popular "B" student, but some of his teachers observe that he is "falling in with the wrong crowd." In English class, Mrs. Cheney assigned a writing assignment that required students to identify and write about a hero in American history. When Lamar turned in his paper, his hero of choice was the fictional movie character Scarface. He wrote about his admiration for the gangster lifestyle and how Scarface had high-powered guns. Mrs. Cheney, along with the administration, knows that Lamar lives in a violent community where guns are prevalent. Lamar was actually suspended twice last year for carrying a switchblade to school. His explanation of the incidents was that he was being bullied on the school bus by some upperclassmen. Lamar never admitted to using or threatening anyone with the knife, but he carried it for an entire semester. Lamar's grades started to slip into the "C" and "D" range, and although it is school policy to inform parents by sending interim reports, administration thought it would be prudent to speak to his parents by phone. Lamar's mother was sad to hear about his performance and indicated that his attitude had changed as well. She explained that Lamar gave away his Playstation II to his younger cousin and wanted to sell all of his favorite CDs. Administrators questioned Lamar's mother about his overall behavior at home, and she responded that Lamar came home a few days ago with some unexplained injuries. Lamar had never been in a fight at school and has never shared with his mother how he got the injuries. Lamar's mother ended the conversation by informing the administrator that he had broken up with his girlfriend and that in a fit of rage he had talked about hurting those who have hurt him. Lamar's mother did not take this threat seriously, but she is now concerned about what may happen next.

"I didn't think that it could happen here" is a statement made too often by individuals who have experienced tragedies surrounding school violence. This statement causes individuals to analyze and dissect the reasons for violent incidents such as school shootings. The school community will question those who may have observed precursory behaviors. Some individuals will also recollect problem behaviors that were earlier dismissed. Why were these indicators that a student may need help overlooked? Are educators, parents, and others oblivious to obvious cries for help? Or do we just not know what is staring us back in the face?

WHAT IS A WARNING SIGN?

Imagine a neighborhood that is awakened by the sound of sirens. It is 2 a.m. Residents look outside of their windows and see smoke billowing from a house. The next thing they see is people running frantically out of the house in their pajamas. What can one assume? All signs lead to a possible house fire. The warning signs are definitely observable, and the situational factors make it easy to determine the problem. However, when dealing with youth, behavior that leads to school violence is difficult to predict, not always observable by all, and complicated. Understanding the root causes of school violence is critical in this discussion, and identifying valid warning signs assists educators and parents in determining if a potential problem or threat is imminent. Warning signs are not the same for each student. For some situations, different combinations of events, behaviors, and emotions may lead to violent incidents or behaviors.[1] Regardless of the individual, the identifiable warning signs provide "red flags" and indicate a need for further analysis to determine appropriate interventions.

There are many warning signs that can be addressed. Some warning signs relate exclusively to depression and/or suicide. The early warning signs presented here are based on research that looks at the signs of potential violence toward others. Many of the signs of potential aggression are also signs of depression and possible suicide, which need to be addressed through early identification and intervention. Practices that are research-based can be valuable in helping schools recognize the warning signs early so that youth can get the help they need before it is manifested in destructive behaviors.[2] It is important to understand what leads to violence and the types of strategies that have been shown to be effective in preventing violence and other troubling behaviors.

There are many early warning signs that could indicate aggression and school violence. None of these signs alone is sufficient for predicting aggression or violence, and it is certainly harmful to use early warning signs as a checklist against which to match individual children. Jumping to conclusions and overreacting are not recommended. Nevertheless, there are principles that should be used as a guide in identifying early warning signs to aggression and school violence. Educators and parents should emphasize the importance of using warning signs for identification and referral to the correct prevention or intervention services. To accurately identify these signs, it is critical to build close supportive relationships. Educators must know each individual youth and his or her normal attitudes and behaviors before they can recognize a problem that arises or sudden changes in behavior.

PRINCIPLE 1: THE RIGHT WAY TO USE EVIDENCE OF WARNING SIGNS

The first principle is that early warning signs are not used to cause harm but rather to assist in getting help. Children who are troubled should be afforded help early in their lives. The warning signs should not be used to punish or isolate a student; doing so can only exacerbate the problem and create a more volatile situation. Harmful identification of early warning signs can lead to mislabeling or stereotyping a student, which can then result in inappropriate interventions and negative reactions by the school community and parents. Under federal law, there has to be an individualized evaluation by qualified professionals for establishing a formal disability. All referrals to agencies outside of the school must be kept confidential and must be done with parental consent, except in cases of suspected child abuse and neglect.[3] Early warning signs are to help, not to harm.

PRINCIPLE 2: UNDERSTANDING VIOLENCE AND AGGRESSION

The next principle is to understand violence and aggression within a context. Violence is an emotion that may be caused by factors within the home, school, or community. Youth who exhibit violence and aggression do so for various reasons. Those who are fearful in their community may feel the need to be aggressive for self-defensive purposes. Other youth may cope with extreme stress by acting out. The lack of positive coping skills can only perpetuate the problem. This principle is most evident during post-reports of a violent school shooting when determining why a student acted in such a violent manner. Acting out so violently is a perfect example of not having the necessary coping skills. Although the violence is not justifiable, many youth who have committed such violent acts have profiles that include intense and repetitive bullying by peers; family neglect, abuse, and rejection; and/or severe depression and emotional distress.

Avoiding stereotypes is a principle that speaks to the need to deal with youth on a case-by-case manner. Identifying warning signs generically can interfere with the opportunity to help youth. For example, the social construct that "boys will be boys" almost justifies violence between young boys and suggests that violence is a normal part of their development. By accepting this assessment, people dismiss any potential intervention on a potential warning sign. Similarly, using any false cue, such as race, gender, socioeconomic status, or physical appearance, to label youth can perpetuate the problem. Stereotyping will also aid in the misassessment of a potential problem. If the school community insists that African American males are the purveyors of most aggression on a campus, then there is a potential to "overlook" other warning signs within other subgroups.

Children have different levels of development based on their different social and emotional capabilities. Youth who are 2 years of age express themselves differently than 12-year-olds. This calls for the need to identify warning signs within an appropriate developmental context. Educators and parents must understand what behavior is typical for elementary, middle, and high school students. Younger students tend to act on their emotions and leave rationality at the door, whereas older students are better equipped to deal with their emotions.

Another important principle is not to overreact to any single warning sign. Educators and parents need to understand that youth who are at risk of aggression and violence typically exhibit multiple warning signs. These warning signs are usually repeated and increase in intensity over time. Constant monitoring is critical when determining appropriate interventions. It is also important to make all who are involved with youth aware of warning signs to assist in the identification and monitoring of any potential problem behaviors.

PRINCIPLE 3: THE COMPLEXITY OF MULTIPLE DOMAINS

The last principle is to understand that warning sings can be observed in multiple domains. Youth who act out aggressively in the home do not necessarily do so in the classroom. Other youth may act out violently in the school but never exhibit these problem behaviors in the community. As alluded to earlier, constant communication between parents, educators, and other youth-serving professionals is critical in the identification process. Early warning signs that are observable must be communicated appropriately to develop prevention and intervention strategies. It is also important to empower all students to report if they identify potential problem behavior in their classmates. Often it is only after a violent incident, such as a school shooting, that students will speak up about observing negative behaviors. Establishing open lines of communication will assist in the accurate reporting of warning signs within the school community and neighborhood.

Understanding and recognizing the various warning signs are important in developing successful intervention strategies. Early warning signs are not equally significant, nor will they be presented in order of seriousness. These warning signs can only be used in the context of their prevalence for a specific student. Some students may have a different combination of events, behaviors, and emotions that could possibly lead to aggression and violent behavior. Whether there is one warning sign or multiple signs, each sign is a serious indicator that an intervention is warranted. The following are some early warning signs.

Feelings of Isolation, Being Alone, and Social Withdrawal

Many children who appear to be "loners" are not violent and will never have violent tendencies. Although experts agree that isolation and social withdrawal could be indicators of internal issues that may hinder the development of needed social affiliations, social withdrawal by itself does not mean that students will be violent. However, in school shooting cases, the youth were described as being socially withdrawn and isolated from others. School and family disconnections were the norm when these incidents were later examined. It is also important to note the students who have many friends and then suddenly withdraw and become distant. This is an obvious warning sign that there may be a problem.

Excessive Feelings of Rejection

Rejection is a normal and inevitable part of growing up. Most youth experience being rejected from a sought-out peer group, while others may experience more emotionally damaging rejection from the family or a parent. Regardless of either or both situations, rejection can lead to reacting negatively, which includes acting out violently. Youth who are rejected from a peer group usually find solace by hanging out with other peers who may encourage negative activities. Substance abuse and violence are normal activities in extreme cases. In these cases, without support and intervention, youth can find themselves thinking that the world is "out to get them" and will potentially react violently against themselves and others.

Being a Victim of Violence

Simply put, students who are victims of violence are at risk themselves of becoming violent toward themselves or others. Research indicates that youth who are victimized or bullied have a high propensity to act out aggressively. This aggression can be foreseen in drawings, writings, cruelty toward animals, and other signs of distress. Regarding the cases of school shootings that involved multiple victims, the FBI reports that the common denominator of all perpetrators is that they were all reported as being the targets of bullying.[4]

Feelings of Being Picked On and Persecuted

Adolescence, emotionally and physically, can be a challenging phase of life for most youth. Because of this development and the ever-changing landscape of emotions, some students have normal self-esteem issues and prevalent desires to be accepted. Students who are frequently bullied or teased usually withdraw from social situations or avoid their persecutors at all costs. Constant humiliation from peers can cause some students to not only withdraw but to also act out aggressively. The mindset that can develop is one of "us verses them." An ostracized youth can find comfort in other students who have experienced similar incidents and can therefore find support for perpetuating antisocial behaviors.

Low School Interest and Poor Academic Performance

Low academic achievement can occur for many different reasons. Building rapport with students will make it easier to assess the conditions that could have possibly led to a drop in achievement or school interest. Those conditions could range from being a victim of school violence to lack of connection with teachers or the school environment. Each situation is different, and it is important to evaluate each student to determine the nature of the problem. Without such interventions, chronic poor academic performance can lead to frustration and potentially violence.

Expression of Violence in Writings and Drawings

It is normal for students to express their feelings and thoughts, whether positive or negative, in their writings or drawings. Such activities are encouraged in normal child development. Students are also encouraged to use art and writing to vent instead of doing the alternative, which is usually a negative activity. When educators or parents find writings or drawings that are directed toward specific individuals and have been consistent over time, this should raise a "red flag" that there are emotional problems that could potentially lead to aggression. It is important not to overreact, but it is equally important not to be passive. Referring a student to a counselor or psychologist can assist in understanding the meaning and intent.

Uncontrolled Anger

Being angry is a natural emotion that everyone exhibits from time to time. The expression of anger can range from shouting at the top of one's lungs to being completely silent; everyone expresses it differently. Educators and parents are tasked to teach youth about monitoring anger and ensuring that it does not lead to destructive decisions. An early warning sign is when students exhibit anger frequently and intensely. Anger that goes unchecked can lead to possible violence toward the self and others.

Patterns of Impulsive and Chronic Hitting, Intimidating, and Bullying Behaviors

Children often engage in mildly aggressive behaviors, and these are usually a normal part of growing up. The warning sign to look for is when the physical aggression is consistent and intensifies, especially when it is unprovoked or out of context. This staircased aggression can certainly escalate and lead to more serious destructive behaviors if left unchecked.

History of Discipline Problems

Students who have consistent behavior and disciplinary problems are commonly displaying a sign that some of their emotional needs are being unmet. If not managed, discipline problems can easily lead to further disconnection from the school, community, and family. Not following the rules in school often leads to not following the rules and norms of society. Once disengaged, youth are at a higher risk of engaging in aggression and violent behaviors.

History of Violent and Aggressive Behavior

Research asserts that youth with a violent past and upbringing are more than likely to repeat those behaviors.[5] If a child is under the age of 12 and is engaging in bullying incidents, cruelty to animals, and other antisocial behaviors, he or she is more prone to exhibit similar behaviors as he or she gets older. It is critical to identify these early patterns in both the home and the school. If no one intervenes, the frequency and intensity of the violent acts can lead to serious harm to self and others.

Intolerance of Differences and Prejudicial Attitudes

Youth who have strong negative feelings against individuals based on their race, ethnicity, gender, sexual orientation, or physical appearance, along with other factors, can be led to violence targeting any of the aforementioned groups. These attitudes should not go unchecked. Sharing prejudicial words and thoughts can escalate to becoming involved in hate crimes and therefore should be viewed as a serious early warning sign.

Drug and Alcohol Use

The use of drugs and alcohol is almost viewed as a normal part of growing up. In fact, drug and alcohol abuse is seen as socially acceptable and is glorified by youth peer groups. Regardless of the perception, substance abuse is not only detrimental to one's health and development but can also lead to loss of self-control. This reduction in inhibitions can lead to increased levels of violence towards self and others, especially when coupled with other risk factors.

Affiliation with Gangs

Students who decide to join a gang or mimic gang activities are more prone to violence than youth who do not engage in these activities. Gang membership supports antisocial behaviors and engagement in high-risk activities. The perpetuation of such activities over a long period of time desensitizes youth, and violence against others then becomes the norm and part of being involved in the gang culture. If youth are validated as gang members early, then interventions must occur to deter any potential aggression and violence. The longer educators and parents wait to intervene, the more difficult it becomes to implement effective strategies.

Inappropriate Access to, Possession of, and Use of Firearms

Youth who have access to firearms have increased likelihood of being violent and also of becoming a victim to violence.[6] Families can reduce inappropriate access and use by restricting and supervising the usage of firearms. Regardless of monitoring, if students have high impulsivity, a history of aggression, or other emotional problems, they could certainly use firearms in a destructive manner.

Serious Threats of Violence

In a frustrated and emotional state, idle threats are a common response. Although it should be taken in all seriousness, often the threat does not warrant intensive interventions. A threat becomes serious only when it is detailed and specific. Understanding the nature and context of threats is critical to taking action. If not handled expeditiously, they could potentially be carried out and become fatal. Idle or not, a response is needed.

PUTTING WARNING SIGNS IN PERSPECTIVE

The aforementioned early warning signs of aggressive behavior require appropriate and timely interventions to ensure that youth do not engage in destructive activities down the road. At the same time, there are imminent warning signs that require an immediate response. Imminent warning signs give educators and parents a view of how close youth are to potentially harming themselves or others. These are overt, serious, and hostile acts that are directed toward educators, students, parents, or other individuals. It is critical to intervene early and immediately so that behaviors do not become an imminent danger to the school community.

Imminent warning signs may include the following:

- Serious fighting with educators, students, or parents
- Written plans or the development of "hit lists"
- Severe destruction of property
- Consistent and detailed expression of violence through artwork or writings
- Severe rage for seemingly minor reasons
- Visits to Web sites that promote and glorify past violent school shootings
- Specific threats of lethal violence
- Possession and/or use of firearms and other weapons
- Self-mutilation or threats of suicide[7]

When any one or more of the listed warning signs is evident, immediate action must be taken; hence, taking the stance of "better safe than sorry" is the best option. Immediate interventions by law enforcement, parents, school authorities, mental health, and other appropriate organizations are warranted at this level.

CONCLUDING THOUGHT

Regardless of the situation, prevention has always been the best solution to ensure that youth do not engage in violent activities or behave aggressively. Schools and parents that act rather than react will fare better when dealing with youth who have the potential to be violent. Although we know that prevention is key, it is just as important to have intervention strategies available. Prior to the utilization of prevention or intervention strategies, recognizing the warning signs is the first step toward ensuring a safe environment conducive to learning.

Chapter 5

Addressing Risk and Building Resiliency

Danya C. Perry

Explaining the realities of risk factors that impact our youth sometimes is a difficult process. In an attempt to make the conversation on risk factors more "real," we incorporate activities into presentations given to community and school groups. Of the many attempted activities, I rely on what is called the "Walk of Life" to speak about the risks youth are faced with and the needed opportunities to build resiliency. The "Walk of Life" is simple; all you need is a piece of tape and a willing participant.

This is how it goes. Lay approximately 15 feet of tape on the floor and explain to the audience that this represents the walk or journey toward success for our youth. The beginning of the tape represents the beginning of life, and the end of the tape represents their measure of success, whether it is graduating from high school, going to college, getting a job, or entering the military—whatever success means to them.

The participant from the audience will represent all youth in America and take this journey. I usually give the participant some preparatory statements before we start the activity, just so that we are in line. I then ask the participant to start walking from the beginning and attempt to make it to the end. The participant steps onto the tape, carefully making sure that he or she walks the line like a tightrope. One wrong move could mean disaster for the youth of America. The participant successfully makes it to the end the first time he or she walks, and I discuss all the protective factors in the lives of youth that gave him or her the strength to make it through.

I then ask the participant to do it again, and this time as he or she walks the tape, I stick my leg out midway through and try to make the participant trip or stumble. With preparation the participant stops, recognizes my leg as an obstacle, and easily steps over it to make it to the end. Seems easy enough. I then ask the participant to walk the line again, and this time I shove the participant once he or she gets to the midway point. As with the last stumbling block, the participant recognizes that he or she is off the lined tape and returns to complete the journey to the end.

Now I ask the participant to make this journey for the final time. At the midway point, I step in front of the participant. The participant attempts to walk around me, and I step back in his or her way. The participant attempts to push me, and I push back. He or she may try a myriad of other moves, but to no avail. The participant cannot get around me; I represent a huge risk factor that seems insurmountable. This is where I bridge the gap in discussion. I indicate that we need to give youth the ability and resilience to hit a risk factor (as big as me) and figure out a way to get around it.

Easy enough and makes a great point, or so I thought.

I tried this very routine activity in Albany, New York, at a conference on dropout prevention and had an opportunity to meet Sam. Sam was a young man who was sitting with a group of young people in the back of my session, and I called on him to be a participant in the "Walk of Life." What better person to assist in explaining the challenges of youth? I went through the motions and I got to the part where I stood in front of the participant, Sam, to explain the seemingly insurmountable risk factor. Sam tried to walk around me; I stepped in front of him. Sam tried to fake me out; I didn't fall for it. I then placed one hand on his shoulder to prevent him from getting around me as I discussed with the rest of the audience the dynamics of risk factors. All of a sudden Sam elbowed me in the chest and quickly crawled under my legs to reach the end of the tape.

I was now befuddled, confused, and a little shocked that I was just punched by some kid in my presentation. I could not believe it. He messed up my attempt to explain this topic in a visible way. As I refrained from making any inflammatory remarks, I thought, this is a great teachable moment. So I took my foot off his neck and picked him off the floor and said "EXACTLY!! This is exactly what we need to do. We need to give our youth the tools to reach their goals, by any means necessary. They need to kick, scratch, fight, and punch through any risk factors that may impede their success. Whatever it takes." So the point was made and everybody was happy. And for the record, I actually didn't step on Sam's neck. Did I want to do it? Well, that's another book entirely.

RISK AND PROTECTIVE FACTORS

Two decades ago, the notion of "risk factors" was a derivative from the health profession and was normally associated with factors that led to heart disease, high blood pressure, and other health problems. "Risk factors" is now used to describe factors that put youth at greater risk for becoming violent. Many factors can contribute and influence a range of behaviors that can lead to incidents of school and youth violence. The National Youth Violence Prevention Resource Center speaks to the dynamics between risk and protective factors in an ecological framework. This model recognizes and supports the notion of domains or complex networks of individual, family, community, and environmental factors that impact youth's ability to avoid risk. Once again, the background of this framework is a public health perspective on reducing risks and preventing diseases, illness, and injury. Understanding these factors will give educators a more comprehensive view of the nature of the problem. This multileveled approach helps in understanding the nature of school violence and identifying points of intervention that are essential in building resiliency. These characteristics or domains originate from the individual youth, relationships with family and peers, the school, and the community. It is therefore important for educators to look beyond individuals who seem at risk and pay close attention to their surroundings.

Across the nation there are educators and youth advocates who do not buy in to the notion of a risk factor that accurately predicts behavior. This is absolutely correct, as there are many examples of youth who have endured seemingly insurmountable risks from various domains and achieved academic and social success. The examination of the risk factors that lead to youth violence should help us develop effective strategies to prevent and intervene. The risk factors that face youth today should not negatively shape the beliefs or behaviors of educators and other youth-serving professionals in their attempt to deliver services.

Research shows that the presence of one risk factor does not in itself cause violent behavior, but the combination of multiple risks can shape attitudes and behaviors over the course of adolescence. Risk factors normally impact youth in a cumulative way. The greater the number of risk factors, the greater the likelihood that the youth will engage in violent or risky behaviors. Research has also proven that problem behaviors and risk factors tend to cluster. The confluence of risk factors can lead to violent behavior, and we need to be cognizant of these risks to provide opportunities to increase protective factors and build resiliency.

The implementation of effective prevention and intervention strategies must take into account the dynamics of both risk factors and protective factors. Protective factors are important because they can decrease the likelihood of risk factors having a detrimental impact on positive youth development. Many of the factors that make it likely that youth will engage in risky behaviors are the opposite of the protective factors that will make it likely that youth will not engage in such behaviors. For example, family dysfunctions and an unstable living environment can enhance the likelihood that a child will engage in delinquent behaviors or substance abuse. Inversely, a protective factor is present if the home provides both a nurturing and structured environment, as it could increase the likelihood that youth will not get involved in risky behaviors. All youth are faced with risks, but the greatest concern is for those who are exposed to constant risk with the relative absence of protective factors. This dynamic dramatically increases the probability that youth will engage in risky behaviors. To decrease school and youth violence, it is imperative to reduce risk factors while increasing protective factors from every domain. The question is, How do educators impact the risk factor of a dysfunctional home? How do we move youth from dysfunctional behaviors to engaging in positive activities? This has been the question that plagues most school officials.

Ron Edmonds stated that "a school can create a coherent environment so potent that for at least six hours a day it can override almost everything else in the lives of children. This being so, schools and educators have a tremendous opportunity to move mountains."[1] In the following discussion, both risk and protective factors will be organized into categories that reflect their level of influence. Understanding that individuals operate in the context of their surroundings, the discussion will start with broader environmental factors and move to specific factors that relate to the individual.

COMMUNITY

First, environmental factors can contribute to a culture of violence among a group of people or a community. The factors at this level that may contribute to violence include accessibility to firearms, media violence, poverty, and an increasingly evident gap between youth and adults. It has always been evident that socioeconomic status directly correlates with the existence of violence. Unemployment, situational and generational poverty, and hopelessness for better economic opportunities—all contribute to higher levels of violence within a community. Youth who are a part of these conditions are more likely to view violence as a necessary evil. This misperception comes from sources such as the media, which reinforce the need for violence as an effective strategy to gain financially and socially. Research has shown that youth who are overexposed to violence in the media may become desensitized to violence. The sound of a gunshot is no longer a cause for panic. Media also contribute to the perception that violence is a normal part of life and reinforce the notion that it is an effective way to solve problems. Educators have witnessed youth who believe that it is a far greater sin to be hungry than to commit a crime that could assist in getting their basic needs met.

Community deterioration and disorganization also contribute to the risk for violence among youth. Community-level factors are a direct result of environmental factors and are closely connected. At the community level, researchers have found that the prevalence of drugs, weapons, gangs, poor housing, crime rates, and the lack of quality educational and recreational activities leads to increased incidents of violence.[2] Limited access to positive and productive development activities can easily make youth succumb to destructive behaviors. It is important to note that these dynamics are not exclusive to communities that are crime-ridden. Suburban, middle-income communities can also include factors that contribute to school violence. Gangs, weapons, and drugs are not restricted to one type of demographic. Early research linked these risk factors to certain socioeconomic conditions, but this is not necessarily the case today. Horrific scenes of school violence in rural, middle America have dispelled the belief that urban, low-socioeconomic areas are largely the perpetrators of school violence. Either way, community factors are instrumental in the playing out of violence in American youth. But even with the risk in the community that youth face, there are also many opportunities in the community to build resiliency.

Creating a strong infrastructure that is supportive of educational attainment is important. Across the nation, communities have embraced the notion that "it takes a village to raise a child." This means providing youth with opportunities to participate in activities that build social competencies, ensure decision-making power, and enable youth to share responsibility. Community engagement in all forms builds new skills, increases self-esteem, and gives youth a sense of power to change their situation. The following community factors and activities can be directly attributed to high levels of resilience in youth:

- Increasing caring relationships with adults
- Providing access to basic necessities, including housing, food, health care, education, child care, recreation, and employment
- Providing opportunities for meaningful involvement and participation
- Creating a culture of high expectations
- Increasing positive relationships with and among families
- Avoiding youth stereotypes and labeling[3]

FAMILY AND PEERS

Risk factors that are prevalent within the family structure or are part of the family dynamics have a direct correlation with youth propensity to engage in violent activity. Millions of youth are faced with families and parents who do not create the supportive and loving environments that are necessary for their positive development. Research has demonstrated that family neglect and abuse have played a significant role in violent outbursts, especially in males. Parents who are overtly abusive physically or verbally can create an environment of distrust and resentment that can lead to youth harboring a "me against the world" attitude. Youth who experience such abuse and neglect are about 50 percent more likely to be abusive as adults.[4] They also tend to develop deep psychological problems that can lead to perpetual victimization and internalization of feelings that can end in severe violent outbursts. Other youth may develop patterns of engaging in bullying incidents and finding comfort in others' misery. Either way, these patterns of behavior that are derived from dysfunctional families are common across all backgrounds.

Youth who feel that they have no familial support will resort to finding a surrogate family through their peers that often supports antisocial behaviors (substance abuse, sexual promiscuity, and criminality). Interestingly, parents and families may also inadvertently create an environment that does not support positive youth development. Physical or verbal abuse and neglect are not always the culprit. Lack of parental interaction and involvement is also likely to increase the risk for violence. Parents that do not set clear expectations, have inadequate supervision and monitoring, and provide inconsistent discipline also contribute to delinquent and violent behavior. Parents who do not engage their youth can inadvertently perpetuate the problem and almost create a feeling within youth that the behavior is acceptable. Lastly, exposure to high levels of marital and family discord or conflict can increase the development of antisocial or delinquent behaviors in youth. Other familial risk factors include the following:

- Family history of problem behavior or parent criminality
- Family management problems
- Poor family attachment or bonding
- Pattern of high family conflict
- Family violence
- Having a young mother or father
- Sibling antisocial behavior
- Family transitions
- Low parent education level or illiteracy[5]

Youth learn vital social competencies primarily from family interactions and parental guidance. There is no such thing as a perfect family structure, but without counteracting support, incidents such as divorce or situational poverty can negatively impact youth.

There is a saying that "birds of a feather flock together." So what happens when a nondelinquent child "flocks" with negative peers? Will deviant peers reinforce antisocial behaviors? Or is the child's association with deviant peers simply another manifestation of the child's predisposition to delinquency? Either way, negative peer influence can lead to increased aggression and violence. Research states that there is a strong correlation between deviant peer influences on nondelinquent juveniles and violence. According to a national youth survey, juveniles between the ages of 11 and 17 were negatively influenced by their deviant peer group. This association led to other crimes as well. This trend increases as youth become more involved with delinquent peers and more serious offences follow, which can lead to the highest level of negative association: gangs.[6]

It is important to note that peer rejection is also a risk factor for aggression and antisocial behaviors. Youth who have been rejected by their peers are significantly at greater risk for chronic antisocial behavior when compared to youth who are not rejected. A case study examined this notion and revealed that peer rejection in the third grade predicted greater antisocial behaviors from the sixth grade onward.[7] These same problem behaviors will persist well into early adulthood. Interestingly enough, peer rejection can lead to a perceived reality that other classmates will do the same. This belief can lead to increased aggression in response. Another explanation is that rejection can cause youth to have less positive interactions with peers and so will become a part of deviant peer groups. Once associated, youth may increase their engagement in negative activities to gain standing in these groups.[8]

Along with developing strategies for positive peer interactions, it is important to relay to the family that they play an important role in the prevention of school violence. Parents, primary caregivers, grandparents, siblings, aunts, and uncles can protect youth and build resiliency by emphasizing the importance of education and offering affection and a supportive infrastructure (see Figure 5.1). The family must provide support via open lines of communication and conversations that surround measures of success and expectations. Former Secretary Colin Powell spoke of his upbringing and being saved from the streets by his family and a system he called the "Aunt-Net." In an interview on CBS's *Face the Nation*, Powell said, "When I set off to school each morning, I had an aunt in every other house, stationed at the window with eyes peeled, ready to spot the slightest misbehavior on my part and report it back to my parents." He added, "The Internet pales in comparison to the Aunt-Net." Powell spoke to the need for the expansion of the family, effective communication, and being proactive to early warning signs that could lead to delinquent behaviors. Other family-level protective factors include clear boundaries for behavior and the enforcement of household rules. Discipline plays an integral part in youth social development. Family discipline is not the enemy of enthusiasm and should be seen as a necessity in ensuring that youth develop proper values.

1. Make connections and encourage friendships
2. Help your child by having him or her help others
3. Maintain a daily routine
4. Take a break—worrying can be counter-productive
5. Teach your child self-care
6. Move toward your goals
7. Nurture a positive self-view
8. Keep things in perspective and maintain a hopeful outlook
9. Look for opportunities for self-discovery
10. Accept that change is part of living

Kenneth Ginsburg, *A Parent's Guide to Building Resilience in Children and Teens* (Elk Grove, IL: American Academy of Pediatrics, 2006), 19–25.

Figure 5.1. 10 Tips for Building Resilience in Children and Teens

Educators must also develop strategies to reduce antisocial behaviors associated with peer influence. Initial strategies should be aimed at creating an environment that does not perpetuate negative peer influence. They should ensure that there is little to no unsupervised time, along with constant conversations and staff developments on the issue of signs of gang activity. Schools should implement policies and codes of conduct that stress respect for others. The implementation of character education classes or themes can serve as a backdrop to the school's approach to creating conducive learning environments, starting with the people in it. Other strategies can include reducing contact with all negative peer associations. If there is contact, students should be prepared to handle any situation by building prosocial skills and learning to resolve peer conflicts.[9] Students can also be encouraged to see their school community as a place where they can be respected for their individuality. Interestingly, adolescents choose friends who "look just like them" or have characteristics or talents they admire. These characteristics can serve as a motivator to act as their friends act. Although this interaction is evident in negative peer associations, it can also be manifested in a positive way. In a Canadian school, friends encouraged each other to study hard and to think creatively. The high-achieving peers had a positive effect on adolescents' satisfaction with school and educational expectations.[10] In Canada, 80 percent of graduates from high school had friends who thought that school was important.[11] Research supports the notion that students who have friends who like school and get good grades are more likely to graduate from high school.[12]

How can educators achieve positive peer association? National events, such as "Mix-It-Up Day," speak to the need for students to break out of their "box" and socialize with others. Strategies such as this recognize the need to accept diversity, but more importantly to stress positive peer interaction, which leads to a more conducive learning environment. Some best practices in creating such an environment that fosters positive peer interactions include the following:

- Providing activities that encourage positive peer interaction
- Engaging in schoolwide activities with positive reinforcement (such as "Fight-Free Days")
- Utilizing "study circles" or facilitated discussions for youth on various topics
- Developing peer mentor programs
- Targeting interventions for students who have problems "getting along" with others
- Developing peer mediation to assist with problem solving
- Providing training for parents on the topic of "knowing your child's friends"
- Giving youth opportunities to become involved meaningfully at school

Building positive peer interactions is not a problem that is limited to the school. Involving the community and encouraging volunteers and mentors to work with youth can yield positive results. Having positive role models to encourage respect and effective management in conflict can assist all educators in their attempt to create safe schools.

SCHOOL

With community and family conditions being as they are for many youth in America, youth frustrations are magnified when they cannot find employment because of limited job skills, insufficient training, or logistics such as transportation. This frustration obviously filters down from parents or guardians to the youth, and a sense of hopelessness ensues. With time, youth tend to view school as a place that does not breed success, especially when there are no examples of success through education within their immediate environment. Youth who are plagued with these thoughts tend not to believe in what educators and other authority figures teach in regard to traditional success through schooling. This distrust goes both ways. Often adults do not view youth as a valuable asset to be utilized. The current youth culture is being painted as violent, unmotivated, unsupervised, and delinquent. As a result of this mutual distrust, youth may find it difficult to involve themselves meaningfully in the school or community. This lack of connection leads to alienation and disenfranchisement from society and breeds the probability of delinquent or violent behavior, even if only used as a way to garner attention.

Poor academics and poor achievement can also result in violence. This relationship is stronger for youth who are consistently absent from school, for whatever reason. Dropping out of school also correlates strongly with increased incidents of violence. In schools that seek to build resilience among their youth, educators should push for incorporating experiences into the school that provide for the following:

- Competency: the feeling of being successful
- Belonging: the feeling of being valued
- Usefulness: the feeling of being needed
- Potency: the feeling of being empowered
- Optimism: the feeling of being encouraged and hopeful[14]

Educators should proceed to integrate these themes in writing, social studies, mathematics, reading, and science. The specific processes of increasing protective factors fall into four general categories: assessing self, building caring relationships, having high expectations, and creating opportunities to contribute to others.

As a best practice, educators and other youth-serving professionals need to always keep in mind that despite of all the risk and adversity, the majority of individuals will be successful. Do most young people considered to be at risk for violence actually become perpetrators? No, only a small percentage of youth become seriously or chronicically violent.[15] This question could lead to the perception that adults have of an individual youth and the subsequent attitudes and behaviors that could possibly impact the youth's achievement. This is not meant to suggest that educators are malicious in their mission to teach, but to assist in understanding how one's perceptions could lead to ineffective instruction. For example, if a student comes to school with a laundry-list of risk—family dysfunction, impulsive tendencies, and crime-ridden neighborhood—does this change the delivery of instruction? Most educators would say that it would not change how the student is being taught; if anything, it would intensify efforts to overcome the risk and build resiliency. At the same time, it is a tough reality to face when one knows that there are educators, knowingly or not, who believe that a student with seemingly insurmountable risks will not achieve to the level of their expectations. With these beliefs and attitudes, teachers' expectations begin to lower, and so does their ability to reach those high-need youth. This is more of a phenomenon than one would think. Resiliency building oftentimes starts with the individual educator. Educators must at all times believe that all youth can be successful, no matter what their circumstances. An assessment of one's attitudes and beliefs is warranted if the resiliency-building process is to be successful. Everybody has strengths and weaknesses, and it is important for educators to realize what they bring to the table and their own areas that need improvement. If one is more tolerant of boys than girls, blacks than whites, primary than secondary students, these dynamics need to be assessed. All of these are important aspects in determining if schools are the perpetuators in the disenfranchisement of our youth. A study looked at the walking patterns of African American boys and came to the conclusion that academic success was directly correlated to how these young boys walked.[16] Does that make any sense? The study continued by defining ethnic walk patterns by saying that European-American boys walk with an "erect posture, leg and arm swing synchronized with posture and pace, a steady stride, and a straight head," whereas African American boys walk with "a deliberate swaggered or bent posture, head held slightly tilted to the side, one foot dragging, and an exaggerated knee bend or dip." Do speed, posture, and pace have a direct impact with student achievement or even IQ? Not at all. The study asserts that it is not the actual walk pattern of these boys that impacts academic achievement, but rather the educators who view the walk patterns and reach a judgment. The assessment process needs to be founded on what resiliency research says about youth development:

- Most youth "make it"
- All individuals have the power to transform and change
- Teachers and schools have the power to transform lives
- It is how we do what we do that counts
- Teachers' beliefs in innate capacity start the change process[17]

Understanding these facets along with assessing one's beliefs is the beginning strategy in the resiliency-building process. Regardless of students' background, demographics, or history, they all should have an opportunity to better themselves, and educators have an unbelievable amount of power in crafting their success.

The next school-initiated best practice centers on empowering caring relationships. Caring and competent relationships with youth are critical in building resiliency. Researchers have stressed the centrality of caring relationships in the educational process and the connection to positive outcomes. Caring, respectful, and participatory relationships are the determining factors in whether a student learns, whether parents become engaged, whether change in education is sustained, and lastly whether youth feel they have a place in their school community.[18] Most youth who cite an educator who is their "favorite" usually do so because of a combination of skillful teaching and emotional support. Youth who do not experience this are more than likely to experience alienation from school. But what can be done specifically to make educators more caring and competent? Can caring and emotionally supportive attitudes be taught, or is it the fiber of a person's being? Educators inherently are caring individuals, much like most humans. But schools have to ensure that there is an organizational capacity to foster these caring relationships. Most research cites that smaller learning communities and class sizes, within larger schools, will help students and teachers build such a rapport. Although many schools logistically may not be able to accommodate such a request, they should provide an opportunity to make healthy connections by creating one-on-one time with students. With high teacher-student ratios, this can prove challenging, but nevertheless it can be done. This one-on-one time is more about quality than quantity. Spending time tutoring youth who need assistance, engaging youth in peripheral school programs, and knowing the "ins and outs" of youth all count in this process. Educators must also be innovative in their approaches. They must think outside the box and determine ways to build bridges to youth by having youth participate in developing classroom rules or lesson plans. In this rapport-building process, educators must use appropriate self-disclosure. Conversations about one's educational achievements, challenges in social development, and even personal bouts with substance abuse can be considered appropriate. Using good judgment regarding one's personal life is important, but it is also important to show youth that educators were in their shoes once, even if it was a long, long time ago.

The next school-based strategy relates to the need to have high expectations and adequate support. Research indicates that schools that convey high expectations for their students have increased rates of academic success and more importantly lower rates of problematic behaviors. To accomplish this, educators must have a "resilient attitude" and believe in the potential of their youth. In a paralleling activity, educators must also provide adequate support to enable youth to reach their potential. Expectations that are high without support will never work and can set youth up for failure. The combination of the two enables youth to believe in themselves and to develop self-reliance, self-esteem, autonomy, self-efficacy, and optimism. In a study of middle schools, it was found that schools can best support the need for competence through positive teacher regard for students and instructional practices that encourage adolescents to view self-improvement, effort, and task mastery as the benchmarks of competence and academic success.[19]

The last strategy is providing youth with an opportunity to contribute. Educators should strive toward finding meaningful opportunities for youth to be involved in the school community. This sense of involvement can be achieved by a range of activities and practices. Asking questions that encourage discussion and participation, using hands-on learning, involving youth in lesson planning, and allowing youth to create the rules of the classroom are all examples. Other approaches that are more cooperative include peer helping, cross-age mentoring, and encouraging civic and community service. Research has shown that empowering youth to work with other youth is an effective violence prevention strategy. According to the International Association for Cooperation in Education, over a thousand studies support cooperative peer learning, and most of them have documented positive outcomes in cognitive, moral, emotional, and social development. The following positive outcomes increase:

- Academic scores
- Empathy
- Social skills
- Acceptance of ethnic, racial, and physical diversity
- Conflict management
- Self-esteem and control
- Positive attitudes towards school
- Critical thinking[20]

Meaningful involvement via peer programs has shown positive effects; this success is due to the ongoing participatory opportunities for youth, a basic belief in youth's ability to contribute, and learning in a social context. Youth have a say in being joint architects, which promotes feelings of control and autonomy. Obviously, this would allow for educators to now focus on instruction rather than control.

The risk factors discussed certainly seem insurmountable, and educators must understand their role in the alleviation of risk. Educators are not asked to take on the whole spectrum of risk, although they are usually exhibited in the classroom and school. It is important to understand that the different risk factors take on greater or lesser importance depending on the different stages of a child's life. Educators can assist in planning for developmentally appropriate strategies to combat risk factors at any level. Schools should not be responsible for societal ills, but they can play an integral role in ensuring that risk factors do not impact academic and social success, while reducing the likelihood of school violence.

INDIVIDUAL

The last factor to examine includes that of the individual youth. Most research on youth violence points to risk factors as they relate to individual characteristics that predict or contribute to violence. In understanding individual risk factors, it is important to not inappropriately label or stereotype youth because they possess a certain characteristic or fit a specific profile. Individual risk factors need to be viewed within a developmental framework to avoid misinterpretation. In other words, one needs to know what is an appropriate behavior at a certain age. Also, one must realize that violent behavior is usually a product of multiple factors that operate on many levels, especially in the absence of protective factors. Youth can simply be acting within the context of their environmental experiences. Research from the U.S. Department of Justice found evidence that suggests a correlation between violent behavior and conditions such as hyperactivity, concentration problems, restlessness, and risk taking. Although more research is needed, this sheds a light on the fact that risk factors may not always be derived from environmental, community, or family sources. They could also be related to mental health disorders, such as depression, among youth with delinquent or violent histories. Another predictor of more serious and chronic violence is aggression from an early onset (ages 6–13). Youth who are engaged in violence during early adolescence are more likely to be more aggressive and exhibit destructive decision making in later years.

Educators understand that those who have difficulty in academics usually find it frustrating to exist in the school environment, especially youth who have not experienced success on any level. As an educator would explain, most youth who have difficulty reading, when asked to read in class, will do anything to distract the teacher from the fact that they cannot complete the academic task. Other individual risk factors include the following:

- Antisocial behavior and alienation, delinquent beliefs, general delinquency involvement, and drug dealing
- Gun possession, illegal gun ownership or carrying
- Teen parenthood
- Favorable attitudes toward drug use, early onset of alcohol or drug use
- Intellectual and/or development disabilities
- Poor refusal skills
- Life stressors
- Early sexual involvement[13]

In offsetting individual risk, protective factors must increase youth sense's of purpose and a belief in a positive future. Protective factors must also improve youth's commitment to education and desire to learn. Youth who feel that education can actually lead to a better situation will engage in fewer incidents of aggression; aggression is the norm for youth who have a sense of hopelessness. Youth who have the ability to transcend an environment, community, or family that perpetuates negativity will have a greater capacity for success. Also, the ability to be adaptable and flexible helps youth develop problem-solving skills and be resourceful. Other skills such as conflict management and critical thinking are factors that could protect youth from the need for violence and delinquency.

CONCLUDING THOUGHT

Despite the number of risk factors that youth face today, only a small number of youth become highly aggressive and engage in violent incidents at the school and community. Shielding youth from risks must be the duty of the entire community, although the schools will be in most instances the initiators. Strategies that focus on the entire child will yield positive results and provide the necessary "bounce-back" ability. With a strong commitment to education, supportive relationships, and strategies to offset the negative impact of the various domains, educators will be able to be instrumental in academic achievement and violence prevention.

Protective factors that could assist in building resiliency and reducing violence must be implemented through policies and programs. Lawmakers and key stakeholders should ensure that programs specifically geared toward combating environmental risks are supported. These programs are necessary from the standpoint of building relationships with youth. Once again, research supports the notion that the presence of caring and competent adults is a pillar of any resiliency-building efforts. To ensure adult-youth connectedness, resources for programs that support this interaction should create a culture of caring instead of distrust. Success depends on adults who understand the plight of young people today and youth who have an opportunity to learn from those who have "lived it."

The nation's initiative to leave no child behind, although with the best intentions, is a directive with little to no support at the school-building level. Changing a teacher strategy in math class does not impact federal funding streams that target after-school programming with a focus on literacy. Understandably, this is a long and arduous process to change laws and policies when educators are looking for what can help Johnny who has violent outbursts in second-period English, tomorrow.

PART II

Problems and Problem Solvers

Chapter 6

Bullying

William L. Lassiter

If you watched the news, read the newspaper, or were around schools much in the last eight years, you most likely heard people talking about bullying. Why is it that this behavior, which has been around since students have been going to school, suddenly has become such a huge interest for school officials? This chapter will seek to answer that question, along with what exactly bullying is, what causes it to occur, and what schools can do about it.

WHY DOES BULLYING MATTER?

After the school shootings at Columbine High School, people across the country were searching for answers to the questions of why and how this could happen in a school in America. Numerous groups have assembled to research that very question, and they have discovered that there are no simple answers. However, one common finding appearing in the research was that the students who perpetrated these and other school shootings were victims of bullying, harassment, and physical assaults by their classmates. In a collaborative report written by the U.S. Secret Service and the U.S. Department of Education, which did an "extensive examination of 37 incidents of targeted school violence that occurred in the United States from December 1974 through May 2000," one of the major findings was this: "Almost three-quarters of the attackers (school shooters) felt persecuted, bullied, threatened, attacked or injured by others prior to the incident." The investigators added,

In several cases, individual attackers (school shooters) had experienced bullying and harassment that was long-standing and severe. In some of these cases the experience of being bullied seemed to have a significant impact on the attacker and appeared to have been a factor in his decision to mount an attack at the school. In one case, most of the attacker's schoolmates described the attacker as "the kid everyone teased." In witness statements from that incident, schoolmates alleged that nearly every child in the school had at some point thrown the attacker against a locker, tripped him in the hall, held his head under water in the pool, or thrown things at him. Several schoolmates had noted that the attacker seemed more annoyed by, and less tolerant of, the teasing than usual in the days preceding the attack.[1]

Numerous other research reports have drawn the connection between more serious forms of school violence and bullying, but it was not until the U.S. Secret Service's report that many in America started focusing on the issue of bullying. The reality is that bullying is not only a precursor to school violence but also a predictor of delinquent or criminal behavior later in life for the bully. A report released by Fight Crime Invest in Kids found this: "Specific studies of bullying also show that bullies' anti-social behavior is not limited to school, but continues in other settings and into adulthood. Approximately 60 percent of boys who were classified by researchers as bullies in grades six through nine were convicted of at least one crime by the age of 24, compared to only 23 percent of the boys who were not characterized as bullies or victims. Even more dramatic, 40 percent of the boys who were bullies—compared to 10 percent of those who were neither victims nor bullies—had three or more convictions by age 24."[2]

Although many aggressive children do not become violent adults, too many do. Criminologist David Hawkins and his colleagues reviewed studies showing the link between early and later aggression and concluded that "these studies show a consistent relationship between aggressiveness in males measured from age six and later violent behavior."[3] Studies of generally aggressive behavior (as opposed to studies specifically of bullying behavior) also show similar results. One study of 10- and 13-year-olds showed that two-thirds of the boys with high teacher-rated aggression scores had criminal records for violent offenses by age 26.[4]

The National Center on Addiction and Substance Abuse found, "Children and teens who are bullied are at a greater risk of suffering from depression and other mental health problems. Bullying behavior has been linked to other problem behaviors such as: vandalism; shoplifting; truancy; school dropout; fighting; and tobacco, alcohol and drug use."[5] The Centers for Disease Control found that students who were bullied were likely to miss school and thus fall behind on their schoolwork. "The 2007 National Youth Risk Behavior Survey indicates that among U.S. high school students 6 percent did not go to school because they felt unsafe at school or on their way to or from school on at least 1 day during the 30 days before the survey."[6]

It is not just adults speaking out about their concerns over bullying; children are seeing the devastating effects of bullying also. A survey conducted by Nickelodeon and the Kaiser Family Foundation found that "more eight to 15 year-olds stated teasing and bullying as 'big problems' than those who chose drugs or alcohol, racism, AIDS, or pressure to have sex. Even more interesting, more African Americans saw bullying as a big problem for people their age than those who identified racism as a big problem."[7]

DEFINING BULLYING

When discussing bullying, it is important to understand what it is. Just as we did with school violence, we must start with an accurate definition. It is important to note that bullying is a form of school violence and should be treated as such, but as with gangs and other forms of school violence, bullying possesses some unique characteristics. When I define bullying, I discuss four major characteristics: repetition, intentionality, being unprovoked, and power imbalance.

Repetition is one of the characteristics that make bullying incidents unique from other forms of school violence. Bullying is done over and over again, and this is important to note because this repetition is what makes bullying so devastating to the victim. Most humans can withstand being put down every once in a while. Please do not misunderstand what I am saying here; I do not think that adults should allow students to put down their classmates every once in a while. What I am saying is that most humans have the resiliency to overcome those put-downs occasionally. What makes bullying so different is that it does not happen every once in a while; it is every day. Targets of bullying behavior usually wake up in the morning knowing they will be bullied at school that day; they just do not know where and when it will happen. Even the most resilient persons have their breaking point, and targets of bullying behavior are often pushed to that point.

Second, bullying behavior is intentional. Simply put, bullies intend to hurt the student they target with their attack. This is important to keep in mind, because the most common excuse you will hear from a bully is that "we were just joking around." The reality is that "we" were not; the bullying might have been joking around, but the target did not see any humor in the bully's behavior. If bullies are going to change their behavior, they must first accept that the behavior they are doing is wrong. Most bullies already understand this fact, but for years they have been getting away with hurting their classmates. They may be shocked to find out that a teacher or a caring adult does not accept that behavior anymore.

Third, bullying is unprovoked. Now this is the one where many people get hung up. Why is this one so difficult to understand? The reason is that it is often easier to ask victims of a crime to change their behavior than it is to get perpetrators to change theirs. This can be illustrated well by examining another type of crime. Often when you watch a report about a young lady being raped in the community, you hear some of the following things: "Well, did you see what she was wearing?"; "Did you see where she was?"; "Did you see who she was hanging out with?"; or "Did you see what time she was out at?" As if any of these things make it acceptable that the young lady got raped. All too often we hear people making these excuses for the perpetrator. The same happens with other crimes; people all too often make excuses for the bully rather than condemning the behaviors of the attacker. Some of these common excuses include the following: "Well, he or she is just a strange kid"; "He or she does smell bad"; "Well, he or she does act gay"; or "He or she is stupid." When adults make these types of statements, they are actually empowering the bully to continue his or her attacks.

I remember working with one young man who had gotten in trouble for stealing a car. This young man was in the gothic subculture, which means that he wore black clothes, dyed his hair black, painted his fingernails black, wore black mascara, and listened to some pretty depressing music. I was asked to talk to him because the young man stated that he stole the car because he was sick and tired of being bullied at school so he was going to run away from home. I remember the first question that I asked him was "Why do you wear all these black clothes?" His answer somewhat surprised me. He stated, "Well, one day I was watching *Oprah*." I thought, "A 13-year-old male into the gothic culture was watching *Oprah*, huh. It just goes to show you, you cannot trust your stereotypes."

He added, "And she had on this fashion expert, who said, if you want to look thinner, wear black." He said, "Now I have been fat all of my life and people have picked on me for it, so I went into my closet and searched for all the black clothes I could find." The next day when he went to school he wore a purely black outfit, and he found that not a single one of his classmates picked on him for being fat.

He said, "Now they did pick on me for wearing all black, but no one picked on me for being fat." Being picked on for wearing all black, he said, was "not so bad, but being picked on because you are fat, that is horrible."

I asked him, "What is the difference?"

He stated, "I can control what I wear, but I cannot seem to do anything to control my weight."

I said, "Well, that explains the black clothing, but why did you start wearing the rest of the gothic getup?"

He said, "Because I wanted people to fear me; see, people do not pick on you when they fear you."

This young man taught me a lot about bullying and how sometimes we make poor assumptions. For example, I assumed he was wearing the gothic clothing to get attention, but in reality he was wearing the gothic clothing to draw attention away from his size. I have often heard adults say that "he had it coming." They say, "If you dye your hair purple, people are going to pick on you." They are really saying that if someone is different then you have the right to pick on him or her. What a horrible message to send to our kids.

So when I say that bullying is unprovoked, I mean that the target did not do anything harmful to the bullies to cause them to pick on him or her. If a child acts differently, talks differently, dresses differently, or is just plain different from other kids, these differences are not sufficient reasons for bullies to attack one of their classmates.

Finally, when defining bullying, it is important to keep in mind that a power imbalance exists. This power imbalance can be physical or psychological. Often we think of bullies as being the biggest kids in the class, but the research does not suggest that this is always the case. A child who believes he or she is better than everyone else can often be a smaller kid that is somehow good at manipulating others.

WHAT CAUSES BULLYING?

When considering the causes of bullying, one can start by breaking the causes up into five major areas: individual; family; school; peers; and community. Often these categories are referred to as the developmental domains in which kids exist. Each domain holds risk and protective factors that aid in development, be it delinquency or resiliency.

Individual Characteristics

Individual causes would be those that relate to characteristics about a child that would make him or her either more or less likely to be a bully or a victim. So what about a person makes him or her more likely to be a bully? Many believe that bullies are insecure and have low self-esteem, when in reality they are generally confident, with high self-esteem.[8] Bullies also tend to be physically aggressive, believe violence is acceptable to meet their goals, are short-tempered and quick to anger, and often lack impulse control with a low tolerance for frustration. Bullies have a strong need to dominate others and usually have little empathy for their targets. Male bullies are often physically bigger and stronger than their peers.[9] Bullies tend to get in trouble more often, and they dislike and do more poorly in school than teens who do not bully others. They are also more likely to fight, drink, and smoke than their peers.[10]

What makes a child more likely to become a target of bullying behavior? I am personally drawn to the argument that it is a difference. That difference could be physical, cultural, racial, intellectual, or economical. I lean toward this argument because of personal experience. Being an albino, I have extremely white skin, white hair, pink eyes, and vision that is not that great. So you might say that I stood out in school just a little bit. These personal experiences are what shaped my view of bullying. The way I see it, most bullies are cowards, meaning they choose targets by looking for the student they think they can get away with bullying and suffer no repercussions. They choose a child that is different as their target because they believe that by picking on the student who is different, they will only offend that student. This is important, because the last thing the bully wants to do is take on a group of people; in those situations the bully would lose his or her power. For example, when kids bullied me in school, they were pretty sure that I would not show up with my posse of albinos the next day to take them out.

This theory is, of course, backed up by research. In a study conducted in 2001, the researcher found that the most frequent reason cited by youth for persons being bullied is that they "didn't fit in."[11] Researchers have also shown that with boys physical size is important.[12]

The Bully's and Target's Home Life

"Children and teens that come from homes where parents provide little emotional support for their children, fail to monitor their activities, or have little involvement in their lives, are at greater risk for engaging in bullying behavior. Parents' discipline styles are also related to bullying behavior: an extremely permissive or excessively harsh approach to discipline can increase the risk of teenage bullying."[13]

Schools Themselves

There are two ways schools play a role in contributing to bullying behavior. The first relates to opportunity theory. Opportunity theory is part of a larger theory known as the Crime Prevention Theory. This framework states that for a crime to occur, the following three elements must be present: an available and suitable target; a motivated offender; and no authority figure to prevent the crime from happening. Schools are unique because there are so many youth gathered together in one place. A bully sees each of those youth gathered there as a potential target.[14] Schools can also cause bullying behavior to worsen by ignoring its presence. When school staff members ignore bullying behavior, they are actually giving the bully an implicit message that the bully's behavior is acceptable.

Peer Groups

Many are surprised to learn that bullies appear to have little difficulty in making friends. These friends typically share their violent tendencies and problem behaviors.[15] Research has also suggested that these friends are often followers who do not initiate bullying but participate in it.[16]

The peer group is an especially integral part of female bullying. Most female bullying begins as isolation or rejection of a girl from a group often known as a clique. By rejecting the youth, the group has made a value judgment about that individual. They are stating that the youth is not "cool" enough to hang out with them. Once this value judgment has been made, the bullying behavior usually evolves into rumor spreading, name calling, gossiping, and insults. The initial rejection by the group made these other forms of bullying possible by creating the power imbalance necessary for bullying behavior.

Society as a Whole

If schools sometimes ignore bullying behavior, communities almost always ignore the behavior. Think about the loud-mouth parent at the little league football game who spends the whole game yelling at the referee and coaches. Does anyone ever call these people out? If they do not, what message does that send to the youth participating in the game? In fact, society actually encourages bullying behavior sometimes. Think about your favorite comedian; doesn't he or she spend half the act making fun of other people? If so, aren't you paying him or her to be a bully?

Although all of these major causes play a role in causing bullying behavior, I ultimately believe that kids bully because it works. Some people call this the "rational choice theory," or the "ideal theory on crime." No matter what you call it, kids or even adults bully because they derive some benefit from doing so. When I was getting my master's degree in public administration, we called this doing a cost-benefit analysis. This basically means that when people decide to take a certain action or participate in a behavior, they do so because the result will be beneficial to them. In other words, they look at the cost of doing the behavior and they look at the benefits of doing that behavior, and if the benefits are greater than the cost, they are going to do it. On the other hand, if the behavior is more costly than beneficial, they are not going to do the behavior.

So let's do a cost-benefit analysis of bullying behavior. What do bullies get out of being bullies? One can argue they get power; respect;

popularity; intimidation so they do not get bullied; money; stuff; and attention, just to name a few. Now, on the other hand, what are the costs? In most cases nothing. Rarely do bullies ever get caught, and even if they do get caught, hardly ever do they get in trouble for their bad behavior. To make the situation even worse, let's say the bully gets caught and someone actually has the audacity to come over and tell the bully he or she did something wrong. How does the bully get punished? You got it: he or she gets suspended from school—a paid vacation, if you will. How many bullies do you know who hate getting suspended from school? Not too many, I am guessing. If you are an educator, you may be thinking to yourself, "How could someone not mind getting suspended from school?" I know that in my household when I was growing up, getting suspended from school would have been just as bad as getting the death penalty because I was taught that nothing is more important than your education. But I grew up in a household of educators. The day that I graduated from college, I went over to my grandmother's and the first words out of her mouth were "When are you going to get your master's degree?" Not congratulations or good job, but rather, when are you going to get your master's degree? Education was important in my household, and if you are an educator, it was probably important in your household as well. We find it hard to believe that there are people out there who just do not care about education or see the value of it, but they are out there. So although suspension may seem like the death penalty to us, to bullies it might even seem a benefit, not a cost.

WHAT CAN WE DO ABOUT BULLYING?

As we discussed earlier in the book, there is no one solution to a bullying challenge, just as there is no one solution to school violence. To have an effective bullying prevention effort, a school must do the following things: involve the whole school; use a common language; raise awareness; involve families; provide staff development to all staff; have top-level support; change the way supervision is done on the school campus; change the bystander effect; and empower adults to intervene effectively when they see bullying.

Involve the Whole School

Too often when I go to a school I find that one staff member, usually a counselor or an assistant principal, has been tasked with the school's bullying prevention effort. This is fine except for the fact that this one person is the only person at the school who is doing anything on bullying prevention. There is no way that a school is going to rid itself of bullying with just one person doing anything about it. If a school has the counselor come in and teach a class on bullying prevention, then the teacher in the classroom should be prepared to follow that lesson plan up with one of his or her own. Students learn best through redundancy. To learn a concept, they must be exposed to it over and over again. Youth are also fairness fanatics, and they expect consistency, but what I find in most schools is that teachers are very inconsistent in the way they treat bullying incidents. Students pick up on these inconsistencies and learn the places in the school where they can get away with bullying and the places they cannot.

Use a Common Language

One of the important elements in ensuring that a school consistently enforces its school policy on bullying is that the school has a common definition for what bullying is. Establishing a common definition can be a difficult process; just look across the country, and you will find a number of state legislatures that have gotten hung up on this very issue. For example, the state of North Carolina has been considering a bullying prevention bill for several years, but because legislators could not decide upon a common definition, the law still has not passed. Having a common language goes beyond just defining what bullying is; it can also go to the heart of the solutions to bullying. For example, character education is often recommended as a program that can target bullying behavior. I could not agree more with those who say that character education makes sense when it comes to addressing one of the root causes of bullying behavior, but what exactly is character education? In the state of North Carolina, a law passed that requires all schools to incorporate character education into their general course of study. So one of the questions that I ask schools when I am conducting a safety assessment is "Does your school have a character education program?" I remember at this one school a counselor said, "Come out into the hall with me." So I did, and she pointed to a poster hanging in the hall. The poster read, "Respect" in big letters and then in a smaller font, "Got to Give it, to Get it."

I said, "That is a nice poster, but where is your character education program?"

She started emphatically pointing at the poster and said, "It is right there."

I said, "Oh, the poster is your character education program." The problem is that in too many schools the poster is the program. The problem with the poster being the program is that the most difficult component of that poster is the word "respect." What exactly is it, and how do you give it to get it? If the students are not taught what these words mean, then posters are very ineffective because the school has not created a common language.

Raise Awareness

Now, on the other hand, every good violence prevention program—or, for that matter, public health program—involves some component of awareness raising. This may sound like I am contradicting what was said under creating a common language and understanding, but I am not. It is important that schools do both. If the school puts up the Respect poster and follows it up with lessons on what respect is and is not, then the poster can be a very effective reminder.

Provide Staff Development to All Staff

Too often when schools provide staff development on bullying, they do not involve the people who need to be there the most: the bus drivers, the cafeteria workers, the custodians, the teacher assistants, and the coaches. These are the very people who are most likely to encounter bullying behavior, and without their buy-in and without training, schools have no chance of consistently enforcing the rules.

Have Top-Level Support

Schools are like most institutions in our society: they rely on top-level support and leadership to make sure a challenge is dealt with effectively. Dealing with bullying is no different. Administrators must stand ready to support teachers who are dealing with students who are bullies, and they must insist upon all teachers consistently enforcing bullying policies.

Change the Way Supervision Is Done on the School Campus

As discussed earlier in the chapter, bullies are effective in choosing students that they think they can bully without repercussions. For this reason they also often choose locations to bully students where they think they can get away with it. These locations tend to be on the school bus, the playground or athletic fields, the locker room, and the cafeteria. These locations are often chosen because they are difficult to supervise. When conducting an assessment of bullying activity at a school, we often recommend that the school conduct a mapping activity. Students in older grades are given a floor plan of the school, and students in lower grades are given pictures of different areas of the school. Students are then asked to mark those areas where they get bullied or feel unsafe. Students in lower grades are often allowed to color those areas, while students in older grades may be asked to use checks or X's. This activity can give a school a quick picture of where the trouble spots are located. Then it will be up to staff to devise a more appropriate supervision plan to cover those areas where students feel that they are getting bullied the most.

Change the Bystander Effect

One of the key factors in bullying is the bystander effect. Bystanders are those students and adults who stand around and watch their classmates or students get bullied. We must consider things that are going to eliminate this effect if we truly want to end bullying. Schools can do this by encouraging students to speak up about bullying. From the first days of students' school career, schools need to explain the difference between students who are tattletales and students who are speaking up. Tattletales are only telling an adult in the hope that someone will get in trouble, whereas students who speak up are trying to help someone who is getting hurt. This important distinction can go a long way toward removing some of the stigma that surrounds speaking up.

Empower Adults to Intervene Effectively When They See Bullying

Kids learn to be bystanders by watching adults. How often as an adult do you step up to help someone who is being victimized? We have all heard the stories of the wife who suffered from domestic abuse for years and all the neighbors knew about it but chose to do nothing about it. Every time as an adult that we choose to look the other direction when a child is being bullied, we are sending two powerful messages. The first is to the bully, and the message is that we think the behavior that you are doing is perfectly acceptable. The second is to the target of the bullying behavior, and that message is that we do not care about you. No wonder so many targets of bullying behavior suffer from depression and suicidal ideations: they believe no one cares about them.

If we are going to end bullying, we must first change peoples' attitudes toward it. This became reality for me several years ago. I got up one morning and was eating breakfast. At the time I lived in a townhouse, and we had a large bay window in our kitchen that overlooked the parking lot and road. On this particular morning I was eating breakfast and three students had gathered to wait for the school bus at the end of the street. While I was looking out at them, I saw one of the young men push another to the ground, and then I saw the two other young men start to kick him while he was down on the ground. I could not believe what I was seeing. I thought to myself, "What are you going to do?" I looked out again, and the young man who was lying on the ground had gotten up and had run back to his house. I thought, "Oh good, I do not have to do anything now."

But all of a sudden this feeling of guilt overtook me, and I thought, "I have got to do something." So I looked back out the window and thought, "Wow, those are some big boys standing out there. What are you going to do about it?" Just then one of the other boys ran back to his house, so now it would be just a one-on-one confrontation with the boy who seemed to have started the trouble by knocking the victim to the ground. The only problem was that he was the biggest of the three, and although he was much younger, he was much bigger than me. I thought, "What can I possibly do about what just happened?"

For some reason I was still compelled to go out there and talk to this young man. As I walked out the door, I could feel my palms starting to sweat. It was not that long of a walk over to the young man, but I walked over to him at a very slow pace so I could think of a strategy of how I should approach this situation. About halfway over to him I decided I could not just come out and say what I saw because that would get our conversation off to a bad start. I decided I would just dance around the issue for a while and see how things went. So I did.

In trying to dance around the subject, I learned a lot about the young man. It turns out he played football, and I could see why; he definitely had the build for it. As the conversation moved along, I thought, "I could just keep talking to him until the bus gets here and as he is getting on the bus yell at him for beating up that other kid." At the moment it seemed like a really great idea, because if I waited for the bus to arrive, at least I would have witnesses around if things got ugly between me and the young man.

So we continued to talk for what seemed like forever, and the kid's school bus still did not come. Finally, I looked down at my watch and thought, "I have got to go or I am going to be late." So if I was going to say something about the fight, I would have to go ahead and do it, or I could still just walk away. I made the decision to say something to the young man, because for years I had gone around the country telling people that you cannot be a bystander to bullying incidents; you must say something. I did not want to be a hypocrite. So I turned to the young man and said, "What happened out here before I came out?"

He responded with a "Huh?"

I repeated, "What happened out here before I came out?" It turns out the young man heard my question the first time; he was just trying to ignore it. He looked at me with the most intimidating look he could give me and asked, "What do you mean?"

Gaining confidence for some odd reason, I said, "I mean it looked like you pushed that young man to the ground and kicked him."

He said, "We were just playing around."

I said, "It did not look like you were playing around to me. It looked like that young man got hurt."

He uttered, "So?"

I said, "Well, the thing is that I live in that house right there, and I was looking out the window this morning as I was eating my Pop Tart and I saw what happened. And to be honest with you, I do not want to look out my window and see people getting beat up."

I thought as I was saying all of this, "Why are you pointing out where you live?"

I then told him, "I have to go to work now, but I came out here today because I care about my neighborhood and I care about you, and I do not want to see this type of thing happening in front of my house again."

As I was walking back to my house, I was thinking, "I am not sure if I did any good here," and I was wondering if he was chasing me back to my house.

The next day as I was leaving to go to work that young man yelled at me from the bus stop, "Hey, Mr. Lassiter!" I responded with a wave and a hey, but then I noticed he was walking over to talk to me. I thought, "Oh no, here it comes." But when he got over to me, he started talking about football practice.

For weeks after that, every time he saw me, we talked. But about a month later he came up to me and said, "Mr. Lassiter, do you remember that day we met?"

I said, "Yes," thinking, "Where is this going?"

He said, "I respected you for coming and talking to me that day." He added, "I know you were scared, weren't you?"

I said, "Yeah!"

He said, "I knew it because your hands were shaking." He said, "Very few people talk to me the way you do. I like that about you, Mr. Lassiter."

Could this story have turned out differently? Of course, if that young man had wanted to, he could have turned me into a little grease spot on the ground, or his mom could have come rushing out of her house asking why I was talking to her kid. But I decided that day to take a risk, and that risk paid off. Too often we do not take the risk to speak up for someone in need; we simply let things happen. If we are going to change bullying, we need to empower adults to intervene when they see it.

RATIONAL CHOICE THEORY

"Rational choice theory sees social interaction as social exchange, modeled on economic action. People are motivated by the rewards and costs of actions and by the profits that they can make."[17] As with any theory that tries to explain delinquency and crime, there are limitations to the rational choice theory; however, it does the best job of explaining bullying behavior.

How does it work? When a child or even an adult is deciding whether or not to participate in bullying behavior, he or she considers the benefits and the costs of doing so. If the benefits are greater than the cost, the child will choose to engage in that behavior. On the other hand, if the costs are greater than the benefits, the child will choose not to engage in that behavior. This may at first glance seem like a sophisticated equation for a young child to consider, but in reality it is very simple, and kids do it every day.

For example, when children are considering whether or not to be a bully, they will weigh the benefits of power, respect, popularity, intimidation of others so they do not get bullied themselves, attention, money, and other stolen property against the costs of getting caught. So what are the costs of being a bully? The first cost would be getting caught, but whether a bully gets caught is a big "if." For the most part, bullies are smart enough to know where, when, and with whom they can bully and not get caught. Second, if they do get caught, what are the chances that an adult that will say something about the behavior? Third, bullies weigh whether the punishment that they will receive is truly costly, and as we have discussed before, we know the most common punishment is suspension. How many bullies do you know who hate getting sent home from school? In many cases, instead of punishing children we are only adding to the list of benefits they see of being a bully.

If schools are going to eliminate bullying, they must change the dynamics of the rational choice theory in their favor. It helps to think of the benefits and costs as being on the opposite ends of a scale. How can a school balance out the scale, or better yet, how can a school make the costs of being a bully greater than the benefits? There are two ways that schools can go about do this. First they can increase the cost by saying to bullies, "You will get caught, you will get in trouble, and most importantly, you will be punished with something you do not like." The other way is to demonstrate to students how they can achieve many of the same benefits they get from being a bully by doing positive behavior.

One example of where I saw a teacher achieve this on a micro level in the classroom was with a fifth-grade teacher. This teacher called me up the day after I had conducted a staff development at her school. She started out our conversation by stating, "Mr. Lassiter, I have the worst student in the whole school in my classroom, and I am a first-year teacher. Can you please help me develop a plan for working with this young man?"

I asked, "How do you know that you have the worst student in the whole school in your classroom?"

She stated, "Because everyone told me he was the worst student in the whole school before the year started."

I must interject this side note. Now how does something like that happen? We put the toughest students with the least experienced teachers. Those experienced teachers are lobbying the schedule makers at their school not to put those students in their classrooms. To me it would make sense to put the best and most experienced teachers with the students who need the most help.

I said, "Tell me what this young man does."

She said, "Well, he pushes people out their chairs, he jumps people in line, he gets into fights, he is late to class, he pulls people's hair, he disrupts class." She said, "I could keep going but I think you get the picture."

I said, "Yes, I think I do get the picture. So what do you do when he acts out like this?"

She said, "Well, I tell him his behavior is unacceptable."

"Good! And what does he do?"

"He argues with me about whether he did anything wrong."

"Hmm," I said, "and how long does this argument go on for?"

"Three to 5 minutes."

I added, "Uh, and how many times a day does this happen?"

She answered, "Five to seven times a day."

I exclaimed, "Five to seven times a day! And the arguments last 3 to 5 minutes each time? I am not a math expert, but that is anywhere from 15 to 50 minutes a day you spend disciplining this child."

She said, "That sounds about right, Mr. Lassiter; that is why I am calling you."

By this point it was obvious to me what this child wanted. Attention! So I asked her, "What do you think this young man is trying to get by acting out in class?" She had to think about this for a minute, but she eventually came up with attention also. I said, "Understanding that he wants attention, what we need to do is find a positive way for him to get that attention. So help me think of a way that you can load him down with some positive attention."

She said, "What do mean?"

I asked, "Well, is there something he does well?"

She said, "Besides beating kids up? I have not really found it yet if there is."

Seeing that this was going to be tougher than I originally thought, I started to throw ideas out there for her. I said, "For example, tomorrow when he comes into class, could you get him to do a homework problem on the board?"

She answered, "No, he does not do homework, Mr. Lassiter."

"Well, could you get him to do some class work and get him to present to his classmates? That would be an easy way for him to get some attention," I responded.

She answered, "I know you probably think that I am just being tough on you, Mr. Lassiter, but hardly ever does he do class work either."

I threw out several other ideas, but I kept running into roadblocks with this teacher. I could tell that she really was at her wits' end, but I could also tell that she cared what happened to this young man. So after thinking about it for a few minutes, I said, "I got it! Tomorrow when he comes into class, have him call the roll."

She said, "Huh, how is that going to help?"

I added, "Well, if what he wants is attention, he will get it. Give him five minutes at the beginning of class to call the roll. Now you will need to set down some simple ground rules. For example, he cannot say anything that hurts anybody in the classroom. Tell him he has five minutes, and if he gets done early he can talk about anything he wants to, but no matter what, he is done once the five minutes is up. When he gets done calling the roll, I want you to call him over to your desk and ask him if he enjoyed calling the roll. I am guessing that he will say yes. If he does say yes, tell him he can do it again tomorrow if he behaves in class today. It is important that you be clear with him what your expectation of good behavior is. I would tell him something like 'If I do not have to call on you at all today for bad behavior, you can call the roll again tomorrow.'"

She said, "I will give it a try, but it seems a little unfair to me."

I asked, "Why?"

She said, "Because it almost seems like I am rewarding his bad behavior from earlier in the year."

I said, "You are not rewarding his bad behavior; you will be rewarding his good behavior, but he has to get a taste of how much he likes it before it is going to motivate any change in his behavior. It would be like someone offering you cake for doing well on a test, but if you are not sure if you like cake, you would not be very likely to work hard to get any of it."

She agreed to try it. I told her, "Call me back and let me know how it is going."

She called back in two weeks. I remember answering the phone and hearing, "It is working, Mr. Lassiter!"

I said, "What is working?"

After realizing who it was, she said, "I have only had to correct his bad behavior twice in two weeks. He loves to call the roll."

I said, "Great!"

She said, "Most days he calls the roll in just a minute or two, and then he spends the rest of the time telling jokes. The only problem is, he does not keep the roll very well. If he does not like you, he will check you as being absent every day, but little does he know that I am keeping my own roll over at my desk."

I said, "Well we most likely need to address that behavior also, but let's not rock the boat right now."

We kept in touch over the rest of the year, and I would like to tell you that this young man became a straight A student, but I would be lying. He did, however, learn something really important that year: that you can get what you want through positive behavior. He also learned how to sit still for a few minutes at a time. Both are skills not tested for on end-of-term tests, but I would contend they are skills that are necessary to be successful in school and life.

This story is an excellent example of how the rational choice theory works. The child in this story wanted attention and was willing to do just about anything to get it. The problem was that he did not realize that there were positive ways to get attention. The other important point is that if children feel that they have nothing left to lose, then it is extremely hard to punish them. With the child in this story, I can tell you he was not motivated by having his education taken away from him. He had told the teacher on numerous occasions that he did not care about school. So why should we believe that by taking education away from him we are going to change his behavior? What the teacher did in this story was give the student something he did not want to lose: the opportunity to call the roll. All of sudden the teacher moved from having nothing to take away from the child to having the one thing he really wanted. This is not to say that having an opportunity to call the roll will motivate every child to behave better. If a child is terrified to get up in front of the class and speak at all, obviously this method will not work. But what will work is finding the thing that motivates that child to want to behave. There are many ways to reward good behavior; this story merely highlights one of those ways.

I believe that this method can work with every child, just not in every circumstance. As you most likely know, not all violent behavior can be explained as rational behavior. In fact, some violence is quite irrational and based on emotions and situations. But remember, in this chapter we are exploring bullying behavior, which tends to be much more methodical and premeditated in nature. That is why for this particular type of violence the rational choice theory seems to be such a strong predictor of behavior.

I have done trainings on bullying with teachers who work in juvenile justice settings and work with some of toughest kids in the country; these teachers have the same complaints as the teachers I talk to in schools every day: primarily, that there are not enough consequences for these kids. I always ask those care providers working in the juvenile justice system, "What do you want? They are already locked up. So what is it that you want, for us to take them out in the courtyard and shoot them?" I tell them, if you want to have consequences for these kids, then you have to give them something first. Only then do you have something they can work toward earning more of in the future.

WHAT CAN WE DO FOR TARGETS OF BULLYING BEHAVIOR?

From what the research has shown us and from the research I presented to you in the beginning of this chapter, we know the targets need as much help, if not more, than the bullies themselves. So what should teachers or school staff members do if they have a target in their classroom?

The first thing is to do something. Targets believe that no one cares about them, so simply by showing that you care you can make a profound difference in their life. Second, it is important for those children to know that they do not deserve to have this behavior happen to them. One of the common things that we find out about children who are bullied is that they actually start to believe that they deserve the abuse. Some people have labeled this behavior the "victim mentality." A child who adopts this victim mentality is more likely to carry the negative effects of that mentality into adulthood. This is why Olweus found that students who are targets of bullying behavior are seven times more likely to be domestically abused later in life.[18] Third, targets must be taught behaviors to help protect themselves from bullies. These would include simple things like walking down the hall with their head up instead of slumping their shoulders; role-playing appropriate responses to bullying behavior; and learning social rules on how to make friends. All of these behaviors will help a target of bullying behaviors to fend off bullies by exerting confidence. As demonstrated earlier in the chapter, bullies are looking for easy targets, so by teaching targets these skills, one will decrease the likelihood that they will be seen as that "easy target."

Here is a final story on bullying and one that is very personal to me, but it demonstrates the perfect intervention you can do with a target.

I am albino, which means that I have really white hair, really white skin, pink eyes, and not the best vision in the world. As you can imagine, this meant that I stood out in the crowd as a child and that I got picked on a lot. But I also was born with a temperament that made it easy for me to deal with bullies. I am anything but shy, and I am perfectly capable of turning a bully's words back around on the bully. These skills served me well throughout elementary school, but when I got to middle school, as it is with middle school kids, things got a bit tougher. The harassment grew, and life was a little tough for the kid who was so different from the others.

The event that changed my life was a day in seventh grade. I remember it like it was yesterday. It was sixth-period English on a Thursday afternoon, and we had a substitute teacher. Now I know being a middle school substitute teacher must be an extremely difficult job, but what happened next shocked my system. This substitute teacher was having a rough day. The students in earlier classes were picking on him because he had a very distinct dialect and was somewhat hard to understand.

The students were questioning, "How can you teach English if you do not even know how to speak English yourself?" I guess by the time sixth period rolled around he was tired of the harassment the students were giving him, so he decided to tell a joke to get class started. So at the beginning of class he told a joke about me being albino. Other students in the class took the opportunity that the substitute teacher gave them to begin picking on me also. Now I am a pretty tough cookie, but after this harassment took place for what seemed like an eternity I could not take it any longer. I started to feel that burn behind my eyes that you get right before you start to cry. I thought to myself, "You have got to get out of here!" What is the worst thing that you can do as a seventh-grade boy? CRY. I tried to quickly grab my stuff, and as I did, I knocked over my desk, causing most of my belongings to spill out onto the floor. I thought I could gather it all up before the first tear started to fall, but I did not quite make it. I remember running for the door as the tears started to fall. As I escaped the classroom, I slammed the door behind me. Then I heard a thunderous roar of laughter in the room.

As I stood out in the hallway, I tried to decide what I was going to do next. As I thought about it, I thought, "I should go tell someone about it," but then I thought, "What makes me think anybody here is going to care?" I had friends in that class, and not a single one of them stood up for me, and the teacher did not stand up for me. In fact, he started it. So I decided to tell no one and to go home.

When I got home, my mom could clearly see that I was upset about something. So she asked me about it. I told her the story. Her first natural inclination was to go to the school and get that substitute teacher fired. But I guess she thought there was something more important than talking to the staff at the school, and that was talking to her son. So she sat me down, and I told her all about it.

After I told her my story, my mom turned to me and said, "I have something really important to tell you."

I said, "Well, if it is really important, I need to hear it."

So she said, "Billy, you are albino."

I responded, "Duh!"

So she said, "Wait, I am not done yet. You are albino. What does that mean?"

I said, "It means that I have really white hair, really white skin, and bad vision."

She said, "Yes, but what else does it mean?"

I responded, "What do you mean?"

She said, "Being albino means that you will stand out in a crowd because you are different, and yes, sometimes that means you will be picked on. But it also means that people will remember you because you are albino. You see, Billy, being albino is actually something really great about you. It makes you special."

With a puzzled look on my face, I said "special?" See, I had always thought of being albino as a handicap, not something that makes you special. I thought, if you could go to the de-albino-fication factory, you would. But my mom was telling me that being albino was something really special about me. I had never thought of it that way. Something strange started to happen; I actually started to believe her. Now I am sure my mom had told me a thousand times before that I was special, but I just was not ready to listen until that day.

She finished our conversation by saying, "Billy, I believe you were created this way for a purpose. I am not sure what that purpose is, but one day I think you will find out."

My mom is a smart person. You would not believe how many people come up to me from elementary school and middle school who remember me. I have no clue who they are, but they sure do remember me.

The next day I walked into that same classroom where I had been tortured the day before, and I walked around to each of the students' desks in that room and said, "I am special." Now most of the students laughed, but I did not care because I believed it. My mom had convinced me that it was true. After that day I carried myself with a new level of confidence that I did not have before. Looking back, I know how blessed I was to have a mom like that.

How can this story help you intervene with a child who is a target of bullying behavior? Targets need to hear that they do not deserve this to happen to them. They need to hear that they are special. I know these sound like simple things, but they work. Remember, targets are often depressed and feel that no one cares about them, and unfortunately too few of them have a mother like mine waiting to pump them back up at home. So that responsibility will often fall on the shoulders of school staff members and other caring adults.

CONCLUSION

The acceptance of bullying behavior in today's society is a major factor that contributes to more complex and devastating forms of school violence. To end bullying, schools must address the bystander effect, they must train all staff on how to deal with bullying situations, and they must not accept any bullying behaviors.

Chapter 7

Addressing Gangs in the School

Danya C. Perry

I make every attempt to speak to parent groups about the dangers of gang involvement. Parents are often the last people to realize that their child is at risk of being in a gang or is currently involved in a gang. This ranking is sometimes self-inflicted, meaning that parents find it difficult to see the "writing in the sky" as it pertains to their own child. One parent gang awareness session in particular stands out in my mind as I was reminded of this parental affliction. As I carefully explained to participating parents the signs to gang involvement, I realized that a few parents had their children sitting beside them. When working with local school systems that organize such parent seminars, I ask for youth not to be present. I try not to share the signs and symbols with youth, so as to not add to their own street knowledge. If they are present, I tone it down a bit. In this particular session I was well into the discussion when I witnessed probably the most disturbing scene ever in my public speaking career. For seemingly no reason, a parent began to take off the pants of her child in the middle of a huge lecture hall. After she tussled with the young man, she took his jeans off and threw them into a nearby trash can.

I tried to remain focused, but for the rest of the session I could not shake the image of this very upset young man sitting in the middle of this group with only his boxers. After any presentation, I normally stay around to answer questions, and with this session that was no different. The mother quickly came up to me, gripping the arm of her disgruntled son. She exclaimed, "Do you know what I saw on my son's jeans?" Of course, I had no clue, and before I could answer she released her death-grip of her son and hurriedly ran to the trash can to retrieve his jeans. She walked back to me with the jeans in the air as if she was selling them on a television shopping show. My eyesight isn't great, and as she came closer I finally made out two words—one word per pant leg—"Crip Nation." I now understood.

She continued, "I never realized it 'til now that my son even knew about gangs." I then asked her how often her son wore the pair of jeans. "This is his favorite pair, and he wears them everywhere," expressed the mother. This did not surprise me, as more parents, educators, and community members are coming to the realization that gangs are prevalent, regardless of where you live. It only takes being aware to start the process of finding effective solutions for your specific gang problem.

The mere fact that gangs are in existence means that there are negative contributing factors to keep these entities sustainable. Community deterioration, socioeconomic climate, family dysfunction, misaligned measures of success, and school disconnections all contribute to the problem of youth gang involvement. The youth violence continuum speaks to where prevention should start (long before deep involvement in gangs has ensued), and the fact that we are dealing with the issue of gangs currently means that the job of prevention has failed. For youth currently involved in gangs, effective interventions are critical to move youth past destructive decisions. This is not to say that prevention is unnecessary. Prevention in gang terms means that the "recruitment line" needs to be stifled. Preventing youth from traveling down the road of gangs is where emphasis should be placed. The question remains, where do we focus attention? Before strategy development and implementation can occur, "gangs" must be properly defined.

WHAT IS A GANG?

Some gang researchers would consider this the "age-old" question. It is difficult to define in specific terms, but easy to define once visible. The difficulty in defining gangs is attributed to the many functions of these "cliques" and their similarities to other organizations. Starting out with a basic outline, gangs can be defined as a group of three or more people who share a common identity or purpose. This common identity usually is recognized by signs, symbols, or colors. For example, the most notorious gang in America, the Crips, identify themselves traditionally with the color blue and a six-pointed star. These groups also utilize unique ways of communicating. Verbally, each gang has its own "slang" or way of speaking and writing in code, and gang members also communicate nonverbally by the use of hand signs. The definition goes further to describe the functions and activities of gangs. One must understand that gang involvement is part of a process that some youth follow in their development and their neighborhood and peer group interactions. Some gangs initially start out as social groups that are neighborhood based. These groups are innocent and the neighborhood and adolescence experiences create a bond amongst the peer group. At the other extreme are adult criminal organizations that could be a result of the normal peer group association as a youth. Either way, there is a range of levels that can define gang involvement. Understanding that there is a continuum of involvement, most consider a valid "gang" to be organized for the purpose of carrying out illegal activity. These crimes can include dealing drugs, extortion, inciting conflict, and a myriad of other illegal undertakings. The criminality part of the definition is the reason people should be careful in using the word "gang" and why it is important to differentiate by using the terminology "street gang." Without the criminal designation, this definition could describe a number of different groups. Athletic sports teams, civic organizations, fraternities, sororities, and construction crews are just a few groups that could be classified as gangs. To illustrate, fraternities are usually a group of three or more persons who identify themselves with colors and signs, and some even have nonverbal ways of communicating through hand signs. Yet these characteristics do not make them a street gang. A street gang is one that involves criminality. This definition is traditionally used by law enforcement and neglects distinct elements of association.

From the sociological perspective, gangs are organizations of the street composed of the socially excluded, alienated, demoralized, or bigoted elements of a dominant racial, ethnic, or religious group. Although most gangs begin as unsupervised adolescent peer groups and remain so, some institutionalize in barrios, favelas, ghettoes, and prisons. Institutionalized gangs often become business enterprises within the informal (illegal) economy, and a few are linked to international criminal cartels. Others institutionalize as violent supporters of dominant groups and may devolve from political or conventional organizations.[1]

Both the law enforcement and sociological perspectives provide a firm foundation for defining street gangs, whether in a suppressive or sociopolitical manner. Either way, educators must accept the fact that street gangs are in existence and can negatively impact the school climate and school violence prevention efforts.

WHERE DOES THE GANG MENTALITY COME FROM?

It is important to note that the idea of a gang is not new, and there are many historical examples of the existence of gangs in various ancient cultures. The word "thug" dates back to India in the year a.d. 1200, and it refers to a gang of criminals that roamed the country pillaging towns.[2] These individuals had unique symbols, hand signs, slang, and rituals. Even in American history, images of "gangsters" were prevalent in the form of pirates who were known for their role in acting illegally outside their sovereign nation. Throughout the 1800s, western outlaws such as the James Gang, Billy the Kid, and Butch Cassidy could certainly be categorized under the current definition of street gangs. Following suit, a new generation of street gangs was created out of the new immigrant populations that competed with newly emancipated African American slaves in the streets of New York in the infamous area called "Five Points." Five Points was considered a slum and was governed by gang-initiated violence. Irish gangs such as the Bowery Boys and Whyos were in competition with Jewish gangs like the Monk Eastman Gang. The social and economic turmoil of the area was evident in the estimated number of murders: one murder a day for 15 years, according to researchers.[3] Interestingly, gangs in the Five Points area helped shape and mold one of the most notorious organized crime entities in American history, the Mafia. The most notorious Mafia gangster in New York during the early 1900s was Alphonse Capone, better known as "Scarface." Gangs during this time started to become synonymous with lower-income classes, and communities started to deteriorate because of the "flight" of people into suburban areas to escape the destructiveness of gangs. All across America, street gangs flourished and became a mainstay for impoverished youth and economically depleted communities.

WHAT ARE GANGS LIKE TODAY, AND WHY DO YOUTH BECOME INVOLVED IN GANGS?

Current notable gangs such as Latin Kings, Vice Lords, Crips, Bloods, and Black Gangster Disciples are all derivatives of America's violent past. Schools are being faced with challenges associated with the inception of these violent entities. Although gangs are often a community-based problem, educators must take the first step in starting school-based initiatives that will deflect the lure of the street gang culture (see Figure 7.1).

In attempts to reduce involvement, educators must understand why youth are seduced by street gangs. As with discussions on risk factors, there are contributory issues that need to be discussed prior to the development of prevention and intervention strategies. Youth gangs that are prevalent in schools are sometimes considered "gang members in training" or "wanna-be's." The connotation is that these youth have not committed themselves completely to an available gang culture but are certainly leaning in that direction.

Youth join gangs and are at risk of gang involvement for various reasons. Researchers view youth gang involvement as consisting of both "pulls" and "pushes." *Pulls* refers to the attractiveness of the gang to the individual. Some pulls include increased status and respect from

LEVEL I   FANTASY
- Knows about gangs primarily from the media (music, movies, and literature)
- May or may not know about "real" gangs
- May or may not like, respect, or admire a gang, gang member, or the gang lifestyle

LEVEL II   AT-RISK
- Knows about gangs and gang members firsthand
- Occasionally associates with gang members
- Lives in or near gang areas (turf)
- May like or admire gangs or gang members as individuals
- May like and/or admire the gang lifestyle, but does not participate

LEVEL III   WANNA-BE / ASSOCIATE
- Knows and likes gang members firsthand
- Regularly associates with gang members
- Considers gangs and related activity as normal, acceptable, and admirable
- Finds many things in common with gang members
- Is seriously thinking about joining a gang

LEVEL IV   GANG MEMBER
- Is officially a gang member
- Associates almost exclusively with gang members to the exclusion of family and former friends
- Participates in gang crimes and most other related activities
- Is not considered hard core by fellow gang members or others
- Has substantially rejected the authority or value system of family and society

LEVEL V   HARD-CORE GANG MEMBER
- Totally committed to the gang and gang lifestyle
- Totally rejects anyone or any value system other than the gang
- Is considered hardcore by self, other gang members, and authorities
- Will commit any act with the approval of a demand from the gang
- Does not accept any authority other than the gang

E. H. Johnson, *Handbook on Crime and Delinquency Prevention* (New York: Greenwood Press, 1987), 1–12.

Figure 7.1. Levels of Individual Gang Involvement

one's peer group. Youth who are involved in gangs view themselves as having authority, power, and popularity. Popularity is an interesting byproduct of gang involvement, but it is understandable when you think of how violence is viewed in the current youth culture. Violence and the usage of violence are viewed by Generation Y as justifiable in many instances. Accepting violence as a viable option comes from the desensitizing and glorification of its existence. Youth are bombarded with images of violence in the media, and to have it reflect everyday life makes for the justification of its usage. Ultimately, media products assist in making it "cool" to be a violent member of a gang. For boys, gang involvement could also serve as a way to impress girls and provide opportunities to be with them sexually. "Bad boys" attracting girls is not a new phenomenon, but it calls for an analysis of why girls possibly choose these types. Either way, sex does serve as a "pull" to potential gang involvement. Gangs also provide opportunities of excitement and rebellion against parents, guardians, and other authority figures. Simply posing as a "thug" provides excitement for some youth. Along with excitement, there are opportunities to benefit financially through the selling of drugs or other profitable crimes, such as robbery and theft. These factors all serve as rational reasons for gang involvement for many youth. Youth are always conducting informal cost-benefit analyses. For gang involvement, there are more benefits than there are costs. The personal advantages listed above are all beneficial, and the costs are never enough to deter involvement. Youth see themselves as impenetrable and indestructible, so the cost of one's life or jail is not enough to distract them from the attainment of these personal advantages.

The opposite of *pull*, of course, is *push*. There are many factors that push youth into possible gang involvement. Those factors include social, economic, and cultural facets that make youth more prone to the allures of the gang lifestyle. These pushes are oftentimes out of the control of many youth. They do not have any control over the neighborhood that they are reared in or the nurturing environment of a family. Family dysfunction is a primary push for many youth who join gangs. The gang often serves as a surrogate family and fills in some of the gaps in the home. Parents and family structures that cannot meet some of the basic needs may push youth into a gang situation, especially if there is an accessible gang in the community that has shown signs of being a supportive structure. The definition of family should include not only biological parents, but also support from grandparents, uncles, aunts, siblings, and other close-knit guardians. The epitome of a supportive and nurturing family structure provides youth with the following: food, clothing, shelter, love, discipline, belonging, identification, security, and status.

Youth who are part of a family that exhibits some type of dysfunction and is not able to provide some of these components will become more susceptible to the lure of a gang. The gang "family" promises most of these components, but it also offers the attraction of money, drugs, sex, and power. These four components alone are enough to steer some youth into gangs. Youth who see this as a way of life and an integral part of their existence will be more apt to stay involved into adulthood, thus creating a more difficult process to intervene.

Another push that impacts youth involvement is the normal tribulations of adolescent development. Youth who may not have enough supports as they move through adolescence are being placed at risk of failure simply because they have not been exposed to the necessary social competencies to be successful. Competencies such as conflict management and problem solving are keys for youth who may have grown up in violent communities and schools. Saving face and "turning the other cheek" may not be a revered practice in some neighborhoods and can be perceived by educators as a liability in building social competencies. Teachers urge youth daily to "walk away," but this strategy, to some youth, is a sign of weakness. Weakness in many environments is detrimental, or at least that is the perception of many youth today. In this regard, youth may sometimes find themselves as victims of incidents of violence, whether perpetuated by a single bullying incident or a gang. For this reason, youth may join a gang for protection from other gangs to avoid being perceived as weak or a victim. Youth have also reported that neighborhood gangs sometimes violently coerce them into involvement. The options being presented to many youth are to either join the gang or continue to be a victim. For many youth faced with this decision, it is easier to choose safety. The youth seemingly have "no choice," and without a supportive family network, this will be the most rational decision.

In the same vein of being coerced, some youth are born into gangs as a result of their family's participation. Familial-based gang structures are an incredible obstacle to overcome, simply because of what they imply. Traditional family structures give youth opportunities in learning about the world around them and how they are to interact. Families are the first educators of our youth and seen as where standards of morals and values are introduced. All families are not aligned the same, but in America most families are governed by certain standards. One example is the golden rule of "do unto others." Unfortunately, not all families in America adopt and teach this rule. This being said, families that rear youth into an existing gang culture are setting youth up for failure. Respect, honor, and other long-standing values may be a part of the rearing process of parents who are involved in gangs. The chronic criminality and destructive decisions being perpetuated by the family's gang involvement will invariably create a mindset that this is normal for youth. Educators who have witnessed youth who are, for example, third-generation gang members understand that these youth are the most difficult to reach. It is an arduous process to convince children that their family is not leading them to be productive citizens. Imagine attempting to change the belief structure of an individual. If that person was socialized in an environment that embraced the gang lifestyle, then the process of changing his or her mindset would be comparable to convincing Americans to abandon the tradition of Thanksgiving.

The final push to discuss is the cultural status of minorities in America. The reality is that major contributing factors to the prevalence of gangs are racism, oppression, and prejudice. From Irish immigrants coming onto the shores of America, to African Americans during the civil rights movement, historically the "minority" population suffers disenfranchisement from the mainstream. This leads to obvious alienation and severe economic deprivation. Gang formation from this perspective is a function of many culminating factors. Young Mexican adolescents to this day speak of the impact of the Zoot Suit riots in 1943 and the formation of many modern-day gangs. Since 1942, growing tensions between servicemen from southern California and Mexicans led to many incidents of violence, robberies, and increased dissent. During the time of war rationing in World War II, young Mexican boys donned flamboyant outfits called Zoot Suits. This act served as a rallying cry for soldiers, who saw it as being unpatriotic, and Mexicans became a scapegoat from the enemy (Japanese). Not being supportive of the war efforts and ongoing prejudices were the catalysts for what was to come. Soldiers, while on leave, assaulted young Mexican boys and set off a series of skirmishes in what is known as the Zoot Suit riots. Because of the assaults, young Mexican boys rallied in self-defense of themselves and community. One of the most notorious gangs on the West Coast was derived from these acts of racism and violence. This is one example of how race and cultural status play into the push of youth being involved in gangs.

Identifying Youth Involved in Gangs

Early identification of gang-related activity and behavior is important. Within the school and community, educators and parents must be aware of specific patterns of antisocial behavior that can signal possible gang involvement. The initial strategy in preventing gang activity is to learn where it is taking place, who's involved, what types of activities are being engaged in, why they are doing it, and what resources the community has. Knowing these dimensions will assist in strategy development and the implementation of policies by administration. Recognizing some of the signs of the presence of gangs means to first understand that members often view their gang as their family. Within this family, gang members must "represent" their family at all times.

Representing their family refers to showing through dress and behaviors their affiliation with a particular gang. Representing is a form of respect and a key facet for gang members in showing loyalty. The most obvious way to represent is by wearing clothes that are the same color or have a common color pattern. Along with recognizing color, one must be aware of sports logos and numbers. For example, the color red traditionally is worn by Bloods. Blood gang members wear red shirts, pants, and shoes, or red necklaces, beads, and jewelry. To also assist in identification, they use the number 5 to represent their gang affiliation. So on a red shirt you may see the number 5 or a five-pointed star. Youth are very innovative in how they represent their gang through dress. For most kids, wearing an innocent Sponge Bob Square Pants t-shirt shows their admiration for the character. For a gang member, it could represent their disrespect for another gang. Blood gang members who wear this particular T-shirt explain that Sponge Bob eats Crabby-Patties, and the derogatory term for a Crip is a Crab. Thus the aggressive tone of Bloods eating Crabs (Crips) is an obvious sign of disrespect. Each gang has their own specific way of representing via the mode of dress. Any piece of garment can be used to represent. It is also important to note that some fashions may not necessarily be indicative of gang involvement. Some of the current fashions emulate gangster dress because the style is looked upon as cool. There is a fine line between the popular culture and gang culture. To this end, being aware of multiple indicators will provide a better understanding of youth involvement or the presence of gangs in the school.

Gang members will also represent the group through the use of graffiti. Graffiti is one of the first indicators of a gang presence in a school or community. Graffiti can be found on the back of business buildings, in alleys, on the back of street signs, and on sidewalks, trash containers, school bathrooms, and school books. Graffiti is used by gangs to show what they may "claim" as their turf or where they reside. In regards to "claiming turf," the graffiti will generally be in more visible areas to ward off any other area gangs. Most people may not be able to interpret graffiti, but one should be intuitive about what one is viewing. There is an obvious difference between "I HATE SCHOOL" and "BGD 187." "BGD" refers to the Black Gangsta Disciples, and the number "187" refers to the California Penal Code for homicide and murder. The graffiti reads that the gang has an intention to commit murder or is ruthless enough to do so at a drop of a hat. If the graffiti is not understood, educators should ask local law enforcement, juvenile officers, and, if present, the local gang task force. Regardless, educators should follow the "3 R's" in dealing with graffiti on school property: Recognize, Record, and Remove. Recognizing the graffiti will assist educators in understanding which gangs are present in their school and other potential threats (see Figure 7.2). Recording it means taking

---

- Skips school or misses work often
- Significant drop in school achievements
- Shows a strong disrespect for authority
- Significant change in attitude
- Spends time with negative peer group
- Desires a lot of privacy and time away from the family
- Refuses to take part in family activities
- Stays out later than usual
- Unexplained injuries, cuts, and bruises
- Drinking alcohol and using other drugs
- Has more money than normal, along with other possessions
- Starts to have an interest in tattoos or actually gets one
- Marks personal property with specific codes and symbols
- Fascination with violence and gangs in media
- Speaks of needing protection and carries a weapon

Figure 7.2. Some Typical Signs of Gang Involvement

a picture and logging the date and time the graffiti was found. Lastly, removing it immediately is critical to prevent any potential problems that may stem from its presence. Removing it also sends a message to the gang that it will not be tolerated. Ignoring it will incite only more graffiti and the belief by nongang members that the school does not care for their individual safety.

Other notable signs of involvement include the usage of hand signs. Recent conversations surrounding the usage of gang hand signs at professional sporting events have sparked a renewed interest in the subculture. Educators have long understood the implications of this nonverbal form of communication. Yearbook pictures, touchdown scoring celebrations, and lunchroom interactions are only a few venues where gang hand signs are prevalent within the school community. Hand signs can simply be used to secretly communicate to fellow gang members without others knowing, or they can be used to intimidate rival gangs. "Throwing" and "flashing" are the general terms used to describe hand signs by gang members. Hand signs are the derivatives of sign language, and fingers are contorted to represent affiliations and communicate messages. Youth who use hand signs are not always involved in gangs. Hand signs such as "bunny ears" and the "peace sign" are common. It is important for educators and parents to understand the context in how the hand signs are being used:

- Is it in an aggressive manner?
- Do others react negatively?
- What is the history of the youth who is "throwing" or "flashing"?
- Are the hand signs one more piece of the puzzle in determining gang involvement?

All of these questions are critical in determining gang involvement and youth who may be at risk of involvement.

ROLE OF THE SCHOOL IN REDUCING GANG INVOLVEMENT

School administrators must develop and integrate gang policies and practices that will prevent gang activity and intervene once a youth has decided to become involved. Schools must first develop a definition of gangs and the dynamics of gang activities on the campus. Educators can utilize definitions set by local school systems or by the state. Either way, most gangs can be defined by the following characteristics:

- A group of three or more persons
- Members view themselves as a gang and they are recognized by others as a gang
- Shares a common identity, usually through a gang name
- Adopts and utilizes certain signs, symbols, and colors
- The group has some permanence and a degree of organization
- Individually or collectively engages in criminal activity

This definition, without the criminal engagement component, can embody sports teams, fraternities, sororities, and organizations. Regardless, it is critical for staff to come to a consensus on what to look for and to be adequately trained on the aforementioned signs of gang activity. Staff developments should focus on increasing the awareness of all staff, and administrators should call on local law enforcement and juvenile justice personnel to determine local trends. There should also be specialized training for administrators, counselors, and school psychologists about working with and intervening with gang-involved youth. Staff should also be trained on how to respond to confrontations, and the crisis response team should be organized to be able to handle the possibility of gang-related violence. The aforementioned trainings and presentations should be provided on a consistent basis, and a concerted effort needs to be made to understand issues that mitigate increased gang activity. Schools should pay attention to their suspension and expulsion rates and be aware of the fact that juvenile crime increases during unsupervised time. An examination of policies such as these is warranted, as they may lead to potential delinquency.

Other policies are needed to implement a code of student conduct regarding gang activity, symbols, and clothing at school. There should be a policy in place that speaks to guidelines regarding bullying, intimidation, and harassment. There also needs to be an emphasis on dress, graffiti, insignias, hand signs, turf claiming, hats, belt buckles, and other ways gang members show affiliation. The consequences need to be clearly established and known by all youth. Yet these discipline policies need to be backed by supportive policies and programs that are geared toward changing and modifying the behavior of gang members. It is not enough to remove the youth involved from the school premises, because they will return with the similar mentality. Schools need to also entertain and discuss the possibility of utilizing a uniform dress code. Schools that have enacted a dress code have found noticeable differences, yet once again this should not be the end-all attempt. Dress codes do not necessarily mean uniforms, but they could address the issues of baggy pants, gang dress, and other ways that youth represent their gang affiliation. Other policy questions that should be answered include the following:

- Is there a system available to staff and students to report criminal incidents?
- Is there a system established to record incidents of disruptive and/or criminal behavior on campus?
- Does this system provide guidelines for differentiating between gang-related and non–gang-related incidents?
- In the event of an actual or suspected gang-related incident, are these activities reported to law enforcement?
- Is there a policy established to ensure a timely and effective response to reporting of incidents?
- Is information from other schools or districts on expelled students shared prior to transfer to this school, for example, on the nature of the expulsion, social history, gang affiliation, etc.?
- Is gang intelligence kept by a central source on campus, such as an administrator, probation officer, campus police, or gang specialist?

The next step is to determine if there is indeed a gang problem and if it is a priority for the school and school system. This can be done by surveying teachers, students, parents, and other staff to determine the extent and dynamics of the problem. Along with surveys, interviews within the school community and even with known or former gang members could provide validity to the assessment. The results from the assessment should guide administrators in the implementation of a response. The assessment should provide educators and community with an understanding of *who, when, what, where,* and *how* gangs are prevalent at the school. Assessing the school's gang problem and evaluating the effectiveness of the response is a continual and cyclical process. Assessment can be done biannually or even at the beginning of each semester or marking period. The selected time frame is not critical. The key point here is that an assessment provides essential information for determining the appropriate prevention and intervention strategies and programs.

BEST PRACTICES REGARDING SCHOOLS AND GANG PREVENTION AND INTERVENTION

The process of being aware of these possible signs of involvement means that educators and parents should be attentive to "red flags" that serve as warnings. There are a myriad warning signs to gang activity that serve as a starting point in developing prevention and intervention strategies at the school and within the community. It is important to understand that the risk factors for general delinquency are the same as for potential gang involvement. Thus the warning signs for gang involvement have to be within the appropriate context to avoid mislabeling. Developing a comprehensive plan that includes the entire the community is essential. It is important for the community to recognize that the school is only one part of the community-wide response to gangs that is needed to be effective.

There are five important strategies, as stated in the Office of Juvenile Justice and Delinquency Prevention's Comprehensive Gang Model (CGM), to consider in any attempt to prevent and intervene a gang problem. The first strategy is to mobilize the community around the problem. This means incorporating support from local citizens, former gang-involved youth, youth-serving organizations, law enforcement, juvenile justice, and educators. This cross section of entities will be critical in assessing the gang problem in the community. The steering committee and task force will be derived from these mobilization efforts. The next strategy is to provide opportunities that are targeted toward gang-involved youth. These opportunities should center on education, training, and employment programs that will assist in diverting gang involvement and filling in the gaps where the gang support system was removed. This leads perfectly into the next strategy of conducting social interventions that will reach out to gang-involved youth and their families. Social interventions require the involvement of the faith community, youth-serving agencies, and others in coordinating and providing services. These services are a necessary part in preventing possible involvement and creating a sense of success outside of the gang. The flip side of this method is suppression. In short, suppression is the formal and informal social control procedures used to prohibit and curtail gang involvement and related activities. Close supervision, monitoring, surveillance, and incarceration are all facets of suppressive strategies aimed at eliminating gang growth.

The last strategy in the comprehensive model is organizational change and development. This strategy focuses on the development and implementation of procedures and policies to address the problem. The proposed change focuses on the current way that communities do "business" and altering it to have a positive impact on gang proliferation. The CGM is not a program to put in place in your community. The CGM is a way to organize silolike institutions (health, human services, juvenile justice, education, community groups, etc.) to band together and create the most comprehensive continuum of services possible to reduce the effects of gang-infested communities.

After the initial assessment, schools need to understand the dynamics of the most opportune time to initiate prevention and intervention strategies. Research shows that there are windows of opportunity, that certain prevention strategies are most effective at particular ages and grade levels.[4] Prevention is most effective for elementary-school-age youth, and the risk factors that need to be addressed surround conduct problems, elementary school failure, and incidents of delinquency. If prevention and intervention strategies are not in place, then once a child becomes of high school age, the window of opportunity significantly closes and suppression becomes a necessary strategy.

Schools should adopt a three-tiered approach to dealing with gangs: primary, secondary, and tertiary. Primary prevention and intervention should focus on the entire school population. Schools that endeavor to make a difference, regardless of the grade level, should start by identifying youth who are at risk of gang involvement or already involved. This identification is not meant to label or stereotype youth. This provides an understanding of whom to provide more targeted interventions. The risk factors or conditions to be identified include personal, social, and/or environmental. All these entities can potentially promote criminal behavior. Schools across America have implemented programs that target violence, drugs, and other social problems.[5] The Gang Resistance Education and Training (GREAT) program is one such program that has garnered much attention for its efforts to provide youth with tools to resist the lure of gangs. Although there is some skepticism about its effectiveness, GREAT employs many best practices such as conflict resolution skills, cultural competency, and exposing youth to the negative aspects of gang life.

Other best practices in primary prevention and intervention focus on increasing the social competencies of the entire school population. Strategies to do so can be framed under opportunities to connect youth to the school meaningfully. This can be done from the administrator's office and in each individual classroom. Principals utilize student government to assist in shaping school policy as it relates to the student body. Positive outcomes can also be attained by involving youth who would usually not be a part of the decision-making process. Having the input of high-risk youth will keep them engaged and make them feel that the school hears their voices. Constant conversations and integration into the daily lessons should include topics such as goal setting, pro-social peers, responsibility at school and community, and overcoming obstacles. Early discussions and high expectations provide youth with a foundation that is securely centered on education. Education, with continual encouragement of parental involvement, can yield results that will surpass the gang prevention objective and will lead to success on a larger scale. Primary prevention is about providing life skills to youth that will empower them to resist peer pressure to join a gang and that will modify attitudes and beliefs regarding any misaligned measures of attaining success.

Secondary prevention and intervention methods target youth who are identified as having greater risk of becoming involved in a gang. School efforts toward secondary prevention should provide opportunities for building recreational, educational, and life skills. These efforts should enhance young people's ability to problem-solve and communicate effectively, and they should also help alter their belief system and skill set to deal with conflict. This population of youth generally is case-managed, and their progress is tracked. Some of the measures to evaluate are discipline referrals, school attendance, contact with the juvenile justice system, and grades. This allows administrators, teachers, and caseworkers to acknowledge improvement in pro-social behaviors or to determine if youth are engaging in activities that could lead to gang involvement, such as associating with delinquent peers.

An example of a successful secondary prevention program is the Montreal Prevention Treatment Program, which addressed early childhood risk factors by targeting young boys from low socioeconomic backgrounds.[6] These youth were exhibiting disruptive behaviors while in kindergarten, and their communities were infested with gang activity. The program offered parents training on effective discipline techniques, crisis management, and other skills related to effective parenting. The young boys participated in sessions that emphasized self-control and the development of pro-social skills. The results were positive: significantly fewer boys were gang members by the age of 15. These targeted approaches can yield positive results and should be a successful accompaniment to any antigang efforts for the entire school population.

The final tier is tertiary prevention, which targets youth who are already involved in a gang and criminal activity. This approach was initially seen as mainly suppressive in nature. But research on nationwide programs that relied on a law enforcement presence showed that although the intent was to hold gangs accountable to the fullest extent of the law, these programs were not going to make an impact unless there was a marriage of prevention, intervention, and suppression strategies. In this attempt, tertiary strategies, from a school perspective, will use a targeted outreach approach. Utilizing community resources and employing a part-time or full-time outreach worker to serve as a "go-between" for the school and community will prove helpful in gang prevention efforts. Outreach workers can serve as mentors and role models, while at the same time working with the youth and family that are impacted by the gang. Providing all of the above-mentioned skills is critical, but the outreach worker will also provide daily assistance with such problems as leaving a gang and responding to crises associated with gang activity. Schools could employ volunteers to serve as mentors for youth involved in gangs, but results are mixed. A mentor with a background in gang outreach can prove to be more beneficial. The best practices to employ include the use of mentors, cooperation with law enforcement, monitoring and surveillance, and intensive family engagement.

CONCLUDING THOUGHT

The complexity of the youth gang issue should not prevent schools from trying to find a solution. Understanding the dynamics of youth gang involvement and its notions of a glamorous lifestyle can hold significant keys toward developing strategies. School and community awareness of the problem will create buy-in and make gang participation a priority for all key stakeholders. Most individuals are oblivious to the prevalence of gangs until it directly impacts their life. This should not be the starting point of action. A proactive approach and open-mindedness that gangs affect all students is where all school-based strategies should begin. The three tiers of strategies are obviously interdependent. Schools that strive to have an impact on potential and current gang involvement need to consider how to pull resources and manpower in creating strategies to fulfill each tier. Educators should understand that all youth are at risk of gang involvement and dispel the belief that some youth are "not worth saving." Gang prevention and intervention is not an exact science, and each situation should be treated as a potential threat to school safety. There is no one "magic bullet" program or best practice, but with the coordination of school staff, parents, and other youth-serving professionals, the factors that make gangs a perceived necessity can be remedied.

Chapter 8

Managing Conflict to Build Positive Relationships

Danya C. Perry

Conflict in and of itself is not positive or negative. Since conflict frequently involves differences that may lead to disputes, it has received a negative connotation. When conflict is viewed as positive, it can be looked upon as an opportunity to learn more about oneself and the dispute. Conflict is a natural part of life. When conflict is understood, it can become an opportunity to learn and create. The challenge for people in conflict is to apply the principles of creative cooperation in their human relationships.[1]

The concept of effective conflict management is one that many youth today do not truly understand. This is evident when we work directly with youth in an attempt to highlight the need to solve problems peaceably. An activity that I use to make the point that youth often think in terms of conflict is called "No-Arm Wrestling." Without giving them the name of this activity, I ask for two volunteers to sit across from each other and clasp their hands together. What's interesting is that when I state this first part of the activity, the nonparticipating youth automatically start to cheer for their friend, while others yell "Uh-Ohh!" This type of bystander effect now starts to affect the two participating youth, and one can see the intensity in their eyes; they HAVE to win! That is their number one objective.

"Now that you have your hands clasped, the objective of this activity is to see how many times you can put the other person's hand onto the table. You have 30 seconds to do this. Whoever puts the other person's hand down the most WINS!!!" I then share with them the prize, which is usually a small trinket or t-shirt, secondary to the ultimate prize of garnering the respect from their peers with a win. "Now here is another stipulation: at the end of 30 seconds, if you tie, then you both win." Then I inform the participants that they have one minute to talk to each other. You can probably imagine that, at this point, the participants are in no mood to talk; they want to battle. In 10 years of conducting this activity with youth, I have never seen a single youth actually decide to use this moment to talk to his opponent. This is quite telling of the current youth culture.

I now turn to the audience and ask them to give me a "on your mark, get set, go," which just magnifies the situation and is a final confirmation to the participating youth that they are in a competition and a win is the only option if they are to be respected by their peers.

"On your mark, get set, GO!"

The two youth begin to struggle with each other as they try to wrestle the other person's hand down to the table. The crowd is going wild, and I am counting down from 30 seconds: "4, 3, 2, 1, STOP!" The two exhausted youth now turn to me to declare the winner, and no matter the outcome my first question to them is "Did anyone tell you to arm wrestle?" At this point, they are completely confused, and I take the opportunity to remind them of the instructions.

1. Sit down across the table from each other and clasp your hands together.
2. See how many times you can put the other's hand down on the table in 30 seconds.
3. You can win by having more put-downs than the other or by having a tie.
4. You have one minute to talk to each other.

At this point the youth are feeling duped, and I ask why they did not utilize the one minute to discuss the possibility of a "tie," which would be a "win-win" strategy. The light bulb now illuminates, and the entire group is ready to discuss the nature of conflict and options to manage the daily occurrence that they will most certainly be faced with.

Conflicts are a fact of life to be dealt with, not a sign of failure. Conflict can help people succeed in relationships, personally and professionally. Experiencing conflict is an opportunity for growth and learning. It allows individuals to communicate their feelings and interests. Sharing opinions and differences enables people to feel that their views are being taken into account. This can motivate individuals to work harder to come to agreement. Conflict that is effectively managed can result in increased creativity, rethinking of goals and practices, and a better-informed and cohesive work group.[2] The opportunity to express feelings, get points of view clarified, and stand up for one's beliefs are all positive aspects of conflict. Other benefits include motivation for change, production of better ideas, development of respect for opposing views, and learning new ways to manage conflict for improved relationships.

CHARACTERISTICS OF CONFLICT

There are also negative aspects of conflict. If not handled correctly, these consequences break down relationships and lead to nonproductive behaviors. Destructive attributes of conflict may include hurt feelings, disagreements, anger, threats, and violence. Negative conflict can result in debilitating emotional experiences, and it can destroy the well-being of individuals. Other characteristics of conflict include the following:

- Decreased productivity
- Frustration
- Decreased morale
- Alienation of individuals
- Unaddressed problems
- Confusion
- Climate of mistrust[3]

Conflict is a natural and inevitable part of everyone's life. At some point, everyone will encounter or face a conflict. It is important to understand that conflict often cannot be resolved. That's why it is critical to emphasize and provide youth with skills to manage conflict as it arises. Students' perceptions of conflict have a major influence on how they deal with it. As it relates to America's schools, conflict is often seen negatively because of its escalation into outbursts and violent incidents. But in many instances conflict can actually bring about change and stimulate ideas. Either way, the occurrence of conflict is not the root problem, but rather how we manage or deal with conflict once it arises. Students today are ill equipped to deal effectively with conflict. Conflict or ineffective ways of dealing with it are acceptable in a culture that supports violence and within negative peer groups. Regardless of the misperceptions, it is critical to teach students how to manage conflict to ensure that the school environment is conducive to learning.

DEFINITION OF CONFLICT

The first step in developing effective strategies is to properly define conflict. Conflict is "an expressed struggle between at least two interdependent parties who perceive themselves as having incompatible goals, view resources as being scarce, and regard each other as interfering with the achievement of their own goals."[4] Conflict has been defined in many ways, but this definition expresses the importance of the relationship between opposing ideas and the inadequate resources that frequently leads to conflict. To illustrate the finer points of this definition, let's analyze a few scenarios.

Scenario One: Struggle between Parties

Billy and Jamal are classmates in high school and play different sports. Billy plays baseball, and Jamal plays basketball. In class, the two get into an argument about their sports passion. Billy's opinion is that baseball is America's favorite pastime, whereas Jamal differs by touting football. This difference of opinion, although viewed as light-hearted by observers, is a conflict that many have experienced in their lifetime. One can easily observe the opposing belief structures. The classmates' goal is to convince the other that "their" sport is more important than the other's choice. The question that comes into play is, can they "agree to disagree" or accept the fact and value the other's point of view? These two incompatible goals could possibly lead to a violent act without proper skill building or intervention.

This first scenario is simple to understand. To focus on resources being scarce, let's look at another scenario.

Scenario Two: Scarce Resources

Billy and Jamal are in art class, and the lesson being taught requires the usage a paintbrush. Billy and Jamal go to the art supply closet and find that there is only one paintbrush left. Billy grabs the paintbrush by one end and Jamal grabs it by the other end. They begin to push, pull, and argue about who should be able to use the paintbrush first. Here the conflict arises because there are not enough paintbrushes for both Billy and Jamal. The paintbrushes are the scarce resource, or at least that is the perception. Once again, it must be kept in mind "how" these youth could deal with this normal conflict without resorting to violence.

The final part of the definition is the interference with the achievement of one's goals. The last scenario illustrates this point.

Scenario Three: Interference with One's Goals

Jamal enjoys going to school and values education. Every day that Jamal goes to lunch, he is approached by Billy. Billy has bullied Jamal for the last year and proceeds to push Jamal so that he drops his lunch tray. Jamal usually does not fight back, but he is starting to react negatively. Jamal's grades begin to drop and he misses class frequently. Teachers and other students both agree that Jamal may become extremely aggressive if these bullying incidents do not subside. In this scenario, Jamal has a goal that most adults strive to give their youth: academic proficiency. Because of Billy's actions, Jamal's goals are being hindered, and he could act out aggressively given the circumstances.

In each of the three scenarios, one can see how conflict is manifested in various ways. Educators are faced every day with scenarios that oftentimes lead to aggression and violence, whether verbal or physical. Yet, in the same breath, one can observe where the students in each scenario could have managed the conflict more effectively. Before moving into opportunities to manage conflict effectively, it is important to figure out "why" youth view violence and aggression as a first resort in dealing with a problem. Simply put, social skills are lacking in youth across the nation. Social skills are socially accepted learned behaviors that enable a person to interact with others in ways that elicit positive responses and assist in avoiding negative responses.[5] Too many youth exhibit negative behaviors at school because they lack the necessary skills to use positive behaviors to meet their basic needs. The question is, why are the skills to interact in a constructive and cooperative manner not developed?

In many instances youth find violence as an acceptable option for resolving a problem. These negative values seem to be embedded in the current youth culture and come from various domains. The home and family interaction is the single greatest influence on how youth mange conflict and problem-solve. Parents are the first models of appropriate problem-solving techniques. In a dysfunctional environment, youth can see examples of how "not" to react to the daily occurrences of conflict. For example, if there is violence that occurs domestically (in the home), then violence may become an option for youth who have to deal with a problem. Any changes in the traditional family structure can also lead to ineffective conflict management. Changes such as separation, divorce, and moving can reduce exposure to parents who model constructive conflict management. In some cases, both parents work and have limited time to interact with family members. In other cases, children live with a single parent. In such cases, and others, children may have limited exposure to positive models of adults resolving conflicts.

The second influence is the peer group. It is not difficult to see where peer influence could steer youth into inappropriate problem-solving skills. Even if youth "know" how to deal effectively with conflict, doing so can be deemed as "uncool," especially for young male adolescents. Walking away from a fight or seeking administrative assistance can be seen as nonmasculine. There is an obvious American culture that speaks to the definition of how a "man" is supposed to carry himself or deal with problems. The peer group, especially for males, will call for dealing with a problem aggressively to ensure that one's respect and status within the school or community are maintained.

The same can be said for when youth are in the neighborhood. Community norms can set the standard for how to deal with conflict. The escalation of violence in America today starts with fists, moves to sticks, knives, then to guns. This progression sometimes happens in communities that have been historically plagued with violence. Youth even justify the use of violence as "the only way to survive" in their environment. This may be a valid point, but to have a community where this is the norm is troubling.

The last domain to discuss is the indirect influence of the media. The long-term effects of media violence on youth aggression have recently been gaining attention. The modes of media include television, movies, music, video games, and the Internet. These various modes can have detrimental effects on how our youth view the world and in some instances desensitize them to violence.[6] From violent movies to music with destructive messages, youth find themselves validating violence because of the pop stars that they idolize or revere. This phenomenon is not just recent. Visions of old westerns come into mind in which John Wayne would deal with a problem by calling a man out onto the street to deal with it aggressively. Yet today, with the advancement of technology and the consistent viewing of the ineffective management of conflict through violence, youth are learning that this is an acceptable practice.

Conflict management is the strategy that must be employed at the school-building level and also in the community. At the schools, it is critical to develop a comprehensive approach. The entire school and local community must be part of efforts that support effective conflict management. Such a program offers members of the school and community the opportunity to learn, practice, and model skills that lead to effective conflict management. It is apparent that this will be a long process and will need coordination with local partners to become truly comprehensive. Taking a phased approach will assist in accomplishing tasks and setting easily reached milestones.

INFUSING CONFLICT MANAGEMENT INTO THE SCHOOL AND COMMUNITY

The first phase should start in the school. Administrators could utilize peer mediation programs, which allow for students to be trained as mediators to help their classmates solve conflict without resorting to unnecessary violence (see Figure 8.1). In addition, administrators could encourage all classrooms to teach conflict management. There are many studies that link classroom disruptions to poor academic performance and increased incidents of school violence throughout the year.[7] This research supports the notion of starting at the classroom level. Over time, as students and teachers experience the benefits of teaching and learning conflict management styles and strategies, these methods can expand into the community.

To ensure that students are being taught appropriate problem-solving skills, it is critical to include both peer mediation and conflict management in the curriculum. Preparing teachers through professional

Student peer mediation programs train students to guide other students involved in a dispute through the process. Mediation is a voluntary, informal, structured process in which an impartial third party, called a mediator, helps disputing parties to generate and evaluate options for reaching a mutually acceptable agreement. A mediator does not have the power to impose an agreement on the parties. The mediation process provides the disputing parties with an effective structure and a set of ground rules for pursuing a negotiated resolution to the problem. A variety of age-appropriate mediation models exist. Most models for grades 6 to adult include the following:

- Explanation of mediation and agreement to and rules
- Agreements among the participants that they will keep the process confidential, focus on the problem, respect each other, and refrain from interruptions
- Each participant shares his/her perception of the dispute
- Each participant summarizes the others' perceptions and feelings
- Participants brainstorm possible solutions
- Participants achieve a mutual agreement or decide that no agreement can be reached
- Participants are congratulated or, if no agreement is reached, participants either agree to disagree peacefully or be referred to the counselor

Student mediation programs may be operated inside or outside the classroom. Some mediation are scheduled and conducted at a table in a designated "mediation room." Other mediations occur "on the spot" where the dispute arises—on the playground, in the lunchroom, or in the hallway. Some schools train all students to be able to mediate anywhere, because they are dealing with disputes involving jealousy, rumors, misunderstandings, bullying, fights, and ending of friendships. Mediators do not handle situations that involve drugs, weapons, or sexual abuse. Most mediation programs report that agreements are reached in approximately 90–95% of the time.

C. W. Moore, *The Mediation Process* (San Francisco: Jossey-Bass, 1986), 24.

Figure 8.1. What Is Peer Mediation?

development and adapting a new teaching pedagogy are the beginning of any successful conflict management initiative. It is just as imperative to teach students. Empowering youth to make a difference in their school environment provides them with a sense of ownership and school pride. Students then feel responsible for their own success, along with their classmates.

The implemention of conflict management programs will vary across school districts. Each entity will have its own set of goals, objectives, and desired outcomes. Regardless of these differences, some characteristics of successful programs need to be contemplated. Educational assessment, planning, and evaluation are important. But of all of these characteristics, "buy-in" is the most important, yet the most difficult to facilitate. Successful programs start out with "buy-in" from the entire school community and community-at-large. Engaging key stakeholders in the community is important, along with gaining input from everyone in the school, including those who may not have been traditionally a part of the process (e.g., bus drivers, cafeteria workers). The goals and objectives must be supported by everyone in order to establish a climate that fully supports the program.

In gaining "buy-in" in the community, successful conflict management programs do a good job in promoting the initiative. Staff development programs, parent education seminars, civic organization presentations, and church-sponsored events can provide opportunities to make the school's mission visible. These awareness activities also aid in teaching adults effective conflict management skills. This is important because chances are increased that the promoted skills will be taught to youth in the homes, community centers, and detention centers to youth-serving professionals and invested community members. This consistent role modeling of effective conflict management skills by adults outside the school can offset attempts by negative peers and other factors that can encourage using violence to solve problems.

Although starting a conflict management initiative is not an easy process, it is paramount to create a strong foundation to ensure its effectiveness and sustainability. The following additional characteristics will provide a solid framework to the success of any conflict management initiative. Once buy-in has been established, the next step is to create a planning committee to conduct a needs assessment to determine which conflict management strategy to employ. Understanding the nature of the problem locally is the first step toward finding possible solutions. For example, if the school community finds that bullying is the priority problem, then it is important to understand the what, when, where, why, and how. In many instances, simple surveillance and placement of school staff in key areas can curb the occurrences of bullying or any other violence-related problem.

Next, determine how conflict management will become institutionalized in all schools in a district. Once again, it is important to have the same message across the board, although there will be slight differences in implementation at the school-building level. A coordinated plan can benefit the entire school system and community. Changing the status quo is difficult, and some educators may need to be convinced. Utilizing evidence-based practices is a sure way to make the argument for such change. Changing the organizational capacity of the school takes time and may mean "contracting before expanding." Regardless, with patience, the plan can take shape and become the new landscape of how the school operates and teaches. This school-initiated plan can then take root in the community.

Next, designate a conflict management coordinator for the school district and each school. This coordinator will be responsible for professional development and staff development workshops, the sharing of new research and trends, and the review of coordinated plans. The coordinator will also assist in efforts to develop in-school curricular materials and training expertise. The school administration should not reposition this coordinator into a disciplinary role. The coordinator has to oversee and monitor the school's attempt to create a successful institutionalized change. The coordinator may also be asked to assist in training student facilitators for the peer mediation program. It may be a difficult process for the school to adopt mediation as an option for resolving all conflicts. The coordinator can be responsible for finding and introducing other methods to derail escalating conflicts. The coordinator can therefore be responsible for ensuring the comprehensiveness, success, and sustainability of such programs.

WHAT DOES A SUCCESSFUL CONFLICT MANAGEMENT PROGRAM LOOK LIKE?

A successful and sustainable conflict management initiative must consistently educate students, teachers, guidance counselors, administrators, school board members, and parents. At the beginning of the process, these same individuals are sought out for input. After the "buy-in" stage, their involvement continues. The education and awareness process is arduous at the beginning but becomes commonplace once the strategies have been adopted into the culture of the school. Actively engaging the entire school community will assist in sustaining conflict management programs, even with administrator and teacher turnover. School systems have long been plagued with programs that end because the school did not invest in enough staff. Investing in all that are involved will alleviate any possibility of this occurrence. In addition, by developing partnerships with parents and leaders of civic organizations, the school system will have an opportunity to assist others in exploring ways in which conflict management concepts and skills can be infused into their activities.

Building the capacity of a school and community to effectively teach and model effective conflict resolution is critical. One cannot stress enough the importance of school- and instructional-based programs and initiatives to teach youth necessary conflict management and social skills. The skills taught must include inter- and intrapersonal problem solving, decision making, and the art of mediation and negotiation. Generically, programs and initiatives should include three major components:

- Appropriate behavior must be modeled, preferably by several people in a variety of situations.
- Learners must be given opportunities to practice the behavior with necessary guidance until they perform it "skillfully and spontaneously."
- Learners must be rewarded for successfully using the new behaviors outside the school environment.[8]

The specific content of any conflict management program should give youth an overview of the reasons for conflict, feelings and attitudes related to conflict, and the styles of dealing with conflict. There are a variety of such styles. A conflict management style is one's natural response. Most people do have a particular style that they usually use, but the ability to choose different styles in different situations is a necessary skill. One must understand that there is not just one best style to use; the styles have to vary from one situation to another. The five most common styles that need to be taught to students include the following:

- Compromising: to bargain and make concessions to come up with a solution in which both sides can be in agreement.
- Accommodating: to work cooperatively with another person without trying to assert one's own concerns or position.
- Collaborating: to assert one's position while still trying to cooperate with the other person. Attempting to find a "win-win" solution.
- Competing: to be very assertive and interested in getting one's own way, with not much interest in cooperating with other people.
- Avoiding: to avoid, evade, or delay a conflict entirely, with no intent to cooperate in finding a solution.[9]

Educators must also teach youth about the importance of communication in effective conflict management and social skills development. Communication can be conveyed in various ways, such as by words, gestures, emotions, and written messages. Communication often reflects "who" we are and "how" we were raised. Most people are aware of how they communicate, yet they give little consideration to the impressions of their words and behaviors. Normally there is a correlation between poor communication and ineffective conflict management. When one cannot communicate effectively, there are more opportunities to be misunderstood. Educators must teach youth to be active and reflective listeners. Active listeners can take an active role in the process of communication. There are four steps in active listening:

- Restatement: restating or paraphrasing a message
- Summary: summarizing the main issues of important points
- Responding to nonverbal cues: acknowledging and verbalizing the presence and effect of nonverbal messages

- Responding to feelings: acknowledging and verbalizing the presence and effect of expressed feelings[10]

Active listening ultimately means to take an active role in communication in the early treatment for conflict. Once students have mastered active listening, they will invariably become honest, compassionate, sincere, and attentive communicators.

Alongside active listening is reflective listening. Reflective listening is an active way of listening that focuses on the feelings of the speaker. Most describe reflective listening as "listening with your ears as well as with your heart." In order to be good at reflective listening, one must engage with the speaker to recognize his or her feelings. This builds up the listener's capacity to empathize with the speaker. Reflective listening allows for true understanding of the speaker's feelings that are being expressed. For example, instead of commenting on content, the reflective listener may add: "I know you were sad and upset when you found out that you didn't pass the test." This allows both parties to agree on the feelings being conveyed and will result in proper communication.

Lastly, conflict management programs should teach students about solving problems. This means working cooperatively to meet the needs of both participants and creating options that will lead to a positive outcome. Strategies that should be taught include the art of looking at both points of view, negotiating to resolve disputes, and mediating to come to a peaceful solution.

EVALUATION AND IMPROVEMENT

To ensure that the implemented strategies are effective, the school must evaluate to determine if it is meeting set goals and objectives. The most immediate measurements of effectiveness include discipline referrals, incidents of school violence, suspensions and expulsions, and other data that school systems collect annually. These are important measures, but the evaluation should go further. Interviews and observations, along with the data, will give countless benefits to a successful conflict management program. These qualitative data will change the landscape of the school community, which in turn affects the quantitative measures. Some of the benefits that schools site include the following:

- Teaching time is increased because less time is spent on managing classroom conflicts
- Knowledge of nonviolent options to resolve conflicts is greatly increased
- The ability to control one's behavior in conflict situations is increased
- Interpersonal communication skills are enhanced

- The ability to identify common interests and achieve "win-win" solutions is improved
- The school climate is improved
- Violence is prevented
- The time spent handling playground and lunchroom disputes is reduced
- The ability to deal constructively with anger and other strong emotions is increased
- Name calling and put-downs are reduced
- The ability to analyze and understand how conflicts escalate and deescalate is increased
- The ability to respect different perspectives is improved[11]

These benefits have been observed by educators on all levels who have implemented successful conflict management programs; they are contingent on being comprehensive. If only one teacher in an entire school utilizes effective strategies in problem solving, then these strategies only benefit the youth in that classroom. To achieve maximum benefit and to impact the greatest number of people, the design has to be supported by all teachers and staff.

CONCLUDING THOUGHT

Building the capacity of the school and community, along with curricular interventions, can affect the attitudes and behavior of youth who may deal with conflict ineffectively. There are many instances in which ineffective conflict management leads to extremely destructive decisions. Improving social skills can assist in eliminating any potential violent threats that may start from a simple misunderstanding. It is certainly possible to intervene effectively and to teach youth (along with educators) how to become better decision makers, which will invariably change the entire school climate. Success in introducing and supporting conflict management strategies will have long-term benefits that will be rewarding for both the school and the community.

Chapter 9

The Need for People, Not Programs

Danya C. Perry

I am a product of people who took time and were invested in my development. There were no formal program standards or evaluations that assisted the caring people in my life that contributed to my passion for learning and desire to help others. In sort of a "Pay It Forward" mode, I now am the mentor of 17 youth: 16 young men and 1 young lady. In my attempt to be a contributor to their development, I have realized a few things. All children need a support system, but they have no capacity to request this necessity. Each one of my mentees has challenged me in some capacity. Whether it be their gang involvement, substance abuse, or absent parents, each child had a unique situation that calls for an independent set of solutions. Undeniably, my presence is doing something that is difficult to measure. The fact that I am accessible at 3 o'clock in the morning is comforting to them. The fact that I get upset and disappointed when they fail to meet the challenge of academics or life is comforting to them. Even the day that I sat and watched one of my kids pass away at the hospital from a gunshot wound, there was comfort. In any situation, the commonality across the board is "I was there." What does "being there" mean? If I operationalize it, I would say "being there" is the basis of many youth-serving professionals. Whether it is in a personal or professional context, it requires taking the time to get to know an individual, providing the individual with a framework of community, and ensuring high expectations from each and every adult an individual comes in contact with. That is "being there." I tell all of my mentees that success is the balance of two factors: preparedness and opportunity. In order to help youth be successful, people need to be prepared to contribute, because we have plenty of opportunities.

PROGRAMS OR PEOPLE?

In an evidenced-based world, measuring effectiveness is becoming an integral part of the ever-changing landscape for entities that attempt to curb school violence. The country has been inundated with organizations, both public and private, that claim to have the solution to school violence by offering a specialized program. This is not to say that these programs do not offer a part of a solution or are ineffective, but our nation has become programmed to believe in programs. Grants and other funding sources are looking for the next "best program" like Tyra is looking for "America's Next Top Model." This invariably creates a "flavor of the month" mentality, where educators have to sort out and balance the implementation of a program with the next glamorized problem in America's schools. Unfortunately, many organizations are opportunistic and prey on the fact that we are always looking for the solution—or at least a solution that has enough "bells and whistles" to keep us interested.

The Center for the Study and Prevention of Violence launched an initiative in 1996 to identify violence prevention programs that were effective. The criteria used to determine if a program was a "model" worth undertaking included evidence of a deterrent effect with a strong research design, sustained effect, and multiple site replications. Other factors included mediating factors and costs versus benefits. The center came up with an impressive list of programs that met their standards or were deemed successful within their own right. After reviewing many of these programs, another commonality of effectiveness became evident: people. Although it may sound like a cliché, the ultimate reason that programs are successful is the people that "run" the programs. Now, one could argue that without a strong program design the program will not be successful, no matter who the "people" are. This would be an accurate statement, but the same goes for the reverse. The argument for "people" and not programs is the nexus for a strategy for effective school violence prevention. Most, if not all, intervention programs for at-risk youth recognize adult interaction as a critical factor for positive youth outcomes and include it as a program component in some way. Adults may serve as role models, educators, authority figures, or counselors. In fact, one of the five critical resources in America's Promise, founded by former Secretary of State Colin L. Powell, is for communities to "provide all young people with sustained adult relationships through which they experience support, care, guidance, and advocacy."[1] What the former secretary is referring to is a mentor: utilizing people to make a difference.

The original mentor is a character in Homer's epic poem *The Odyssey*. When Odysseus, king of Ithaca, went to fight in the Trojan War, he entrusted the care of his kingdom to Mentor. Mentor served as the teacher and overseer of Odysseus's son, Telemachus. During his voyage, Odysseus irritated a few gods, who, in their effort to destroy him, kept him at sea for many years. Upon his return home, Odysseus found that Mentor has molded Telemachus into a fine young man through his mindful instruction. Enough of the history lesson; mentoring can be simply stated as a structured and trusting relationship that brings young people together with caring individuals who offer guidance, support, and encouragement aimed at developing competence and character in the mentee. Traditionally, mentoring might have been described as the activities conducted by a person (the mentor) for another person (the mentee) in order to help that other person in life. The mentor is someone who has "been there, done that" before. Today, there seems to be ongoing debate about the definitions and differences of mentoring. For our purposes, we will focus on a mentoring relationship between an adult (mentor) and youth (mentee), with the goals of increasing academic achievement and reducing incidents of violence.

HOW CAN MENTORS BE EFFECTIVE?

One effective way to reduce incidents of school violence and reach underserved at-risk youth is by establishing a positive adult-youth relationship through mentoring. Another definition, from the National Mentoring Partnership, defines mentors as adults who, along with parents, provide young people with support, counsel, friendship, reinforcement, and constructive examples. They are good listeners, people who care, and people who want to help youth bring out their strengths.[2] Mentors help youth by creating learning opportunities and by applying learned skills to life situations over an extended period of time.[3]

Mentors have been shown to help youth increase their self-confidence and decrease their delinquent behaviors.[4] In their national sample of over 1,000 mentors, McLearn and colleagues found that 62 percent of the participating mentors reported they were effective in helping the youth overcome negative feelings about themselves, and 50 percent reported they helped the youth decrease the amount they skipped school and how often they were in trouble at school. Nearly half of the mentors felt they had helped decrease the amount of trouble the youth were in outside of school, had helped the youth improve their grades, and/or had decreased their level of substance abuse.[5] The mentors also indicated they had assisted the youth with other problems the youth wanted to discuss, including family and friends, sexual activity, running away from home, abuse, or eating disorders.

Other studies on mentoring using objective indicators have also shown positive outcomes in reducing problem behaviors and fostering positive development. The strongest evidence to date comes from a large controlled study of youth in Big Brothers/Big Sisters, which showed that youth who had a mentor had fewer problem behaviors and improved academic performance compared to youth who did not have a mentor.[6] Other outcomes include the following:

- A greater likelihood of seeing an improvement in the quality of their relationship with their parents
- A better chance of going on to higher education
- Better attitudes toward school with a higher value placed on education
- Reduced negative behaviors related to delinquency, including fewer misdemeanors and felonies
- Improved positive social attitudes and relationships toward school, the future, the elderly, and helping behaviors[7]

Educators who endeavor to implement mentoring as a strategy to reduce school violence should adhere to best practices of school-based mentoring. These best practices were gathered from organizations around the country and on research findings. This practical information provides a basis for educators and other youth-serving professionals in their attempt to bring "people" back into the schools.

First, it is important to establish the goal of a school-based mentoring program. In most school improvement plans, focus should and will always be squarely on academics and behavior. Safe School Plans have ultimately had the same focus. Most schools list mentoring in the same vein as character education, Teen Court, or some other club that instills school pride and meaningful involvement. The end goal is to increase end-of-term scores and graduation rates and to decrease incidents of violence. School administrators must understand that youth mentoring works best when the overall goal is to develop long-lasting trusting relationships with adults.

Relationships are hard to measure, but they should be a goal for all schools. Mentoring programs that focus solely on behavior will show modest gains. Although the research strongly supports the impact that mentoring has on behavior, it is almost deemed a side effect of the most prevalent positive outcome. The focus is on trying to assist youth in developing social competency skills, simply because these social skills benefit the child in other areas. This goal of increasing social competencies will invariably impact grades, behavior, and a myriad other measurable factors. This is a hard concept for most administrators, yet many would agree that mentoring is anecdotally effective. Once again, in an evidenced-based world, mentoring is considered to have soft-research backing its effectiveness. The proof is in the pudding.

Daryl is 19 years old and from a rural community in North Carolina. He is the youngest of four kids and has never met his father. Daryl's mother works two jobs and is struggling with an alcohol addiction. To recover the lost guidance from a father figure, Daryl befriends a local drug dealer and gang leader. At the age of 10, he joins the notorious Blood gang and is now part of a surrogate family. In and out of school, Daryl meets Mr. Campbell, a mentor who was assigned to him via a project called HOPE. Initially meeting with Mr. Campbell was not a high priority for Daryl, but over time he became a confidant. Although Daryl still participated in a gang, Mr. Campbell's guidance became more and more important to the daily life of this young man. Eventually Daryl left the gang and currently is seeking permanent employment while attending a local community college. From Daryl's words, "Mr. Campbell was a role model, father, and friend all balled up in one. If it wasn't for him, I would either be dead or in jail."

This true account is simply one story from many similar stories of the positive impact of mentoring. Though hard to measure, we certainly can see the cost savings for a potential wayward youth who could have been incarcerated or a menace to society. It is hard to argue against the impact of this approach.

The best practices for successful and effective mentoring can be grouped under the following headings: building school and organizational capacity; working with mentors; working with mentees; and involving the family. To build the school's capacity to create successful mentoring, it is important to start with building the case for mentoring. Working with administrators, teachers, the school board, and parents is the first step in gaining buy-in. The argument being made rests squarely on the fact that mentoring needs to be considered an integral part of services for youth. Increasing the awareness of key stakeholders should not be a difficult challenge. Most adults can think back in their lives to when a caring adult or mentor had a positive impact. Using personal experiences, along with explaining how mentoring will compliment the school's mission and reduce incidents of violence, will assist in this process. Explaining the logistics of providing mentoring will be the challenge. Finding a primary person(s) whose job will be to administer the mentoring program may be difficult, and it must be an individual who has passion and ambition. This position may be repositioned from other responsibilities, but the job description should be clear about specific tasks. It may be a more effective endeavor if administrators consider a two-person mentoring team that should share in the responsibilities. Once these person(s) are identified, they should be encouraged to attend training workshops and peer networking events to find others who have implemented successful school-based mentoring initiatives. The fact-finding process will assist in determining if the site-based model is effective or if another direction is warranted. Regardless, the discussion on the framework will be the basis of its success and for positive outcomes for youth.

ACQUIRING AND SUPPORTING POSITIVE ROLE MODELS TO MENTOR

Another best practice has to deal with the actual mentor. The first obvious piece to discuss is how to recruit the mentor. There are many ways to recruit and encourage members of the community to participate. The most effective mode of recruitment is "word of mouth." Once there are a few successful mentoring experiences, those individuals can be utilized to invite family and friends to volunteer their time. Schools can also provide mentors with "Join Me in Mentoring" badges, which could invoke discussions at the workplace and around the community. Along with "word of mouth," schools should utilize meaningful relationships with churches, businesses, civic organizations, and others to recruit. Exposing these groups to successful mentoring relationships and actual youth who have been positively impacted can be a powerful motivator in recruiting efforts. One could also use the mainstream local media and increase visibility by using public awareness campaigns. Being innovative in the approaches and understanding how to motivate people will yield positive results.

Once the recruitment process starts to bring people to the school's doorstep, administrators need to have in place a screening process. This process includes a mentor application and an interview that gives the prospective mentor and school an opportunity to examine the relationship and commitment level. The mentor should be required to provide two to three references; most importantly, a criminal background check is required. Once the successful screening process is complete, the next step is to train volunteers. In the training, there are some principles that need to be included. Mentors need to understand the following:

- School rules and guidelines
- The nature of risk factors in the lives of youth
- The vitality of their mentoring efforts in creating conducive learning environments
- The importance of building trust
- Signs of neglect and abuse, and what to do about them
- A clear set of roles and responsibilities
- Matters of confidentiality
- Appropriate self-disclosure, empathy, and the ability to celebrate successes
- A focus on strengths and activities to build resilience[8]

These principles should be part of comprehensive and ongoing training for prospective mentors. If possible, provide a concise training manual that includes procedures and contact information. To give mentors a

"real-world" experience, utilize role-playing activities to provide hypo-
thetical scenarios. These scenarios will help mentors explore various
ways of responding to their mentees and will test their ability to effectively communicate. To accompany activities at the training, there
should be a current mentor or mentee to speak about his or her personal experiences. This will give potential mentors an opportunity to
ask questions that could alleviate any hesitation or fears. Also consider
organizing a "mixer-type" event for the first meeting between mentor
and mentee to reduce anxiety.

Volunteers also need to be screened for their outlook on the mentoring process. The most suitable mentors see their goal as supporting the
child and helping him or her foster positive relationships in life, rather
than simply achieving good grades or staying out of trouble. Good
mentors are willing to allow the child to make decisions about activities or lessons and to refrain from being too judgmental or "preachy."
Overall, they should see their role as a trusted friend rather than as a
teacher.

Volunteers should receive more than two hours of training before
they begin mentoring. Training should emphasize building a trusting
relationship with the child and should provide the mentor with general
information about youth development, as well as specific information
about the youth in the program. The program should also give the
mentor strategies for coping with a child who will test the limits and
patience of a mentor. Programs should also support mentors throughout the process. If possible, youth mentoring programs should have a
staff member committed solely to mentor development who will contact the mentor at least once a month. Staff can also assist mentors
more directly by writing lesson plans or suggesting activities. Mentors
do their best work when their effort is focused on the mentor-child
relationship rather than on logistics or administration. Overall, mentors
who are screened, trained, and supported properly are likely to stick
with mentoring and have a positive impact on youth.

The final piece in working with mentors is supervision and administration. Administrators and mentoring facilitators should create a form
that tracks information such as the following:

- Number of meetings between mentor and mentee
- Meetings of coordinator with mentors and mentees
- Progress reports and notes

Administrators should also create opportunities to observe mentor-
mentee interaction through field trips, holiday events, and other related
activities. It is also critical to emphasize the importance of attendance
at debriefing sessions for mentors. This regularly scheduled meeting

will allow for the identification of any miscues, opportunities to improve, and feedback regarding the mentoring process. Being supervised is the least attractive piece in the process, but it is just as important as the mentoring relationship.

The next best practice deals with actually working with the mentees. The administration needs to specify how they are to refer youth to the mentor program or whether it will be available for all youth. It may be more effective to look at a priority list of youth who may benefit from working with a mentor. Recruiting youth to participate should not be a problem, but there should be some equity if there are a limited number of mentors available. If the demand is higher than the supply of mentors, then the school should do group mentoring. This would allow for capable mentors to work with a group of youth at the school.

There are other modes of mentoring to service the needs of the school, such as e-mentoring, which is facilitated via e-mail. Once the "how" is answered in regards to recruiting youth to participate, the matching process should be well planned. Matching adults to youth should take careful consideration. Although it is not a perfect science, administrators and mentoring facilitators should try to match the needs of youth and the capabilities of the mentor. There needs to be parental and youth consent before the match is made, along with a review of student individual education plans (IEPs). Many educators have existing relationships with students, so these are far easier to match. But if there is no rapport, the IEP, along with an interview and perhaps a short mentee application, can assist in the matching process. When working to make this match work and the mentoring initiative a success, administrators need buy-in from the mentee in order for it to be an effective experience. Some important points include the following:

- Explain the basis of the mentor-mentee relationship and the benefits of having a mentor
- Arrange for a current mentor-mentee match to speak
- Stress that the relationship in itself can be its own greatest reward
- Allow mentees to debrief and share their experiences[9]

Being innovative in how to recruit and serve the youth population is paramount. Administrators should create a climate that is accepting of what a mentor brings to the table, and the logistics should be well thought out. This will ensure that the mentor does not have a poor experience that will distract from the main purpose of working with youth.

Most purveyors of mentoring also indicate that parental involvement is another beneficial goal. In an effective program model, parental involvement is critical. Mentors who help youth, in many instances, are also mentoring the family. Once the mentor communicates his or her intentions and goals to the family, it is important to have them involved, to not threaten the youth-parent relationship. In many instances the mentor provides stability for a youth who may be part of a dysfunctional family. However, mentors should never usurp the power of the parent, but rather be complementary to the heads of each house. A conversation with parent(s) at the beginning of the mentor-mentee relationship is warranted so that there are no misperceptions.

CONCLUDING THOUGHT

Although the goals will vary from program to program, the goal of mentoring is to build resiliency within youth and give them a sense that they can "reinvent" themselves: that anyone can enhance his or her situation, surroundings, and level of success. Mentoring can be the pillar of prevention and intervention strategies in any school system's attempt to make the school climate more conducive for learning. Yes, programs should match mentors and youth based on their shared interests. Yes, the most successful mentor-youth relationship exists for at least one year, with meetings of at least an hour a week. And yes, the mentoring sessions should involve structured activities. We can determine all the specifics that will drive the success of a mentoring initiative. But lest we forget: the most important and undeniable program component that will impact program effectiveness and efficacy is the people.

Chapter 10

The Role of Parental Involvement in Prevention

Danya C. Perry

Let me set the mood for you. It is 6 p.m.; parents are just getting off work and have been asked to participate in their child's school by attending a PTO/PTA meeting. Parents are tired and have to figure out a few logistical issues:

1. Should I bring my child to the meeting?
2. If I have more than one child, should I bring them all to the meeting?
3. If I don't bring them, who will watch them?
4. What will I make for dinner when I get back from the meeting, or even, should I make dinner?
5. Should I even go to the meeting?

You get the picture.

At the request of administrators and other community organizers, we have been asked to come as special guests to speak to youth on various topics surrounding school violence prevention and positive youth development. Our goal is to get parents to be engaged in the conversation, while understanding that their minds may be thinking of everything else except a presentation on school violence.

My most memorable presentation request from a PTO/PTA was in a Laundromat. Yes, a public Laundromat—you read correctly. I looked around the room and went to an area that I quickly considered the front of the room and started to prepare for my presentation between a folding table and a broken dryer. As I waited for people to arrive, I slowly began to realize that there was a packed house. This was amazing; it was filled to capacity with parents greeting teachers and administrators as if they were long-lost friends. The parents actually looked happy to be at this meeting. Another interesting note: most of the parents in attendance had a basket of laundry, and so did some of the teachers. I then noticed one of the teachers handing small cups of quarters to the parents to start their loads.

OK. This is stranger than I expected. The only thing I could think of was, how can I compete with the sounds of clanking buttons in a dryer and the spin cycle with loose ball bearings? Regardless of the obvious distractions, I gave a compelling argument for the employment of prevention strategies in 30 minutes. After completion of the discussion, the administrator of the school walked up to me smiling. She asked me, "Was this your first time presenting beside a dryer?"

I pretended that this was normal and said, "Yes, ma'am, and I hope that this will not be my last."

She then explained to me that the location of the meeting was important to increase parental participation. "This is just one strategy for getting our parents to come out," she said.

What is important here is that the school had taken into account the logistics of its parent audience: location, time, and need. Yes, need. The particular demographic challenge was low socioeconomic status, and simple tasks such as doing the laundry could be taxing. So the school used the lure of paying for a few cycles to entice parent participation. Gimmicky but very effective. The administrators even eliminated the obstacle of the "us versus them" mentality by having teachers do their laundry as well. What a great way to make parents feel that educators are normal, just like them. We all have dirty laundry that needs attention.

On April 20, 1999, the unthinkable happened at Columbine High School in Columbine, Colorado. Eric Harris and Dylan Klebold walked into their high school, committed heinous violent acts, and became what is now being termed "superpredators." This school shooting assisted in the emergence of many conversations surrounding "why?" What could lead two students to such violence, and were there any warning signs that could have predicted this destruction? What happened on the grounds of Columbine High School evoked debates regarding gun control and violence, the incidence and severity of bullying, understanding youth subcultures such as Goth, and the role of violent movies, music, and video games. This incident single-handedly refocused America's attention on school safety. But in all of these conversations, the most prevalent question that remains on the minds of many is "Where were the parents?" Reports indicated that the parents of Harris and Klebold were aware of many of these warning signs: increased isolation, associating with negative peer groups, and fascination with firearms and explosives. There were even incidents in which the youth were building home-made explosives, and apparently the parents had no clue.

The aforementioned school shooting is one singular incident that highlights the importance of parental responsibility in the school's attempt to ensure a safe environment that is conducive to learning. In the past, the parents' role in the school was a passive experience that involved going to an occasional meeting and monitoring the progress of their child(ren). The role of parents in the school has changed because of the increasing challenges associated with maintaining safe schools. With increased risk factors and destructive messages, the parent becomes a vital component of the school-parent partnership.

The responsibility associated with parenthood is vast. Caregiver, disciplinarian, provider—all these words we associate with the position of parent. If we decided to develop a checklist of criteria for what a "successful" parent should look like, we would have to include involvement. It sounds easy enough, but what exactly does "involvement" look like, and how does one measure whether parents are sufficiently "involved"? There is an obvious Likert scale from the perspective of some parents. Some people feel that a successfully involved parent only needs to provide food, clothes, and shelter, whereas others include engagement and investment in every aspect of the child's life. Seeing that there is such a range of attitudes and beliefs regarding the subject, what should educators expect from parents?

The lack of parental involvement in the academic process has been a long-standing problem that school systems across the nation have endured. Parental involvement has been an enigma for educators and a calling card for programs that tout increased parent participation. School improvement research studies show that parental involvement contributes to academic excellence and achievement for students. Since the 1980s, a new dimension of this research has emerged that focuses on the school climate and a conducive learning environment. Safe schools have been in the forefront of most educators' minds, and there has been a strong outcry for increased involvement from the family and community. Given the volatile circumstances that could lead to possible school shootings, parent connections have become a top priority of administrators. There is a direct correlation between youth success and family connectedness. School systems have taken proactive steps toward increasing school-family connections and are always searching for better ways to motivate and engage parents. It is critical to assist school systems in building the capacity to engage parents in a meaningful way, taking into account their attitudes and beliefs. Conveying the message and highlighting the positive outcomes of parental involvement are the key steps.

HOW CAN SCHOOLS INTRODUCE POSITIVE PARENTAL INVOLVEMENT?

Parent involvement can mean many things. Basically, it means participation in the educational process. This process includes being engaged in anything that can lead to the possible attainment of education. Schools can start the process of involvement by being proactive. Activities such as calling parents before school starts to begin the rapport-building process can prove to be a catalyst to increased involvement. Educators can also establish open lines of communication and show parents that they are truly vested in their child's development. Most parents with children who are having a difficult time in school are pretty familiar with phone calls from the school. These phone calls, of course, are to report discipline problems and poor performance. Throughout the school year, educators can also keep parents updated and inspired by sharing success stories of their children. Once again, this assists in drawing parents closer to the school building to participate in a meaningful way (see Figure 10.1).

Parents can also be involved by helping their children with their schoolwork and encouraging them to be proficient academically. They can support children during study time, monitor class assignments and homework, and provide tutoring when needed. These are all "home"-based examples of being involved. Inside the school, parents can serve as advocates for the school. They can volunteer to work within the classroom or with general school activities. Field trip chaperoning, bus duty, and lunchroom monitoring are all examples of involvement in the school building. There may also be opportunities for parents to be involved on a policy or governance level. Parents at this level can influence the planning, development, and provision of education for all youth in a community. By sitting on education boards, strategic planning committees, and reform meetings, parents can shape the practices and policies of a school and school system.

RESEARCH ON PARENTAL INVOLVEMENT

Research from various sources has pinpointed the reasons for ineffective parental involvement at schools. The two most common reasons

---

- Telephone and written home-school communications
- Attending school functions
- Parents serving as classroom volunteers
- Parent-teacher conferences
- Homework assistance/tutoring
- Home educational enrichment
- Decision making and other aspects of school governance

I. Warner, "Parents in Touch: District Leadership for Parent Involvement," *Phi Delta Kappan* 178 (1991): 372–75.

Figure 10.1. Forms of Parental Involvement

are (1) lack of planning and (2) lack of mutual understanding. Educators need to be both open-minded and well organized in order to institute effective programs to engage parents. Other research speaks to the changing landscape of accountability in the country. Parents are becoming more dependent on social institutions (such as school) to take responsibility in the rearing process. This notion is clearly evident as the summer ends and school starts. Educators jokingly say that parents hand children over to the school and say, "I had them all summer; it's YOUR turn." Regardless, communicating with parents and understanding their perspective are critical in ensuring a successful school-parent partnership.

The most successful parent participation efforts offer parents a variety of roles in the school building. To become well-organized and long-lasting partners, parents need to be given a range of activities that will accommodate different schedules, preferences, and capabilities. It is not just the parent who is responsible for "coming through the door." Teachers and administrators need to assess their own readiness to involve parents and determine how they wish to engage and utilize them.[1] Following are several guidelines:

- Communicate to parents that their involvement and support make a great deal of difference in their children's school performance and that they need not be highly educated or have large amounts of free time for their involvement to be beneficial. Make this point repeatedly.

- Encourage parent involvement from the time children first enter school (or preschool, if they attend).

- Teach parents that activities such as modeling reading behavior and reading to their children increase children's interest in learning.

- Develop parent involvement programs that focus on parent involvement in instruction: conducting learning activities with children in the home, assisting with homework, and monitoring and encouraging the learning activities of older students.

- Provide orientation and training for parents, but remember that intensive, lengthy training is neither necessary nor feasible.

- Make a special effort to engage the parents of disadvantaged students; these students stand to benefit the most from parent participation in their learning, but their parents are often initially reluctant to become involved.

- Continue to emphasize that parents are partners of the school and that their involvement is needed and valued.[2]

Effective utilization of the aforementioned guidelines and complete buy-in from staff will yield positive outcomes for students. Research has found that effective parental engagement produces outcomes in the following areas: general achievement; achievement in reading, math, or other specific curricular areas; IQ scores; and most importantly, behavior. Before focusing on the impact on student attitudes and behaviors, it is important to determine the effect on student achievement, which correlates with a student's outlook. The effectiveness of meaningful parent participation can be determined by examining the decrease in violent outbursts and negative attitudes toward school.

A 2003 analysis of more than 25 public opinion surveys by Public Agenda, a nonpartisan public opinion research organization, found that 65 percent of teachers say their students would do better in school if their parents were more involved, and 72 percent of parents feel that children whose parents are not involved sometimes "fall through the cracks" in school.[3] It is clear that parent involvement in youth learning is positively related to their individual achievement. Research in this area shows that parents who are more involved will observe more benefits in regards to academic excellence. Regardless of the socioeconomic status, ethnicity, or any other demographics, these results will stand true.

However, it is important to note that different types of involvement will yield different results. There are strong indications that the most effective forms of parent involvement are those in which parents work directly with their children on learning activities in the home. There are several successful programs on general tutoring that involve parents in reading with their children and supporting their work on homework assignments. These home-based activities are obvious to some when the discussion is centered on improved academics, but they are not commonplace in every home. To improve academic performance, parents must not only be willing but must also have the capability to assist with academics. Children with illiterate parents usually struggle in the academic process. Having illiterate parents does not necessarily mean that the parents are not willing to be engaged and involved. They simply lack the capacity to do so. When encouraging home-based involvement, schools must take this into consideration as well. As already mentioned, schools must be cognizant of the various modes of parental engagement.

As with home-based activities, research also speaks to the difference between active and passive involvement. Ultimately, active involvement yields greater achievement in students than passive involvement. What is the difference? Passive involvement is receiving calls, signing written communications from the school, and attending parent-teacher conferences. It is important to note that passive involvement is far more beneficial in academic achievement than no participation at all. But it pales in comparison to parents who are actively involved. Active participation yields considerably greater achievement benefits.

Active roles include working with children from the home, supporting school activities, assisting in field trips, helping out in the classroom, and other similar tasks. Active involvement and being involved early in the child's academic process make the parents' impact more powerful. Educators know that the family role is critical early in children's education. The many successful early childhood education programs that have strong parent involvement components prove this point: early and active parental involvement makes a difference.

Schools can provide opportunities for parents who are willing to become more involved in their children's learning and improving the school climate. Schools can start by providing orientations and training for parents. This orientation can take the form of a day-long event or a series of events over a school year. It can be simple written directions with a send-home instructional packet or "make-and-take" workshops in which parents construct, see demonstrations of, and practice using instructional games.[4] The important point is keeping parents actively involved and engaged. Many school systems have gone as far as creating "Parent Universities" that give parents the sense of expanding on their current background. These activities give the school an opportunity to provide workshops on topics surrounding literacy, conflict management, neglect, bullying, and other critical points of emphasis. They also give parents an opportunity to interact with administrators and teachers.

Research indicates that activities such as orientations and trainings will enhance the overall effectiveness of parent involvement. Generally, parents want and need direction to participate with maximum effectiveness. It is also important not to overdo these orientation and training activities. Although they are beneficial, educators have found that parents have limited amounts of time and should be given the flexibility of involvement. Offering too much can be overwhelming for those who do participate and intimidating to those that do not. Most research on this topic reports that a little is better than a lot. Ultimately, parent involvement programs with extensive parent training components do not produce higher student achievement than those with only basic training.[5] The same research found that the schools with the most successful parent involvement programs are those that offer a variety of ways in which parents can participate. Recognizing that parents differ greatly in their willingness, ability, and available time for involvement, schools should provide a continuum of options for parent participation.

EFFECTS OF PARENTAL INVOLVEMENT

Student achievement academically is paramount, but there are other outcomes that are also positively affected by parental involvement. The most important outcome aside from achievement is behavior. Student behavior directly influences the entire school climate and sense of school safety. In regards to behavior, the focus should also include attitude toward school, self-concept, time spent on homework, class-room interactions, expectations for the future, truancy or absenteeism, motivation, and retention. Research that focuses on these outcomes favors the necessity of parental guidance in reducing incidents of school violence. Student attitudes and social behavior are incredibly impacted by parents' engagement, whether it is passive or active. It should be noted that active engagement yields far better results. The same activities that impact achievement will do the same for student behavior.

Educators who have a long-range goal of reducing fights or discipline referrals should look at additional strategies to engage parents meaningfully. Passively or actively, parents should be encouraged to have conversations about violence in the home, community, and school. There are many destructive messages being conveyed to youth on a daily basis. These messages, without conversation with the parent, can have long-lasting negative effects. Discussions in the home about setting expectations become the parents' first and foremost responsibility. Recognizing early warning signs to aggressive behavior is another opportunity for involvement. Educators can prepare parents by offering workshops or trainings specific to this topic.

Other opportunities are for parents to serve as actual monitors or surveillance agents at the school building. Although these roles are not the most popular for the child, they do indeed send a message that violence will not be tolerated and the parent is committed to ensuring that this is achieved. Also, parents can be part of the safe school planning process. Most public schools across the nation are expected to prepare an annual safe school plan (see Figure 10.2). These plans map out the necessary goals and objectives that need to be accomplished to ensure a safe learning environment. Parents' input in this process is certainly warranted.

It is critical to reach beyond the traditional mediums of parental involvement. School systems that have yielded positive benefits from engaging parents have persisted in making their activities innovative. Educators across the nation are attempting to determine ways of motivating parents and developing flexible engagement activities for parents who are traditionally unwilling or unable to become involved.

ENGAGING PARENTS TO BE INVOLVED: WHAT TO DO

To avoid ineffective and alienating policy and strategy development, it is important to understand the barriers that hinder effective parental involvement:

- Logistics: Some parents have nontraditional work schedules, work long hours, or may work more than one job. Parents who are willing to be

- Safe School Planning Committee
- Telephone and written home-school communications
- Attending school functions
- Parents serving as classroom volunteers
- Parent-teacher conferences
- Homework assistance/tutoring
- Home educational enrichment
- Decision making and other aspects of school governance

P. G. Fehrmann, T. Z. Keith, and T. M. Reiners, "Home Influence on School Learning: Direct and Indirect Effects of Parental Involvement on High School Grades," *Journal of Educational Research* 80 (1987): 330–36.

Figure 10.2. Parental Involvement in School Safety

involved may be prohibited because of their work schedule. Other logistics include location of the school and mode of transportation. Finding accessible transportation for some parents is a perpetual challenge. In these instances, parents have to prioritize and make concessions based on their ability to be mobile. School engagement often suffers because of this hardship. A final logistical challenge is from within the school. Schools that are inflexible and only offer set times to become involved will oftentimes see decreased parental participation. For example, schools that traditionally meet in the evening will always lose participation from those parents who work in the evening.

- History: It is important to note that the lack of parental involvement may be connected to the educational attainment of the parents or the value placed on education. Education has to be seen as valued in order for parents to put it on a priority list. This value system can be familial, passed down the family line. The value system can be based on the parents' experience while in school. If parents had a poor experience, then they will be apt to be uninvolved, especially if they perceive the school system and educators as a threat. Fear was also a recurrent theme for most parents. Some parents had a fear of appearing "stupid" or foolish, so they would rather divert the attention away from them or not even show up. Educators speak frequently of the intimidation that usually occurs in the school building. At a parent-teacher conference, the parent sits across the table from a panel of educators that includes the teacher, administrator, and counselor. Depending on the reason for the conference, this can be a very intimidating experience for parents and can create disengagement and defensiveness.

- Inability to navigate: Parents who are willing and able to participate may be "turned off" by the complexity of the process. If parents are not familiar with "how" to be involved in the school, then that lack of knowledge will distract them away from any potential engagement. It is critical to operationalize the entire process. Other parents may take for granted what it takes to be involved. Either way, educators should be cognizant and respectful of parents' knowledge base. Parents operate at a disadvantage when it comes to how a school operates, until they are informed. Being supportive of their need to tear down barriers must become paramount.

- Perception: The perception of educators also plays an important role in parent participation. Oftentimes, schools don't engage parents because they don't think they can. Educators perceive that families don't want to be involved, when, in fact, families don't know how to be involved. The assumption that absence means noncaring will invariably impact the attitude and behavior of educators when reaching out to parents. Educators must understand the barriers that hinder some parents from participating in their children's education. If teachers are sincere in their approach and desire for parental engagement, this can be translated positively in how the parents are "well received." Parents who feel slighted, disrespected, or ignored will become less inclined to participate. The perception works both ways. Parents can have the same misperceptions about the intentions of some educators. Either way, this does not establish the needed rapport for ensuring increased parental involvement and youth success.

- Cultural competency: Parents sometimes feel that they are not welcome because of the differences in culture. The formal definition for culture includes age, ethnicity, geography, and other facets that encompass an individual. Many parents feel culturally, linguistically, and ethnically different. Oftentimes their body of knowledge does not match the institutional knowledge of the school, and they are therefore excluded from home and school conversations. For some parents, it can be as simple as not being fluent in English. Non-English-speaking parents invariably become more hesitant if the school does not create an environment that facilitates acceptance. Failure to recognize and prepare educators to become culturally accepting will create larger disconnections between the school and families. The same feelings of being "unwelcome" are intertwined with the parents' own education history. Once again, if they have a dissatisfying experience, then they will not feel that being involved is guaranteed to be a good experience.

Understanding the aforementioned barriers will assist educators in determining an innovative approach to support the parents' role in the school. Thinking outside the box, while understanding how to overcome the barriers to success, will be a great start in a long-lasting, beneficial relationship.

Utilizing convening points in a community is also critical to increasing parental involvement. Convening points are locations parents normally frequent, and flexible school systems could encourage teachers to use these places to meet. Some natural convening points are churches, community centers, civic organizations, restaurants, and even Laundromats. As the example in the beginning of this chapter shows, the school decided to utilize the local Laundromat in a community to convene parent-teacher conferences. Unconventional, yes, but at the same time effective. Teachers were able to meet the parents "where they were," and this approach overcame transportation barriers. Additionally, administrators thought this would alleviate any intimidation factors or misperceptions of the teachers' and school's intent. Parents felt that the middle school was going the extra mile to build a relationship. This in turn created increased participation in other school activities requiring parent involvement.

Another convening point worth discussing is the church within the community. The church historically has always been the "center" of many communities. School systems that have met with local religious leaders to discuss ways that the faith and school community could partner have yielded remarkable results. Utilizing church facilities to hold school fund-raisers, PTA meetings, and other school-based activities will assist in gaining ground in the school-parent partnership. At the church, educators can clarify how parents can help. Parents need to know exactly how they can help. Some are active in church and other community groups but lack information about how to become more involved in their children's schooling.

Innovative strategies from the school can come in the form of technology. E-mails, school blogs, electronic surveys, and chat forums are all ways that educators can be more connected to parents. Parents who may be busy can sit in on "conference calls" and be provided with updates on their child's performance and grades. Educators can also utilize what is being termed "webinars"—Web-based seminars—on various topics that are of importance to parents. Educators who can offer various modes of getting information and utilizing technology will be a new platform that can reach more parents.

In this effort, schools should use a strength-based approach. Utilizing parent expertise underscores the importance of empowering parents to contribute in their own unique way. Some research calls this using the "funds of knowledge" in the community.[6] For example, if a parent in the community has an expertise in the field of construction, the class could develop a unit on construction. This lesson could cover all points surrounding reading, writing, speaking, math, and carpentry. Other examples are parents cooking ethnic foods with students while sharing information about their cultural heritage, or having a parent who is a talented musician. The school could have parents participate in school plays or concerts. Another example is of parents who have special hobbies, such as model cars; these parents can serve as mentors or helpers in art, carpentry, or automotive car classes. There are a myriad ways to utilize the strength of parents. School systems should provide opportunities that cater to the strengths of the parents. Educators can collect information about parents' "likes and dislikes" by having them complete questionnaires or even have the students complete one for their parents. This could be used as a "getting to know you" assignment for students. Thinking outside the box will assist educators in making parents feel completely engaged and provide them with the feeling that they have something meaningful to contribute.

It is also important to provide a menu of opportunities to be engaged at the school building. This once again speaks to operationalizing parental involvement. Providing parents with a list of options that can fit with their schedules can avert any logistics challenge. Educators should also encourage parents to be assertive and proactive in their child's education. This assertiveness can be misconstrued by teachers as challenging their expertise. Teachers have to understand that this advocacy and a positive dialogue serve to keep parents included. Teachers should not only encourage assertiveness, but they should also develop a trust that they have the child's best interests at heart. Teachers should reassure parents that the school is open to them and that it is "OK" for them to drop by anytime.

Lastly, educators can build on the home experiences. The incorrect assumption is that the home environments can sometimes sever potential links and relationships. Assuming that certain kids do not live in good environments can destroy the partnership that educators want to create. Educators should not tell parents "what to do" without understanding the rich social interaction that already occurs in the home. School personnel should ask general questions about home activities and how these activities could build upon what happens in school. Activities such as reading the Bible, being outdoors, and writing to out-of-town relatives can all assist in building the school-home partnership.

CONCLUDING THOUGHT

The benefits from parental involvement are countless. Becoming engaged in the child's education yields both positive results in academic achievement and behavior; these are critical parameters to ensuring a safe learning environment. Whatever attempt is made to ensure the safety of a school, parental involvement can be seen as one of the single most powerful approaches. This involvement benefits not just students but also school personnel. Improved rapport with educators will generally increase parents' willingness to support the school and increase their involvement with activities. The same goes for the inverse. Parents' attitudes toward educators and the school generally improve when they are involved in their children's learning. Parents often begin their participation doubting that their involvement can make much difference, yet they are generally very gratified to discover what an important contribution they are able to make. In this connection, it is important for educators and parents to be aware that parent involvement supports students' learning, behavior, and attitudes regardless of factors such as parents' income, educational level, and whether or not parents are employed. Parents should be considered the backbone to the school, and involving parents means having them on your side. Once on your side, youth success will far surpass even their wildest imaginations.

Chapter 11

Building Successful Family and Community Partnerships

Danya C. Perry

Recalling my childhood, I can reasonably say that I was not a problem child. Or at least that is my perception. The only instance that I would deem problematic was when I orchestrated the launch of a gang, rather a social club, in a small rural town in eastern North Carolina. This adventure was not too bad, but bad enough to get the attention of the entire community. This particular moment in my life was the only time that I recall my community coming together to address a problem.

Let's start from the beginning. A couple of my friends and I decided one day to start a "social club," simply to create a bond between us, something similar to Blood Brothers. You know, Blood Brothers: scraping your arm with a bottle cap until you bleed and rubbing it with another one of your friend's bleeding limbs. This act alone created a bond that seemingly could not be broken, even if it was completely dangerous for obvious reasons. We decided to start this group and make it to reflect our favorite cartoon show, the *Thunder Cats*. The Thunder Cats were awesome felines with the ability to perform uncanny martial arts. The cartoon motivated us to create this family structure that included an initiation process that would make sure that we picked the right members. This initiation process was not too stringent when compared to that of traditional street gangs. Simple tasks included drinking a two-liter soda without taking a break; scaling a tree in 30 seconds or less; and most impressively, holding your breath under water.

With such a promising infrastructure, we needed a great name. We did not want to break any copyright laws and use the Thunder Cats moniker, so we picked something different, but eerily the same. We were known as the Karate Kats Klub and were one of the most notorious gangs, rather social clubs, in eastern North Carolina. How did we get so popular? It was easy: our first duty was to advertise our existence, and what better way to do this than with spray paint and clean walls? This bunch of whizzes also had the foresight to make sure that the name was short and catchy enough for branding purposes. So, in some areas we decided to shorten up the name of our group and use initials. You got it right, and you might have heard of us as well: the KKK. Genius!

Fast-forward: about two weeks after creating this insignia, I recall hearing my mother on the phone. She was speaking with my aunt, and I could hear flecks of concern and rage in her voice. I tuned in on the conversation, and I heard my mother say these words:

"Did you see what is on the wall at the library and park?"

After hearing that statement, I knew that they were talking about my social group, the KKK. For some reason she confused my innocent social group with a more notorious hate group that used the same initials: Ku Klux Klan. I can see how she misinterpreted it.

She continued, "We are not going to let nobody come into our community and do this: we HAVE to do something!" The next few days were a whirlwind. My dear mother organized a meeting in which everybody attended. Teachers, preachers, business men and women, people from the Elks Lodge—everybody was represented; and to add insult to injury, they met at my house. She had no clue that the president, CEO, and head-honcho of the KKK (Karate Kats Klub) was upstairs, scared out of my mind. We shortly afterwards disbanded, but please note how the community came together to figure out this problem. We decided to quit our endeavors simply because of the invested and interested people who showed up to solve the problem. I recall being scared that not only my parents but the entire community would know what we had done. Yet a small piece of me felt almost "wanted," in that the community was reaching out in a very substantive way.

COMMUNITY INVOLVEMENT: NUTS AND BOLTS

Think about the last time you recall community and family mobilizing to deal with a problem. Across the country, the only time you may experience such mobilization efforts is on the heels of a tragedy. From terrorist attacks on 9/11 to a school shooting on the campus of Columbine High School, we are more prepped and ready to respond to a crisis after it has occurred. This is the norm in our society. This is not to say that there are not attempts to be proactive, but few people usually discuss these proactive and prevention measures.

Violence in America's schools does not just affect the youth, educators, and parents of school-aged youth. The problem of school violence is a social problem, and thus by the very definition it concerns the greater population. If this problem affects the greater population, then the question becomes: Why do government officials, interest groups, or community leaders often define the problem and how the problem will be solved without the involvement of the communities that are impacted? Historically, the communities that have had long-standing problems with gangs or violence are usually the last to contribute to the solution.

There are many variables that can lead to community inactivity. One variable that is a block to community involvement is the fading hope for change. Some communities have seen people who want to "help" come and go without witnessing much positive change. Other variables are impoverished communities and the inability to be a part of change because of work schedules, transportation, or even lack of interest. There can be similar variables in middle- to high-income communities. Regardless of the demographics, the resounding challenge is how to gain input from the community so that it will be engaged in the development of a solution to school violence.[1]

Being left out of the process can be disheartening. Once a person or community feels powerless, then it will take some effort to regain its trust and commitment. So why should the community be involved in strategy development? The reason is that it is critical to get the point of view from people who are or have been directly impacted by the problem. Let's say that you have a pain in your back from lifting a heavy object. There is nobody who can know exactly what you are experiencing except you. Some people may have experienced back problems, and others have read about and studied the issue. But since you are the one experiencing it at that moment, you are the expert. The same goes for dealing with school violence. Communities and families that have directly experienced violence will have a completely different perspective on dealing with the problem. A woman who is attempting every day to keep her son out of gangs will have a different outlook than a politician who has only read about the problem.

Those communities that have a long-standing history of being negatively impacted by violence are usually the last to have a "say" in strategy development. If previous attempts to involve these communities were merely "token" attempts, then the communities will not be interested in any future endeavors. Once people come to expect that they will be ignored, they are less likely to even attempt to be involved in the planning, organizing, decision-making, and evaluating process. To get citizens to remain involved, it is important to help them feel that their involvement is worthwhile.

How does one do this? Author and orator Booker T. Washington once spoke to the importance of "drawing up from one's water-well,"[2] meaning it is important to draw on the "people" resources in the community to make a difference. Community organizers often start by getting a few people in the community involved and also making them a visible part of organizing efforts. This allows the community to see that "one of their own" is invested in the effort. Keeping this mindset is critical when deciding to endeavor upon mobilizing the community around school violence.

There are two important points to discuss when attempting to involve a community that has been plagued by violence that has spread into the schools. First, one must listen to both school and community members to get a better understanding of the causes of the problem, the barriers to prevention, and their ideals about solving the problem. There are many ways to "listen." Community or town forums in the neighborhoods are great opportunities for key stakeholders to listen. An interesting activity to engage in to solicit input at such meetings is something called GRITS (see Figure 11.1). No, it does not stand for "Girls Raised in the South," but rather "Getting Right into Their Shoes," which ultimately means to look at the problem from the

What are some of the challenges that face your community?	
Challenges	Supporting Factors

Figure 11.1. GRITS: Getting Right into Their Shoes

community's perspective. This facilitated activity will assist community members in mapping out the dynamics of a problem and properly documenting their offerings for a solution.

Second, community members must participate in the actual initiative or program that is being offered to prevent school violence. This will ultimately empower them to be change agents and part of the sustainability efforts to ensure a positive impact for years to come. Community members can be involved by doing the following:

- Get involved in the planning process and assist in defining the problem and goal development
- Donate money or time to school- and community-based fundraising efforts
- Become a volunteer at the school office: answer phones, make phone calls, assist in facilitating meetings
- Research the problem, write grants, or talk to other potential community partners
- Attend community events such as town hall meetings, rallies, and community hearings
- Serve on committees that focus on the problem of school violence or positive youth development
- Take leadership roles in community partnerships

This is only a start, but a good start in building a rapport with the community to solve the problems of violence. When examining a problem, perspectives from all types of people and sectors of the community are necessary. Unfortunately, those people who are directly impacted by the problem are oftentimes ignored or serve in minor ways in strategy development.

So the question becomes: who exactly should participate? It is important to include everyone, whatever their race, social class, gender, sexual orientation, religion, or culture. For example, if the school endeavors to work on the problem of youth street gangs, then it would be important to involve as many youth as possible. The school should also involve community members who are impacted by the gang problem, such as mothers who have lost children due to gang violence or parents who are dealing with a youth who is being coerced into gang involvement. Special attention should be placed on those individuals who would be traditionally overlooked, including minority and economically disadvantaged populations.

There are a few things that one must consider when reaching out to those who are directly affected by the problem. The following are recruitment strategies that could increase participation in "listening" sessions and empower people to get involved in organizing and advocacy:

- Familiarize yourself with the community in question. Every community is different, so it is important to know where most of the people work, socialize, attend church, volunteer, receive services, shop, or convene for recreation.

- Assess what existing civic groups, advisory committees, councils, social movements, or neighborhood associations are gaining ground in involvement. It may be beneficial to build on the efforts of a preexisting entity.

- Make sure these initiatives are easily accessible and visible. Provide information to the mayor's office, city manager, chamber of commerce, minister's council, referral agencies, United Way, YMCA, YWCA, and others. These convening points will draw different people and ensure that everyone is in the "know."

- Consistent and regular public hearings, meetings, and State of the Child seminars are all effective in reaching people who are not involved in any aforementioned group. Be creative when advertising to reach the maximum amount of people in the targeted population. Hold events at convenient times and locations. Also, it is important to plan carefully so that the events are not too large. To be effective, plan for no more than 20 people per event so that everyone has a chance to be heard.

To increase the participation of members in a community, one must minimize the number of obstacles. Obstacles to participation can stifle any attempt to make a substantive change. Educators may blame the lack of involvement on lack of motivation or apathy, but there is generally more to the story. It is easy to get discouraged in attempts to mobilize the community and parents, so much so that one might conclude that individuals don't care about the problems of violence that permeate the hallways of schools today. Once the obstacles to involvement are identified, educators and other community mobilization facilitators can assess whether it is a case of being "unwilling" or "unable."

BARRIERS TO COMMUNITY AND SCHOOL EFFORTS TO REDUCE VIOLENCE

The first obstacle is the preconceived notions and attitudes of educators and others who attempt to mobilize the community. Are there sentiments that the community does not care or that one will never be able to get working parents involved in violence prevention efforts? Most likely there are. This pessimistic attitude will always be visible, and if community members see that you are not excited or optimistic, then little will be offered in the way of support. In every situation and initiative aimed at bringing in local stakeholders, treat it as if it is the first attempt. Do not use past failures to shape a current mobilization effort. This is one of the more difficult obstacles to overcome. Engaging the entire community is not a single event, but a process that takes time.

The next challenge is inadequate community communication. Decreased participation can be as simple as members being unaware of opportunities to be involved. Regardless of community members' availability, if they do not know of any efforts or conversations around the issue, they will never show up. Utilizing familiar convening points, such as churches and recreational centers, can be helpful. Local television stations are recommended partners in conveying the messages, along with an underutilized medium such as the Internet. Corporate America and other innovative organizations are using not only e-mail information "blasts" but also other popular sites such as YouTube, MySpace, and Facebook in communicating to community members and parents. An administrator decided once to have a student set up a YouTube account and downloaded videos of students giving public service announcements, weekly updates, and even talent shows. The talent shows were mainly recorded and uploaded for the parents who were unable to attend because of work or being stationed overseas in the military.

This is another way to get the word out. Setting up a "blog site" and keeping the community "in the know" on events is another way to use technology to its potential. Lastly, one can partner with other organizations that may have had success in this area and get their advice in increasing communication. There is no need to reinvent the wheel if another entity has found success. Regardless of the mechanism, improving communication will always yield better results.

Understand also that the population that you are reaching out to may have limited experience in being involved in such initiatives. This alone can prove intimidating to many. Community members may not truly understand their place in efforts to prevent school violence. Their role needs to be operationalized, and activities need to occur that will assist in educating the community about the problem and the opportunities for them to develop solutions. In the same way, some community members may feel that they do not have the qualifications to make a difference. Educators who often speak of involving the entire school community in addressing school violence may not solicit input from janitors or cafeteria staff. If this is a long-standing practice, then this segment of the school will start to believe that they have nothing to bring to the table. This mindset needs to be eradicated, and those who seek to make a difference in the community need to solicit all input and lessen the anxiety of those who are not traditionally part of local initiatives.

Once community members show up, make sure they know what to expect and what will be expected of them if they get involved. Lastly, make sure that the event planners and "staff" are approachable, friendly, and clear should community participants have questions regarding the process. Facilitators also need to be trained in dealing with any community feelings of hostility and despair, especially if people have been dealing with violent neighborhoods and schools for years.

The problem of school violence is complex and already difficult to address. The complexity of the problem is enough to be discouraging, but the process should not discourage or instill a sense of powerlessness in the community. Most community members are intimidated by the complexity of politics, which is what prevents them from getting involved. The same goes for the strategy development phase. Community members may not know where to begin, whom to approach, and how to be influential in the decision-making process. Making the community aware and educated in the process will help individuals gain confidence to begin to work.

This confidence also spills over into "speaking up" on issues that are important to the individual. People who speak up have confidence in their information and perspective.[3] People do not want to appear foolish, so they opt to remain silent. One should think about teachers who put students to ease with statements such as "There is no such thing as a dumb question." John Q. Public should be encouraged to speak up and out regarding topics. In many situations where violence is derived from a specific neighborhood, the residents become the experts to "their" own situation. Educators and facilitators alike should ensure that the community is empowered to speak up, regardless of their experience, or lack thereof.

One school had a long-standing problem with bringing parents and other community members into the school. The administrator recognized that the school was not perceived as "reaching out" into the community to create such a bond. To change the climate, the school opened its doors to the community when the school was out and offered a variety of programs and activities. Some of the events included seminars on topics such as gang awareness, financial literacy, and even job readiness. When the school started building a real sustainable rapport with the community, parents and others felt more comfortable in engaging, simply because the school had engaged them first.

Logistics also play a part in the lack of community participation. To overcome time constraints, educators and facilitators need to organize convenient meeting times for people. For example, if you want a lot of people who work the night shift to be involved, then you will need to have times available that don't coincide with their work hours. Additionally, meetings and other events should not last longer than necessary and should take into account attention spans (especially after work). Lack of transportation is another logistical challenge for potential community participants. To overcome these obstacles, planners should either provide transportation to events or hold events that are not far away. Schools, libraries, community centers, and neighborhood association clubhouses are all viable places that can be utilized.

Next, child care is a good reason for participants to opt out of being involved. Not being able to find reliable child care or having to pay for a babysitter can be obstacles for parents who would otherwise get involved. Event facilitators should consider ways in which child care can be made available. It is also important to take into account the need to feed participants. This will be beneficial in gaining participation from the community.

Another challenge in community involvement is the poor organization of existing initiatives. If there are any groups that are taking action on the issue school violence, there have to be assurances that activities are not being duplicated. If there are several simultaneous attempts to convene and solicit input from the community, then these overlapped efforts from the school or other organizers will more than likely see less-than-favorable results. If the groups are poorly organized and utilized, then some reorganizing may be warranted. An option to reduce the effect of "too much at once" is to join forces with other groups if your goals are aligned. This may ease the public's possible confusion about the school's attempt to mobilize people around the issue of school violence.

At the same time, it may be beneficial to convene in smaller groups. The bigger the group of people involved, the less likely that each individual will have an opportunity to be heard and feel important. Smaller groups allow for the detailed examination of the dynamics of school violence from the community's perspective. By having multiple entities addressing the same problem, one can coordinate efforts to get input from the community at different locations at the same time. Spreading efforts geographically would certainly increase effectiveness. Of course, this would require some careful planning and total commitment from leaders and concerned citizens.

It is important to realize that groups should not do more than what is realistic. Taking on too much could stifle progress, so it is important to set a steady pace that is reasonable for educators and facilitators. With a poor community mobilization experience, community members may become cynical about the effectiveness of efforts. It is equally important to convey why the school system believes that the initiative will be helpful and productive.

MOTIVATION, MOTIVATION, MOTIVATION

Understanding the challenges that are inherent in mobilizing the community is a critical step in building successful partnerships to address school violence. Yet there still needs to be an effort to motivate the community to be involved. There are two basic ways to motivate individuals to be involved in prevention efforts: extrinsic and intrinsic. Extrinsic motivation refers to the motivation that comes from outside the individual. The factors are external or outside, such as money, gift certificates, or food. These types of factors provide satisfaction and pleasure that the task itself may not provide. An extrinsically motivated person will oftentimes be involved in an activity because of the reward and will have little interest in the cause. Educators use extrinsic factors to motivate students to achieve and value education, such as stickers for the completion of an activity or a good grade. Being extrinsically motivated does not mean that people will not get any satisfaction from working toward community goals. It just means that they receive more gratification from some external award, even when the task to be done holds little or no interest.

The complete opposite is to appeal to an individual's intrinsic motivation. Intrinsic motivation comes from the inside of an individual rather than from an external reward. These individuals get satisfaction from the action itself. Intrinsically motivated people will serve on a committee because it is enjoyable or because they enjoy the challenge of problem solving. Being motivated intrinsically does not mean that an individual will not seek a reward. It basically means that external rewards are not enough to keep the person motivated.

Using either extrinsic or intrinsic methods, educators and community facilitators need to determine how to motivate the community into action. The first part of motivating citizens to become involved is to generally know your audience. It makes sense to focus on the uniqueness of each person and to help people realize that what they have to offer is important and appreciated. The message needs to be conveyed that by being involved, they can benefit in ways that are significant to them. Organizers need to be familiar with the physical, social, cultural, economic, and political environments that affect participation. They must also recognize individual strengths, skills, talents, and experiences. Each individual tends to learn differently and to have different values. It is not only important for each person to have an opportunity to contribute; it is equally important to recognize, appreciate, and utilize strengths. This will enable participants to see how their participation is helpful and important.

In addition to recognizing individual strengths, organizers should seek out the strengths of the entire community. For example, if working with members from a predominantly Asian American community, educators and organizers should recognize the strengths that they possess. How do they already organize to get things done? Perhaps they already have an effective system in place that can be used. Even if they are unfamiliar with this problem, they may already have the capacity and feel comfortable in organizing a big cultural event or church fund-raiser.

It is important to recognize the needs of those who want to be involved. Those reasons often coincide with or respond to the basic needs that the individual wants to fulfill, including the following:

- The need to improve or maintain self-esteem
- The need to feel that one's contributions are genuinely useful and helpful

- The need to have some influence
- The need to have some level of control of self and the environment
- The need for friendship
- The need to be recognized for one's efforts[4]

It is equally important for leaders in education to be involved in other initiatives that affect the community. This type of support will instill confidence in the educators' attempt to deal with problems within the school walls. For example, if hoping to get support from the African American community, be prepared to lend expertise and voice to their causes. Speak out publicly against racism and discrimination in the community or discuss issues related to closing the minority academic achievement gap. Be visible at local events and prove to be a reliable ally. An occasional rally or fund-raiser may not be relevant to school violence prevention efforts, but if it's relevant to the interests and concerns of the people you want to reach, then it should be relevant to you.

A 1990 Gallup poll showed that the main reason that has kept most people who are interested in volunteering from doing so is that nobody ever asked them. Already vested individuals should invite people individually. One should reach out to as many people as possible, but one should also pay attention to "one-on-one" relationships. This eliminates the feeling of being a faceless number in a community. When people interact on a personal level, especially as friends and neighbors, involvement appears to be less intimidating. Inviting individuals can be done in a myriad of ways. One could ask directly or have employers invite their employees and coworkers, have teachers ask their students and families, ask friends to ask their friends, ask neighbors to ask their neighbors, and so forth. Individual "asks" also aids in matching individual talents, skills, knowledge, and experience with the group needs. For example, one could ask someone who is detailed oriented to assist with planning and ask someone with an outgoing personality to speak publicly.

A volunteer coordinator from a school once decided that she was going to be innovative in inspiring others to be part of efforts at the school. The coordinator decided to make "I Volunteer at School" buttons and ribbons. She hoped that these individuals would go out to their respective communities and workplaces and that their friends and families would ask them about the buttons. In fact, the school almost doubled the number of participants in the next event. Word of mouth and individual "asks" do make a difference.

Next, make participants feel welcome by listening to them, and when new people arrive for the first meeting or event, recognize their presence. Once again, this will strengthen their confidence in being useful in the process and will sustain future endeavors. Try to get them involved in small projects that will spark their interest and bring them into the discussion. Active listening is a big part of successful involvement from the community. This will prevent alienating certain people and help in understanding different perspectives and opinions. Active listening includes clarifying things that do not make sense, summarizing what is presented, and allowing the participants to finish without interruptions (see Figure 11.2). Allowing people to speak is a big part of showing appreciation for their contribution. Recognition is essential for people to feel wanted, helpful, and important. Other opportunities to show appreciation come through certificates of appreciation, recognition parties or banquets, special attention in newsletters, and simple phone calls and conversations thanking them.

Another important thing to remember is to remain organized. Ensure that individuals do not walk into a disorganized or unclear situation. Disorganized efforts are sure to stifle motivation and long-term violence prevention efforts. Educators and community leaders must help participants feel more secure and confident in their efforts toward goals and outcomes. In this connection, it is paramount to define and clarify the plans, goals, and purposes of the initiative early. The people you are attempting to enlist need to have a sense of direction with goals that are attainable.[5]

In goal development, it is equally important to set milestones in the process. For example, if one of the goals is to decrease bullying incidents at the middle school, then a milestone may be that all of the leaders in the faith community are speaking about the issue to their respective congregation. There can be many milestones in the process, but it is important to communicate the goals and maintain motivation through the completion of milestones. Working toward a common goal is sometimes enough to motivate, simply because it gives people a special bond and enables them to work together as a team.

It is also important to set practical and achievable timelines. If participants see that nothing is happening or they feel rushed, this could have a negative impact on their future involvement. Creating a timeline will allow everyone to see what is completed and what work remains to be done. In addition to keeping people informed, a timeline keeps the efforts moving at a steady pace. There is nothing worse than "wasting time." Once the community decides to be involved, educators and community facilitators should take great care in using time wisely. Anytime people decide to be involved, they are committing personal or professional time and are sometimes sacrificing work time or time spent with family and friends. For example, when people show up for town hall meetings, they expect to have their time used wisely. When facilitators do not plan effectively, it will be evident and can possibly stunt the potential impact of school violence prevention efforts. Remind participants about the goals, objectives, and timeline to keep a focus and to ultimately inspire change.

1. Give your undivided attention. Look at the person, and suspend other things you are doing. Put down the newspaper, turn off the cell phone, look at the person who's speaking, and listen intently.
2. Listen not only to the words, but the feeling content. A large part of human communication is nonverbal. It includes the tone of voice, gestures, body language, and inflections. They often reveal unspoken messages—such as anger, irritation, sadness, or fear—that can be far more important than the words used. Be sensitive to them.
3. Be sincerely interested in what the other person is talking about. Remember that you can always learn something from anyone, and that you are doing service by really listening.
4. Restate what the person said. This is a way of letting the person know that you understood not only the words but also the intent of the speaker. This is very important, especially when there is conflict or when the other party is hostile. Your instinct may be to answer the allegation immediately, but this only creates further tension and distance.
5. Ask clarifying questions once in a while. This will let the other person know that you are actively listening and that you are really interested in what he is saying.
6. Be aware of your own feelings and strong opinions. When we are not aware of our own feelings and strong opinions, we tend to express our immediate reactions when we're listening. Such reactions may cut off effective communication. For example, someone may be stating a religious view you disagree with. Your initial impulse may be to express your disagreement, which may only start an argument. Be aware then that while you disagree, this may not be the time to say so.
7. If you feel you really must state your views, say them only after you have listened. Let the speaker finish first, and if you feel it is helpful, then relate your own experience.

P. J. Donoghue and M. E. Siegel, *Are You Really Listening? Keys to Successful Communication* (Notre Dame, IN: Ave Maria Press, 2005), 164–78.

Figure 11.2. Seven Tips for Active Listening

CONCLUDING THOUGHT

The community must be involved to make a positive change in the school climate. In any attempts to mobilize the community, it is important to look at the problem from multiple perspectives. To gain such insight, educators cannot rely on input from some but should be as inclusive as possible. Acts of violence at school occur because of contributing factors spanning from the individual to the neighborhood, and solutions must target the same sources. Finally, while dealing with issues as tough as community involvement, maintaining a positive attitude in the process and learning from mistakes will make for a more effective mobilization effort.

PART III

The Reality of School Violence

Chapter 12

Safety by Design

William L. Lassiter

Designing a safe school is no simple task, but if you are reading this book, you are probably not thinking through how to design a new school; you are trying to decide how to improve what you already have. This chapter focuses on what can be done to existing schools to make them safer and more secure.

During the 2005–2006 school year there were 97,382 public, 28,384 private, and 3,294 public charter elementary and secondary schools operating in the United States. During that school year 2,291 new public schools opened, and an additional 951 schools were being constructed to open within the next two school years.[1] In 1999 the average age of the main instructional buildings of a public school was 40 years, and on average the schools had not had a major renovation in over 11 years. These facts paint a picture of an education infrastructure that is mostly aging and that was designed long before school violence concerns were addressed through school design. To add to these problems, schools also have to deal with an ever-growing population, which necessitates additional classroom space. This space often comes in the form of portable classrooms. In fact, during the 2005–2006 school year, 33 percent of principals reported using portable or temporary buildings for classroom environments to help cope with the rapidly increasing need for classroom space.[2]

CREATING WARM AND WELCOMING ENVIRONMENTS

One of the first things I notice about a school when I walk in the door is that it is normally easy to tell whether you are walking into a elementary school, middle school, or a high school. When you walk into the front door of an elementary school, you expect to see pictures on the wall, student artwork and school assignments, murals of the school's mascot, and other bright and colorful things. When you walk into a high school, what do you expect to see? Usually one strip of paint running down the hallway, and it is normally green or brown or some other drab color. Sorry if that is your school color. But besides that one strip of paint running down the middle of the hallway, there is nothing up on the walls that say "come on in." High schools look more like institutions than like fun and exciting places of learning. I have done hundreds if not thousands of school safety assessments, and I can tell you, if you walk into an elementary school to do an assessment and you are not feeling your best, when you walk into those doors something changes. It is hard to be depressed or upset when you are surrounded by all those bright, cheerful colors. When I walk into a high school feeling great, my mood often changes as I see that old trophy case sitting out front with all those trophies from 1922 but nothing that relates to the kids who currently attend the school. When you walk into a high school bathroom, you wonder what kind of science experiment they are conducting that is generating that smell.

Why can we not create high school environments that feel warm and welcoming? I ask that question to many high school principals and teachers, and they say "Well, if we put something nice up on the walls, the kids will just tear it down." Although this may be true, wow, what low expectations we are setting for our kids. I think high school kids often do not care about the school environment because they have not seen anyone else in the school or community care about that school environment either. Let me demonstrate this point through two stories.

I was working with one high school in which a students' group got together and decided they were going to beautify the school and school grounds. The young ladies in this group decided they would start with the girls' restrooms. So they went out and had a bake sale to raise money to buy supplies to fix up the girls' restroom. With the money they raised they purchased paint, a plant, a radio, and a small couch that they found at a yard sale. They went to their school on a Saturday and painted the girls' restroom purple. Not only did they paint the restroom, but they also gave it one heck of a good cleaning. On Monday morning when students returned to school, the restroom was all the buzz. Students were asking if you've seen the new girls' restroom and adding they are even playing classical music in there. Teachers actually told me they preferred using the students' new and improved restroom over their private teacher's lounge restroom, which was not in as good a shape.

But as the students came in the next morning to inspect how their restroom was holding up, they were dismayed to find that someone had come in and destroyed it all. I remember one girl called me up crying her eyes out as she told me what happened. In the back of my mind I was thinking about what all those principals and teachers had told me over the years about why they do not make the effort to fix up the high school hallways. I asked the young lady, "What are you going to do next?"

She said, "We are going to fix it!" She added, "Even if it takes another fund-raiser and even if it takes some of my own money to do it. We are going to fix it."

I was surprised by her resiliency and how much this restroom meant to her, but she was bought in. Through her leadership the group went out and did it all again. It took them two weeks, but they did it. This time the restroom stayed nice for several days, but again someone came along and vandalized it. I thought for sure after this second blow the group of girls would give up, but they didn't; in fact, they were more resolved than ever to make this thing work. So after fixing the restroom up for the third time, the students asked the principal if they could make an announcement about the new restroom. The principal obliged, and the students made an announcement about how this was their restroom and that they spent their own money on fixing it up and if you did not know how to respect their restroom you could go somewhere else. For the rest of the year no one messed up their restroom, and in fact they created a duty roster for students to assist in its upkeep. By the end of the year the students had over 100 volunteers who had signed up to help out with that restroom or one of the five other restrooms the girls had adopted by the end of the year.

Another example of students getting involved to create a warmer and more welcoming environment was evidenced at an alternative school I visited. I was going to the school to meet with the principal, and I remember I was running late for my meeting. So, of course, instead of staying on the sidewalk I took off walking rapidly across the grass. As I got about halfway to the building, a rather large young man came running out of the building, looking none too happy. He yelled at me, "Get off my grass!" and since he was a rather large student, I turned around and got back onto the sidewalk. When I got inside, the young man was giving me a horrible look, so I told him, "I am sorry about the grass," which seemed to calm him down some. As I eased my way past him to the principal's office, I asked the receptionist, "What is going on with that student?"

She asked me, "Did you walk across the grass?"

I said, "Well, maybe."

She said, "I will let the principal explain it to you, because he is waiting on you, but I would not advise you to do that again."

When I sat down with the principal, he started to explain to me how his school works. He said, "This is an alternative school. We have the worst kids in the county here, but we do not treat them like they are the worst kids in the county. We have high expectations for our students, and we expect that they take care of their own school. To help drive this message home, we ask them to do the landscaping, everything from mowing the grass to trimming the bushes, and you better believe these students take pride in their school."

I said, "So I have noticed. I thought I was going to get assaulted by one of your students on the way in because I walked across the grass."

What do both of these stories have in common? They are both about how students were empowered to create school environments that are warm and welcoming, and in the process they became more connected to their school environments.

CRIME PREVENTION THROUGH ENVIRONMENTAL DESIGN

The purpose of Crime Prevention through Environmental Design (CPTED) is to "harden the target" or, in other words, to create the perception in one's mind that the school will not be an easy place to perpetrate a crime. Many who believe in CPTED also believe that most crimes are crimes of opportunity. Therefore, they believe that crime can be prevented by reducing opportunities. How does a school go about reducing opportunities for crimes to be committed? Any good CPTED plan will cover the following concepts: natural surveillance, natural access control, and natural territorial reinforcement.

Natural Surveillance

Natural surveillance involves making it easier to spot potential trespassers upon entering a school building. Natural surveillance provides two benefits to a school environment. First, it allows school staff members to spot potential trespassers or criminals before they have access to children or staff members. Natural surveillance may allow a school enough time to take critical steps during an emergency to save lives and property. The other major benefit of natural surveillance is that it creates the perception that this school may not be as easy a target as the criminal(s) originally thought.

Some of the specific things schools can do to increase natural surveillance are the following:

- Do not block windows with artwork or school work, so that clear lines of sight are possible from the school building.
- Follow the 3–7 rule. Do not have any bushes taller than three feet tall, and trim tree branches so that they do not hang lower than seven feet.
- Where visual surveillance is not possible because of the lack of windows or an obstruction, consider using a surveillance camera system.
- Use well-placed lighting to help eliminate blind spots.

- Have designated visitor parking spaces, and locate these spaces close to the building and in view of the front office whenever possible.
- Try to avoid using covered walkways that block visual surveillance.

Natural Access Control

Natural access control decreases the opportunity for crimes to occur on a school campus by clearly creating in one's mind a separation between public and private spaces. Natural access control seeks to limit the number of people who accidentally trespass on a campus and to increase the challenges faced by one who is intentionally trying to gain access to a campus. Schools can do the following things to increase natural access control:

- Use a single, clearly identifiable point of entry. Most schools have multiple entrances to their buildings, and by locking all but one entry, the school limits its exposure to unwelcome visitors. For every entry that is left unlocked, the school should try to provide adult supervision.
- Use signs to direct visitors to the front office, where they should be asked to sign in. Upon signing in, visitors should be issued a visitor name tag that will identify that they have been signed in and have the right to be on the school campus.
- Lock as many exterior doors as possible to limit access to the school building, and use structures to direct the public toward the front office.
- Incorporate maze entrances to restrooms.
- Consider the placement of short bushes, especially thorny or prickly bushes below ground-level windows.
- Secure roof access.

A good access control policy has more to do with the staff than with the building itself. Most schools have what I call the "official door opener," which is a rock that sits on the ground beside the door that staff members leave propped up. Obviously, allowing staff to leave doors propped open defeats the purpose of having an access control policy that requires a single point of entry. Even if the door is not currently being propped open, the rock still can be used to open the door by smashing through a window.

Staff also must be trained on how to challenge visitors on the school campus. The purpose of issuing visitor passes is to make it easier for staff to distinguish between visitors who are supposed to be on campus and people who are not supposed to be on campus. Most staff members state that they do not challenge visitors because they are scared they will be embarrassed to find that the person they are challenging is someone that they already know. For this reason a uniform identification badge policy should be enforced on school campuses. That way, even if the superintendent is strolling down the school halls, the expectation is that he or she will be wearing a badge. If a person does not have a badge, staff should ask that person to report to the front office to receive one.

Natural Territorial Reinforcement

Territorial reinforcement makes it easy for the public to determine where a school's property boundaries are. By clearly defining these boundaries, the school accomplishes two things. First, it creates a sense of ownership. Owners are interested in their property and are more likely to challenge intruders or report them to the police. Second, these clearly delineated boundaries create an environment in which intruders stand out and are more easily identified. Natural territorial reinforcement involves using buildings, fences, pavement, signs, lighting, and landscape to express ownership and to define public, semipublic, and private space.

- Maintain grounds, buildings, and landscaping so they communicate that an alert and active presence is occupying the space.
- Display security system signs at entryways.
- Schedule activities and use all parts of the school campus to encourage proper use and increase the perception that these areas are used and therefore controlled.
- Place amenities such as seating or refreshments in common areas to help attract more students and visitors to those areas where they can be observed easily.
- Avoid cyclone fencing and razor-wire fence topping, as it communicates the lack of a human presence and a reduced risk of being detected.

Maintenance

Maintenance demonstrates ownership of property. Deterioration indicates that the owner of the property does not have control over their property and therefore indicates a greater tolerance for disorder. The theory of maintenance has been best expressed through the Broken Windows Theory, which states that "it is easier to solve a small problem before it becomes a big problem. For example, if one person tags (graffiti) the side of a building, a small area, you want to clean that area up before more people add their tags to the building, making it a big issue."[3] Broken Windows Theory proponents support a zero tolerance approach to property maintenance, observing that the presence of a broken window entices vandals to break more windows in the vicinity. The sooner broken windows are fixed, the less likely it is that such vandalism will occur in the future.

CPTED QUESTIONS

Some of the common questions that should be raised by doing a CPTED analysis of your school would include the following:

What Are the Threats That Students Face on Their Way to and from School?

No matter how nice a school you have in your community, if students encounter problems with traffic, crime, or other hazards on the way to school, they are put at great risk of physical danger, getting involved in delinquent behavior, and emotional trauma. In 2005, 6 percent of students surveyed feared being attacked while traveling to and from school.[4]Students get to school in many different ways, whether by walking, riding a bike, riding a school bus, taking public transportation, or riding with a parent. Each of these methods presents its own risk.

Schools may feel that unless students are riding one of the school buses, they have little control over and therefore little responsibility for students' travels to school. This can be a misconception. Most school administrators that I talk to tell me that many of the conflicts that occur in their schools start in the community and spill over into the school environment.

When considering how to address the threats that students may face on the way to school, administrators should not only look at the threats students face, but also at what untapped resources exist in the community. These resources may include law enforcement agencies, businesses, faith groups, and community organizations. Often after simply asking these groups if they could be more active participants in making sure students arrive at school safely, schools find they are generally willing to assist. If you do not ask, you will never know. These groups want to help but just do not know the best way to get involved.

In addition, if schools mention the concerns of students to the local law enforcement agency, department commanders may decide to patrol these areas more often. Businesses can be encouraged to become safe places for students who may need a place to flee criminal activity. They can also be encouraged to be a part of a community watch program that will report crimes to the appropriate authorities. Faith groups and community organizations can set up safe passage programs in which adults volunteer to walk with a group of students to and from school. Schools may need to get these efforts started, but often these community partners will take them over.

Can Administrative Staff Observe Visitors as They Are Approaching the School Building?

Being able to see a threat coming is a basic tenet of CPTED. Without prior visual surveillance, visitors and trespassers can easily surprise a school and leave school officials and students with little time to respond. Unfortunately, many schools are built with poor exterior visual surveillance, so schools often need to take additional steps to compensate for this problem. This can be done by stationing a receptionist at the front door, even if the front office is not in that location. Schools can also invest in a surveillance camera system. Although most schools that have a camera system do not use it for prevention but rather for solving crimes after they occur, cameras have been shown to have a deterrent effect in the locations where they are used.

Do School Staff Members Have the Ability to Restrict the Access of Visitors or Trespassers?

It really does not do the school any good to have the ability to spot intruders on campus if they do not have any way to respond to these threats. Some schools are moving to electronic locking systems, which can allow all the school's external doors to be locked with the press of a button. I would not recommend this system for all schools, but all schools should have an access control policy and a procedure for locking down exterior doors if a threat is approaching the school building.

What Kind of Visual Surveillance Can Take Place within the School Building?

If someone wanted to hide in your school, how hard would it be? The best way to improve visual surveillance within your school is with people. During class changes, do your teachers step out into the hallway to monitor what is going on? This simple step can reduce everything from bullying behavior to the selling of drugs and other contraband on the school campus.

Can School Staff Members Immediately Lock Down Their Classroom, Office, or Other Location on the School Campus during an Emergency?

In a previous question we discussed the ability to limit access to the school building, but what happens if the intruder does gain access: does your school have the ability to easily lock down? Because many classroom doors can only be locked by a key that works on the doorknob in the hallway, many times during a lockdown teachers are forced out into the hallway, where the intruder is, to lock their classroom door. I recommend that classrooms have internal locking doors so that teachers are not exposed to the threat while trying to protect their students. Schools should also think about support staff members and substitute teachers and ask if they have a way to get behind a locked door during an emergency.

Has the School Identified Trouble Spots around the School Campus?

As was discussed in the bullying chapter, school officials should do an analysis of where the most frequent problems occur around the school campus. Once schools have determined these locations, they should use people and technology to monitor those areas.

OTHER LOW-COST SOLUTIONS

In a document prepared by the National Clearinghouse for Educational Facilities that I helped to write, the following low-cost solutions to creating a safer school were suggested:

- Prevent access to windows and roofs by trimming trees, relocating objects near the building that can be used as climbing devices, and ensuring that downspouts, covered walkway supports, light posts, and other building or site features are not scalable.
- Keep trees well trimmed if they are located near building exits, access roads, and utility wires so they don't block site access and building entry and egress in an emergency.
- Ensure that fire hydrants on and near school grounds are visible and unobstructed.
- Routinely inspect exterior lighting for damage and bulb wear, and make immediate repairs.
- Fence off or otherwise enclose niches and blind spots in exterior walls that provide hiding places.
- Clearly mark and separate visitor parking.
- Keep bus and car access separated from school buildings and play areas with curbs, removable bollards, or gates that allow emergency vehicle access but keep other vehicles at a distance.
- Place traffic calming devices—stop signs, pavement markings, bumps—in parking lots and driveways.
- Give each school building a distinctive marking to help emergency responders, new students, and visitors quickly find their way.
- Clearly mark the main entry to the school, and post signs on other entries redirecting visitors to the main entry.
- Ensure that the fresh air intakes for the school's mechanical systems are screened and located at least 12 feet off the ground or are otherwise inaccessible.
- Ensure that portable classrooms are adequately identified, lighted, and tied down and that trailer hitches and tongues have been removed and access beneath them is restricted with fencing, siding, or other materials.
- Routinely inspect exterior doors for damage and faulty hardware, and make immediate repairs.

- Where appropriate, number or renumber doors and rooms in a logical, sequential, floor-by-floor pattern so emergency responders can locate them quickly.
- Consider displaying room numbers on classroom windows so they are readily visible to first responders from outside the building.
- Keep unoccupied rooms and spaces locked when not in use.
- Ensure that corridor and restroom lighting controls are protected from unauthorized use.
- Ensure that all spaces in the school that require two exits have, in fact, two functioning exits.
- Routinely check that fire alarms, fire extinguishers, and other fire safety components are in good working order and that staff are trained in the use of fire extinguishers.
- Post clear and precise emergency evacuation maps in classrooms and other major building spaces and at key corridors locations.
- Ensure that all classrooms, including portables, have two-way communication with the office.
- Use caller ID on all school phones to help identify and deter threatening callers.
- Ensure that medical supplies are locked in an observable part of the school nurse's office or health room.
- Install a battery or portable generator backup power supply for telephones and emergency communications.
- Restrict access to all rooms and spaces that contain building wiring, equipment, and controls.
- Provide backup emergency lighting in stairs, hallways, and rooms without windows.[5]

CONCLUDING THOUGHT

Usually when schools think about improving safety through physical design, they believe it will be an expensive endeavor, but hopefully this chapter has shown that high expense does not have to be the case. Sometimes doing the small inexpensive things can give you just as much, if not more, bang for your buck than the large expensive things. Schools should focus on the tenets of CPTED and use their people to address the needs of the facility.

Chapter 13

When a Threat Is Made

William L. Lassiter

A young man or woman walks into a school and threatens to shoot up the school. What is the proper response to this type of threat from school officials? This was the case in several of the school shootings that occurred across the country in the last few years. The normal response from administrators has been to suspend the child and turn the case over to law enforcement. In one such case in my home state of North Carolina, the school officials did that very thing. The student threatened to shoot up the school, so the school suspended him for 10 days. The only problem was that while that student was out on his 10-day suspension, he was receiving no services and no supervision. When he returned to school 10 days later, guess what? You got it, he shot up the school. Fortunately for the school and the community, a brave school resource officer was employed at the school and stopped the young man from hurting anyone. It did not hurt that they also had a well-constructed emergency plan, but if they had relied on a strong threat assessment plan, maybe the shootings would have never happened.

People often tell me that when they were kids they made threats all the time about hurting a classmate at school, but those threats were ignored. Then they say sadly, I guess we cannot do that today. To which I reply, Is it really all that sad? First of all, think of our myth that kids are much more violent today than they were a generation or two ago. It would appear that they are not; in fact, they may be less violent than the generation before them. The problem is that the tools of violence are far more deadly than they were a generation ago, and the access to those tools has been greatly increased. But is it really sad that we teach children at a young age that they cannot walk around making threats? I think that is actually a good thing. Everyone knows it is a skill that they will need when they get older. If a child did not learn at a young age that it is unacceptable to make threats, what would their airport experience be like? So although it may be sad, one must understand how to deal with these threats, because kids are much more capable of carrying out a threat today with their increased access to weapons. I do not believe it is sad that kids learn early on that making threats is an unacceptable behavior.

In this chapter we will explore how schools should react to a child making a threat. It is important to note from the beginning that the threat assessment process is very different from the process of profiling students. In separate reports, the FBI and Secret Service have condemned the use of student profiling to recognize potentially dangerous students. Profiling uses a checklist of signs considered common among violent or dangerous youth, but this methodology has been criticized for overidentifying youth as "dangerous." On the other hand, the basis for using a threat assessment protocol is quite different, because the fundamental principle of threat assessment is that, in most cases, threats precede violent acts in schools. The approach requires school officials to investigate any apparent threatening behavior by students and to determine the seriousness and legitimacy of the actions before imposing disciplinary consequences.

One set of guidelines gives the following statement: "One of the defining features of the threat assessment approach is that school administrators do not have to take a zero tolerance approach that results in severe punishment for any kind of threat. If a threatening statement can be identified as a joke or figure of speech—for example, 'I could just kill you for that'—it can be resolved quickly with an explanation and apology. If a threat is considered very serious, it triggers a law enforcement investigation and a mental health assessment of the student. The guidelines include criteria for school administrators to use in determining the seriousness of a threat."[1]

BUILDING A THREAT ASSESSMENT TEAM

The research on creating a threat assessment team repeatedly emphasizes that the team should be multidisciplinary. Two examples include the National Association of School Psychologists and the FBI. In a publication released by the National Association of School Psychologists, it was stated that an "effective threat assessment is based on the efforts of a threat assessment team that is usually composed of trained school-based personnel and select members of the broader school community, such as law enforcement officers, faith leaders, and representatives of social service agencies. School personnel that should be on the team include top administrators, mental health professionals, and security staff members. The interdisciplinary team approach improves the efficiency and scope of the assessment process (which can be time consuming), provides diverse professional input, and minimizes the risk of observer bias. Specific training for all members of the team is essential."[2]

The FBI described the multidisciplinary team in this manner: "Schools could draw team members from school staff and other professionals, including trained mental health professionals. The team would constitute an experienced, knowledgeable group that could review threats, consult with outside experts, and provide recommendations and advice to the coordinator and to the school administration."[3]

One of the team members should be designated as the primary point of contact for the threat assessment team. As the U.S. Secret Service recommends, "Individuals who have information about students that is cause for concern should know how to refer this information and to whom. The threat assessment team should designate a member of the team to serve as the initial point of contact for information of possible concern. The availability of this point of contact should be made known community-wide."[4] The FBI titles this position the "threat assessment coordinator" and describes the role in this way: a "person in a school—or perhaps several in a large school—should be assigned to oversee and coordinate the school's response to all threats. The designated coordinator may be the principal, another administrator, a school psychologist, resource officer, or any other staff member. The school should find appropriate threat assessment training programs for whoever is designated."[5]

Whatever a school ends up calling the position, there needs to be someone at every school who is the threat assessment expert. This person will be the primary point of contact for staff and students who have heard or seen a threat being made. The school's threat assessment coordinator will decide when the whole threat assessment team needs to be called together to handle a situation.

THE THREAT ASSESSMENT PROCESS

The U.S. Secret Service stated, "The primary purpose of a threat assessment is to prevent targeted violence. The threat assessment process is centered upon on analysis of the facts and evidence of behavior in a given situation. The appraisal of risk in a threat assessment focuses on actions, communications, and specific circumstances that might suggest that an individual intends to mount an attack and is engaged in planning or preparing for that event."[6] In other words, the purpose is to identify those students who are a real threat to the school population.

Identifying a Threatening Student

The first step in conducting a threat assessment is to identify a threatening student. Although this may sound like the school staff will be identifying any student who is at risk of committing a violent act, that is not what conducting a threat assessment is about. When conducting a threat assessment, a school is only trying to identify those students who have made a threat. This is not to say that all at-risk students are not in need of help, rather that the threat assessment process is only appropriate for situations in which a threat has been made.

There are several ways that students can come to the attention of school officials that would lead those officials to conduct a threat assessment. The first would be through direct communication of a threat. This could take the form of a student verbally making a threat to another student or staff member, or it could be more abstract, such as a student turning in an English paper threatening to harm another student. No matter in which form the threat is made, it is clear who is making the threat.

The second way that students could come to the attention of officials at the school would be through second- and third-hand reports. An example of this would be a student reporting to the administration that he or she has heard that a group of students are planning to bring a gun to school.

The final way that students can garner the attention of school officials is through anonymous communication. This form of threat could appear as a hit list written on a restroom wall or as a phoned-in threat. An anonymous threat may need to be investigated by law enforcement officials to help the school identify the student or students behind the threat. Although anonymous threats tend to be false more often than directly communicated threats, they should not be taken lightly and should be investigated to determine their source and legitimacy.

The Threat Inquiry

It is important to make a distinction between a threat inquiry and a threat investigation. The U.S. Secret Service draws the distinction between the two by stating the following: "threat assessment inquiries are initiated, conducted, and controlled by the school threat assessment team; threat assessment investigations are initiated, conducted, and controlled by law enforcement agencies."[7] The school conducts an inquiry for the purpose of determining whether a threatening student presents a danger to the school population. If the threat does pose a danger to the school population, that would be an appropriate time to turn the case over to law enforcement so they can conduct an investigation.

Threat inquiries should be conducted as soon as possible after school officials have learned of a threat. If the threat represents an immediate danger to the school population, law enforcement should be called to assist in the investigation of the threat. An example of an immediate threat would be that a student or parent was on the way to school with a weapon to hurt a classmate or a staff member.

When conducting a threat inquiry, school officials should gather the following information:

1. The facts that drew attention to the student:
   - How was the student identified?
   - What type of threat was made?
   - Who are the witnesses?
   - What was the context surrounding the threat?
   - Did any of the witnesses have a reason to lie or to misinterpret the threat?
2. Information about the student:
   - Basic demographic information, such as name, age, date of birth, address, and student ID number.
   - Background and current life situation of the student, such as past history of violence or discipline problems, stability of home life, mental health history, substance abuse problems, any academic problems, and recent life changes such as the loss of a family member.

   Note: During the information-gathering process, school officials may want to seek out a caring adult who is close to the student so this adult can be involved in the threat inquiry process. This adult could provide insight into why the student is making threats and may be able to suggest or be a part of an effective intervention with the student.

3. Information about behaviors related to attacking the school:
   - Has the students communicated multiple threats?
   - Has the student threatened suicide?
   - Has the student sought to purchase or steal weapons?
4. Motives, and some of the reasons the U.S. Secret Service has discovered have been past reasons for school attacks:
   - "Revenge for a perceived injury or grievance"
   - "Yearning for attention, recognition, or notoriety"
   - "A wish to solve a problem otherwise seen as unbearable"
   - "A desire to die or be killed"[8]
5. Target selection:
   - Consider why a student has selected a particular target.
   - Most attackers alert their friends of their selected targets.
   - The targets may be able to give the assessment team some insight as to why the threat has been made.

Once the threat assessment team gathers all the information it needs to continue with the investigation, the U.S. Secret Service recommends that the team consider the following 11 questions:

1. What are the student's motive(s) and goals?
2. Have there been any communications suggesting ideas or intent to attack?

3. Has the subject shown inappropriate interest in any of the following?

4. Has the student engaged in attack-related behaviors?

5. Does the student have the capacity to carry out an act of targeted violence?

6. Is the student experiencing hopelessness, desperation and/or despair?

7. Does the student have a trusting relationship with at least one responsible adult?

8. Does the student see violence as an acceptable—or desirable—or the only—way to solve problems?

9. Is the student's conversation and "story" consistent with his or her actions?

10. Are other people concerned about the student's potential for violence?

11. What circumstances might affect the likelihood of an attack?"[9]

The answers to these 11 questions should allow the threat assessment team to make a determination about the most important question facing the team: Does this student present a real threat to our school's population? Once that primary question has been answered, school officials must determine their next steps. Does the child need to be referred to mental health? Does law enforcement need to be called to help handle the situation? Does juvenile justice need to get involved? Or do we need to do all of the above? What makes the threat assessment process so different from profiling is that once the process is completed, the school should be able to easily develop a comprehensive plan for the student who made the threat. This plan will include dealing with the root causes of the threatening behavior. This may include punishment and taking a look at treatment options.

Threat Levels

Having helped many school districts over the years craft their threat assessment policies, I would suggest that school districts use a decision tree that the threat assessment team can use to help them decide how they should proceed. Many districts are basing their decision trees off the three threat levels described by the FBI: "Schools should adopt a threat assessment process organized around a decision tree that leads school administrators through a step-by-step process of investigating student threats, determining how dangerous a threat is and then planning what actions are necessary to prevent it from being acted upon."[10]

There are three levels of threats, the first being a spontaneous utterance. An example of this behavior would be a student who is playing a game of basketball and who says to the other team, "We are going to kill you guys!" This is most likely a harmless way of saying they will beat the other team in the game. However, as with any threat, the full situation should be considered to determine if the threat goes beyond just playing basketball. The FBI defines this type of threat as a "low-level threat": "a threat which poses a minimal risk to the victim and public safety." According to the FBI, a low-level threat is vague and indirect, contains inconsistent information, is implausible and unrealistic, and sounds as if the person will not carry it out.[11]

So exactly what should staff members do when they hear this type of language used? First, they should determine whether this was truly just a spontaneous utterance or something more. If they determine that it was just a spontaneous utterance, they should call the student over and correct the behavior. It is important to make sure the student understands why it is not acceptable to make such threats, not only at school but also in the community. It is always important to teach students how we expect them to behave and then hold them accountable. So if this is the first time you have had to correct a particular student's behavior for making a threat, you should use this as a teachable moment.

The second type of threat is much more serious and goes beyond the spontaneous utterance; with this type of threat, the person intends to do real harm to another student or staff member. How do you know when you have passed that threshold? Usually the threat involves some type of plan of how the student wishes to carry out the threat. A plan demonstrates that students have thought through exactly how they might carry out such an attack. The FBI defines this type of threat as a moderate threat: "a threat which could be carried out, although it may not appear entirely realistic."[12] According to the FBI, a moderate threat has the following elements:

- "The threat is more direct and more concrete than a low-level threat."
- "The wording in the threat suggests that the threatener has given some thought to how the act will be carried out."
- "There may be a general indication of a possible place and time (though these signs still fall well short of a detailed plan)."
- "There is no strong indication that the threatener has taken preparatory steps, although there may be some veiled reference or ambiguous or inconclusive evidence pointing to that possibility—an allusion to a book or movie that shows the planning of a violent act, or a vague, general statement about the availability of weapons."
- "There may be a specific statement seeking to convey that the threat is not empty: 'I'm serious!' or 'I really mean this!'"[13]

The last type of threat, or a level-three threat, is the most serious threat that an individual can make. The level-three threat includes specific details and describes the means to carry out the threat. These threats require immediate attention. The FBI defines this type of threat as a high-level threat, "a threat that appears to pose an imminent and serious danger to the safety of others." The FBI's definition of a high-level threat includes the following components:

- "Threat is direct, specific and plausible."
- "Threat suggests concrete steps have been taken toward carrying it out, for example, statements indicating that the threatener has acquired or practiced with a weapon or has had the victim under surveillance."[14]

If a high-level threat is made on the school campus, school officials should involve law enforcement in the investigation process immediately. In most cases a high-level threat will justify the search of a student's home and personal items and may require that the student be held in protective custody to protect the student and the school population.

CONCLUDING THOUGHT

If school shootings have taught us anything, they have taught us that threats should not be taken lightly, but by overreacting to a threat we may actually do more harm than good. For these reasons schools should seek to create a threat assessment process that will allow them to react appropriately. It is also important to remember that disciplinary action may not deal with the root cause of why a student is making a threat on a school campus. The threat assessment process allows a school to truly consider all the factors that may have caused a behavior to occur, and it helps school officials develop a comprehensive method for dealing with those precipitating factors, such as the student who is being bullied and threatens his classmates so they will leave him alone.

Chapter 14

How Columbine Changed Everything

William L. Lassiter

Where were you the day that Columbine happened? I was working for the North Carolina Center for the Prevention of School Violence. The Center was a small organization with six or seven staff members at the time. All of us were squeezed into a small copy room where we had a little 12-inch TV set up. The TV did not have cable, so we adjusted the bunny ears to try to hear and see what was happening. Just as the picture became clear, the phone started ringing, and I do not think it stopped ringing until about six weeks later. In the month after Columbine, the Center responded to over 1,000 requests for information from the media, the public, schools, elected officials, parents, students, and anybody and everybody else who was disturbed by the incident. It was immediately after Columbine that the questioning began and we all started to search for answers.

The massacre at Columbine High School was a wake-up call for many in the United States that school violence can occur in any school. Two students, Eric Harris and Dylan Klebold, went on a shooting spree at the high school, killing 15, including themselves, and wounding 23.

As horrific as the events at Columbine High School were, it was not the most deadly incident of school violence to occur in an American school. On May 18, 1927, the Bath School disaster occurred in Bath Township, Michigan. This event remains and hopefully always will remain the most deadly school violence event in American history. The Bath School disaster left 45 people dead and 58 injured. Most of those victims were children in the second through seventh grades. The assailant in this case was a school board member who was upset over a tax that had been leveled on the community to build the school. Many believe that school violence is a recent occurrence, but as one can see, that is not the case.[1]

So what is it about Columbine that rang alarm bells in the American public's psyche? First, although it is not the most deadly event to have occurred in an American school, it is the second most deadly. Second, the perpetrators of those crimes were students, and although other students had come to school and shot their classmates before Columbine, the United States had never seen anything quite like this. Columbine was planned by two students in great detail, and they wanted to hurt many people. Third, the media attention given to this particular event was unprecedented. The 24/7 cable news networks told us everything we wanted to know about the event and much we did not want to know. These three things led the public to focus increased attention and resources on the issues that cause school violence, and for that, we should be thankful.

Having talked to many of the relatives of loved ones lost during the incident at Columbine, the resounding message I have heard is, Let something positive come out of this tragic event. In this chapter we will examine the lessons learned from that day and look at how response tactics have changed in the years since the shootings at Columbine.

LESSONS LEARNED FROM COLUMBINE

Lesson One: The Priorities of Law Enforcement Must Be Adjusted during an Active Shooter Scenario

Before Columbine, the priorities of law enforcement during an active shooter scenario were to contain the incident and to wait for the SWAT (Special Weapons and Tactics) team to arrive to engage the shooter. Columbine demonstrated that in the 45 minutes leading up to the arrival of the SWAT team, innocent people were dying. According to a *60 Minutes* investigation of the Columbine incident, "By the time Klebold and Harris committed suicide at 12:08, at least 75 police officers were surrounding Columbine High School. The first SWAT team had been in the building only two minutes. It would be nearly three hours before they would know the gunmen were dead."[2]

After Columbine, many law enforcement agencies started to adjust their policies and procedures to a new technique called rapid deployment. Rapid deployment is basically having the first two to four officers who arrive on campus engage the shooter. These officers form a contact team whose first priority is to contact and engage the shooter. The theory behind this tactic is that it will change the dynamics of the scenario by changing the focus of the shooter. At Columbine the two shooters were able to focus their full attention on harming staff and students because they were the only armed individuals in the school building. As one parent stated on CBS's *60 Minutes II*, "The police claimed they were outgunned, you want to talk about being outgunned, my daughter was armed only with a pencil. That is all she had to defend herself."[3]

Lesson Two: Communication Is the Key to Crisis Response

Columbine is just one of many crisis situations that have taught us this valuable lesson. One may remember that after the attacks of September 11, 2001, a number of articles were written on how law enforcement and fire responders could not communicate with each other. Although we know that communication is a key, we still have not figured out a solution to this problem. Often law enforcement officers, firefighters, and first responders arrive at a crisis situation operating on different radio frequencies and with equipment that is not interoperable. With school situations, a fourth party can be added to this complicated equation, school officials. Almost any officer who works in a school can tell you that getting radio waves to pass through walls made of concrete and rebar is almost impossible. So even if officers, firefighters, emergency responders, and school officials had the interoperable equipment, what are the chances that their equipment would actually reach through the walls of a school?

Many schools have developed techniques such as using red and green cards to communicate the status of a classroom and thus overcome the inherent communication problems that come with a school emergency. Red and Green cards are displayed in the classroom windows during an emergency to communicate to first responders about the need for immediate medical attention. The red card lets first responders know that an individual in the classroom is in need of immediate medical attention, while the green card means all is well.

This system was developed out of the Columbine tragedy so that there would never again be a case like David Sanders. David Sanders was a science teacher at Columbine who on the day of the incident was shot while trying to shepherd students to safety. From all accounts David was shot very early on in the incident and was moved into a science lab, where he waited to be rescued by emergency responders. According to *60 Minutes II*, "SWAT officers finally reached David Sanders in Science Room Three at 2:42—more than three hours after he'd been shot. They evacuated the kids right away, but held Sanders there to wait for a paramedic. That paramedic didn't arrive for another 42 minutes ... by the time a paramedic finally got to David Sanders, at 3:24, he was already dead. Sanders was the last of 15 people to die at Columbine that day. Twenty-three wounded were taken to hospitals. Six had brain or spinal injuries. Several nearly bled to death. Doctors at six hospitals worked on wounded children all through the night, and saved every one of them."[4]

Lesson Three: The Incident Command System Must Be Better Defined

Today known as NIMS (National Incident Management System), the Incident Command System establishes a chain of command for who will manage an emergency incident at a school. Without a chain of command, there will be complete chaos on the day of an incident. Schools must realize that during an active shooter scenario (or other forms of criminal acts), law enforcement officers are best suited to deal with these types of incidents. Likewise, when it comes to fires, hazardous chemicals, or explosive devices, these are situations best suited for fire and other emergency responding agencies. Incident Command Systems establish who will handle which parts of an emergency response: who will be talking to the media, who will be handling transportation, and who will be handling evacuation and reunification.

The Federal Emergency Management Agency, a division of the U.S. Department of Homeland Security, described NIMS in the following way: "While most emergency situations are handled locally, when there's a major incident help may be needed from other jurisdictions, the state and the federal government. NIMS was developed so responders from different jurisdictions and disciplines can work together better to respond to natural disasters and emergencies, including acts of terrorism. NIMS benefits include a unified approach to incident management; standard command and management structures; and emphasis on preparedness, mutual aid and resource management."[5]

To understand how NIMS works, it is important to understand how state and local government plan to use it. The New Hampshire Department of Safety defined NIMS as "the first-ever standardized approach to incident management and response."[6] Developed by the Department of Homeland Security at the request of the president and released in March 2004, it establishes a uniform set of processes and procedures that emergency responders at all levels of government will use to conduct response operations. NIMS integrates effective practices in emergency response into a comprehensive national framework for incident management.

NIMS requires the following:

- Standardized organizational structures, processes, and procedures
- Standards for planning, training, and exercising
- Personnel qualification standards
- Equipment acquisition and certification standards
- Interoperable communications processes, procedures, and systems
- Information management systems with a commonly accepted architecture

- Supporting technologies: voice and data communications systems, information systems, data display systems, and specialized technologies
- Publication management processes and activities[7]

Lesson Four: Schools Should Practice Their Plans

Far too many schools go out and hire a consultant to help them put together an emergency plan, but they never test that plan to see if it will actually work in their school. Columbine should have been the wake-up call for schools all across America that they need to be prepared for a critical incident such as a school shooting, much as Our Lady of the Angels school fire was a wake-up call in this country for schools having fire drills and taking basic precautions to prevent fires.

On December 1, 1958, a fire broke out in the basement of Our Lady of the Angels Catholic school in Chicago. The school housed approximately 1,600 students in kindergarten through eighth grade. The school had only one fire escape, no sprinklers, no automatic fire alarm, no smoke or heat detectors, no alarm connected to the fire department, no fire-resistant stairwells, and no fire-safe doors from the stairwells to the second floor. Although the building's exterior was brick, the interior was made almost entirely of combustible materials. The floors had been coated and recoated many times with flammable petroleum-based waxes. There were no fire alarm switches in the north wing and only two in the entire school, both located in the south wing. Although there were four fire extinguishers in the north wing, they were mounted seven feet off the floor, out of reach for many adults and virtually all of the children. The single fire escape was near one end of the north wing, but to reach it required passing through the main corridor, which became filled with suffocating smoke and superheated gases. With its 12-foot ceilings, the school's second-floor windows were a daunting 25 feet from the ground, should someone decide to jump. Thus, the scenario for a tragedy was set.[8]

After the Our Lady of the Angels fire, Percy Bugbee, the president of the National Fire Protection Association (NFPA), said in an interview, "There are no new lessons to be learned from this fire; only old lessons that tragically went unheeded."[9] Major changes in school fire safety regulations were enacted nationwide. Over 16,000 older school buildings in the United States were brought up to code within one year of the disaster. After the fire, states across the country began to mandate an increased number of fire drills throughout the academic year.

Other major school fires in U.S. history include the following:

- The New London School explosion (March 18, 1937). The disaster killed at least 295 students and teachers.

- The Babbs Switch fire (December 24, 1924). This fire killed 36 people on Christmas eve, over half of whom were children.
- The Lakeview School fire (March 4, 1928). In the fire, 172 students, 2 teachers, and a rescuer lost their lives.

Many are comparing the lockdown drills of today to the "duck and cover" drills of the 1950s and 1960s. What make lockdown drills different are several key components. First, lockdown drills have been shown to be effective at saving lives during active shooter incidents, whereas many young Americans were highly suspect of whether ducking below a desk during a nuclear attack would save their life.

Why does lockdown work? What we have learned about the mentality of active shooters is that they want to hurt as many people as they possibly can in the shortest amount of time possible. Although a locked door may not seem to provide much protection from someone armed with an automatic weapon, it does seem to provide just enough. Again, this is because active shooters do not want to waste their resources trying to break into a door where they may or may not discover children. In those schools that have experienced an active shooter in the last few years and have implemented a lockdown procedure during the incident, evidence shows that lives were saved.

An example of where lockdown procedures saved the lives of innocent children would be the shooting at Orange County High School in Hillsborough, North Carolina. The incident was described by a local news channel in this manner.

> Hillsborough, N.C.—(Aug. 30) A 19-year-old who allegedly opened fire at an Orange County high school in late August was obsessed with the April 1999 Columbine High School shooting where 12 students were killed, authorities said.
>
> Alvaro Rafael Castillo was wearing a T-shirt with the phrase "Remember Columbine" when he was arrested outside Orange High School on Aug. 30, and he kept repeating the phrase when he was taken to jail.
>
> Hours before the shooting, authorities said Castillo sent a grisly e-mail to the Colorado high school to announce his intentions. The day before, he also sent a letter and video to local newspapers explaining his alleged actions.
>
> The letter refers repeatedly to school shootings and ends with the words, "I will die. I have wanted to die for years. I'm sorry."[10]

Corporal London Ivey, who was the school resource officer at Orange County High School, stated in a phone interview with me in July 2008 that "if it were not for the training I received on rapid deployment and the training the school received on lockdowns, I do not know how many lives would have been lost that day." I was part of a team that trained Orange County High on how to respond to lockdowns only months before this incident, and talking to Corporal Ivey about how this training saved lives was one of the most gratifying moments of my career.

Second, we know that school violence occurs in American schools every year. Some claim that those in the school safety community who advocate lockdown drills are alarmist and overhyping the problem. This means that school violence that claimed the lives of more than 20 students in schools across America for each of the last 10 years is over-hyped, but schools across the country are mandated to practice fire drills once a month. When was the last time a student or teacher lost his or her life to a fire at a school in the United States? If you answered 1958, you would be correct. Now this is not to say that we should stop doing fire drills; in fact, it implies quite the opposite. Fire drills are working. If fire drills work to save lives, then why not other types of drills? Do schools really need to do 10 fire drills every year, or could we do 8 fire drills and 2 lockdown drills?

CONCLUDING THOUGHT

In this chapter I have highlighted just a few of the lessons learned from the horrific events that occurred at Columbine. We should all be inspired to do more to prevent another Columbine from happening. As the relatives of the ones lost that day often tell me do not let the loss of my son's or daughter's life be in vain; please let people learn from this event. Many of the lessons are simple and cost little money to fix, but they require agencies talking to each other and planning together. This investment of time is well worth the lives that can be saved.

Chapter 15

"You Must Prepare for the Day You Hope Will Never Come"

William L. Lassiter

"You must prepare for the day you hope will never come." This is a quote from a school resource officer in Tampa, Florida. This particular officer had just become a school resource officer after spending several years as a patrol officer. As with many new officers, he immediately starting looking for ideas to prevent crime at his school, and he thought that he had found "it." While at a conference he heard about a new way of doing CrimeStoppers, a program that many law enforcement agencies across the country use. CrimeStoppers uses rewards to try to get citizens to provide information about crimes in their community.

The problem with using CrimeStoppers in a school setting is that it is very reactive: you have to wait until a crime is committed before a reward is offered. But this officer heard about a new way of doing CrimeStoppers by which students would call their school resource officer if they knew about a crime that was about to happen. The officer thought, "What a great idea." So he started working with his school officials to put the program together. To kick the program off, he had a big assembly of all the students at the school at which the student body president demonstrated to his classmates how the program worked. The officer was extremely excited about the idea and even invited the media to the assembly. Of course, since this was a positive story, only one representative from the media came.

The officer thought that he had found the silver bullet to preventing all school violence. But he quickly came to realize that there is no such thing. Later that day, a student shot another student in the parking lot, and of course every media outlet in the county came for that event. He said, "I realized right then and there, you have to prepare for the day you hope will never come."

Even if a school has an excellent school violence prevention plan, you never know when something is going to go wrong. In this chapter we will look at how a school makes sure it is prepared for the day it hopes will never come.

CRISIS PLANS: 101

Almost all schools and school districts have some form of a crisis plan these days, but you should ask some important questions about your plan to make sure it is a useful document.

First, when is the last time your school or school district updated its crisis plan? The correct answer to this question can save your school from some intense embarrassment and possibly save lives.

I remember visiting a school that had not updated its plan the way it should have. While doing the site assessment, I reviewed the school's safety planning documentation. I remember reading through the plans and discovering that it appeared that the plan had not been updated in a while. This was most apparent when I was reading through the school's plan for responding to a tornado.

The plan started out pretty well. It stated that an alarm would sound followed by an announcement telling staff and students that the school was under a tornado warning. At this time the students and staff would move to the hallway and get into a tucked position to protect their vital organs from falling and flying objects. But then I saw it: the next line of the plan read, "The assistant principal will climb a ladder and go on top of the roof to try to spot for tornados; if a tornado is spotted he/she will alert other staff to its presence." Of course, I had to show this to the assistant principal, who stated, "I am not surprised. They ask the assistant principal to do every other crazy thing around here." Needless to say, this plan had not been updated in a while. I am not sure that spotting for tornados on top of your school's roof is accepted practice, but the point remains, many of the practices used throughout the years to respond to emergencies have changed. Every school should review its plan at least once a year to make sure it has made any adjustments that are necessary.

Second, schools should consider whether or not their plan is simply a document that sits on a bookcase somewhere and collects dust or is a living document. A safe school plan should be more than just a document; it should be a process that is implemented by a school. That process should include taking steps to prevent, mitigate, and prepare for a crisis. The planning process must be a whole school process and should include programs to prevent incidents and trainings that prepare for an incident. A school that chooses to never test its crisis plan through practice drills and tabletop exercises really has no evidence of whether the plan will be effective.

While observing a lockdown drill at a school that thought it had an effective plan for responding to an intruder on campus, I noticed that several teachers did not lock their doors. During the debriefing I asked the teachers why they did not lock their doors. The teachers explained that they did not have keys to their rooms. At this particular school, in order for teachers to lock their classroom doors, they were required to go out in the hall and use their key to lock the door. First of all, I have a problem with forcing teachers to go out into a hallway during a lockdown to lock their classroom door. This school thought it had an effective lockdown plan, but it quickly discovered that it could not even meet one of the basic essentials of the plan: securing classroom doors.

Who are the stakeholders who need to be invited to the table?

At the school district level a crisis planning team should be formed, and if you live in a jurisdiction where there are multiple districts in one county, you should consider creating a collaborative crisis planning team that includes all the districts within the county. This can be important because law enforcement will want all the schools in a particular jurisdiction responding in similar methods. Members of the school district planning team should include a school administrative representative from each of the schools in the district, district administrators, school nurses, school counselors and psychologists, local and state law enforcement representatives, fire and emergency responders, a hospital representative, businesses in the area that may pose a hazard to the schools, such as a nuclear plant or a chemical plant, other community partners, and parents.

The crisis planning team develops a plan that can be implemented throughout the district. Many times when I am conducting site assessments, I discover that schools right down the street from each other have very different crisis plans. This is because of what many in education call "site-level management," meaning that most decisions are made at the school level and not the district level. The problem with site-level management when it comes to crisis planning is that a number of external partners will have to be involved when a school is experiencing a crisis situation. The districtwide crisis planning team will do the following:

- Develop standardized crisis plans for every school in the district
- Develop a schedule for practicing the plan
- Develop local partnerships with external stakeholders
- Ensure proper funding is available for schools to develop their plans
- Develop code words if any are to be used by the district (it has become accepted practice to only use plain English)

Let's look at the roles of each of these partners in the crisis planning process.

School Administrative Representative

The school administrator serves on the crisis planning tam to be the reality check. In other words, the administrator is there to make sure that anything developed by the planning committee is possible at the school level. Also, the school administrator will take the plans developed by the team back to his or her school to train its school team.

District Administrator

The main duty of the district administrator is to organize the meetings of the crisis planning committee. This is, of course, no easy task when one considers all the stakeholders and their busy schedules that must be planned around. Another major task of the district administrator will be to ensure that the proper funding is available for a school district to implement the plan developed by the committee. Finally, the district administrator should be charged with organizing the practicing of and testing of the plan.

School Nurses

If your district is fortunate enough to have school nurses, it will be imperative to involve them in the planning process. Nurses can be invaluable in a crisis because of their training and experiences dealing with crises on a daily basis. A plan should be developed of how school nurses will be notified during a crisis and what role the district wants them to perform during the crisis.

School Counselors and Psychologists

During a crisis and when recovering from a crisis, the mental health resources of your community will be stretched. The counselors and psychologists on your committee should develop a plan of how the mental health needs of the school community will be met. One extremely important role for these professionals is determining how mental health clinicians who want to volunteer will be handled and how students and staff seeking spiritual counseling in the aftermath of an incident will be served. After a number of school crises, people claiming to be counselors came to schools offering assistance, when in reality they only wanted to proselytize. As one can imagine, these so-called counselors actually made matters worse. Many districts have set up vetting processes to screen volunteers before a crisis occurs.

Local and State Law Enforcement Representatives

During a crisis, having an effective relationship already formed with law enforcement will be a huge advantage. Depending on the type of crisis occurring at a school, there is a high likelihood that local law enforcement personnel will be your incident commanders: once they arrive on campus, they will be calling the shots. For principals this can be an uneasy feeling because they are used to being in charge of their schools, but much of this discomfort can be removed if a relationship with law enforcement has already been created. Law enforcement should help in writing the parts of the crisis plan that deal with a criminal incident such as a hostage situation, a school shooting, a bomb threat, or a riot.

Fire, Emergency Management, and Other First-Responding Agencies

As with law enforcement, during certain emergencies firefighters will become the incident commanders. Firefighters in your community have most likely already thought through how they would handle a fire emergency at your district's school. For this reason it will be important to gain their perspective when writing your plan.

Parents

In most states, laws protecting crisis plans from becoming part of the public record have passed. Just because these plans are protected does not mean that you should not let parents be part of the process. This does not mean that you have to share every detail with parents, but parents watch the news also, and they want to know that school officials are taking all the steps necessary to protect their children. Parents can help the district think of goods ways to educate other parents on what will be expected if a crisis were to occur. Parents also often serve as reality checks to your plan. They can tell you whether what you will be asking parents to do is something they will do, or whether they will ignore that order and do what they want anyway.

Having a parent on the crisis planning committee can also help you after an incident. It does not hurt to have a parent saying "I was involved in writing the district's crisis plan, and I can tell you they did do everything they possibly could to protect your child."

COMMUNICATION

When preparing for a crisis, it will be important to develop an effective communications plan. This will not be a step that any one agency can do on its own, but it could be the most important objective the crisis planning committee completes. Over and over again we hear that the greatest obstacle to effectively responding to crisis is communication, whether it be the firefighter and police officers not being able to communicate on 9/11, or school officials and law enforcement during the incident at Columbine High School.

From a school's perspective, administrators will want to be able to effectively communicate with staff, students, families, law enforcement, first responders, and the media. During a crisis, how will the administrators at the schools in your district communicate to your staff? Do all the classrooms, offices, gyms, athletic fields, and cafeterias have two-way communication? If not, how will you spread the information across your campus in a fast and effective method? If you do have two-way communication in every place you may have staff and students, what happens if that system fails? For example, if you rely on an intercom system and the power goes out, what will be the backup form of communications? It seems like such a simple thing—communicating—but the reality is that communication can completely change the dynamics of a situation. People feel more reassured if they know what is going on and that they have taken every possible precaution they can take to protect themselves from danger.

What should be communicated to students? Whenever I present on crisis preparation, school officials always ask how much of this they should be telling the kids. The answer, of course, is, that depends. Communications with students should be based on age-appropriate levels. For example, you certainly do not want to tell a five-year-old that a mad man is roaming the school campus with a gun. As students get older, they can handle the truth better, and they tend to respond better to direction if they know why they are doing something. While the crisis is taking place, the people who will be communicating with the students will most likely be their teachers. How prepared do they feel to handle these situations? Often when schools go over their crisis plans with their staff, they review what teachers should be telling their kids. Recently while evaluating a lockdown drill at an elementary school, I noticed that all the teachers were quietly reading a story to kids while the drill was occurring. This was an easy way to keep the kids quiet and distracted from what was going on in the hallway.

During the aftermath of the crisis, it will be important to keep the lines of communication open with students. Teachers will once again serve as the front line of defense for referring students to get additional counseling. School counselors can often help teachers think through the best ways to discuss a crisis with their students and help them identify the warnings signs that a child may need additional assistance. When it comes to the recovery process, the research is very clear that students need to return to the structure and consistency they experienced before the crisis as quickly as possible.

Communications with parents is an often difficult but important task the school administrator must undertake during an emergency. What should the administrator be telling parents about the situation? Good preparation can make this process much easier. Administrators should set the foundation of good communications by explaining to parents before a crisis occurs how the school will respond and how the school will get information to parents about what parents need to do.

A number of technological advances in the last few years make it easier to communicate with parents during a crisis. Schools have invested in systems that allow them to call all the parents in their school through an automative system. These systems can call thousands of numbers in a matter of minutes and provide whatever message the school is hoping parents will hear.

Finally, communicating with the media can be challenging during a crisis. One of the keys is for school officials, law enforcement officials, and first responders to speak with one voice to the media. A media spokesperson should be chosen through the incident command system. This person should update the media on what each of the agencies is doing to respond to the incident. A key to working with media is to do your best to provide them with information. A media staging area should be set up where representatives from the media can receive regular updates form the incident spokesperson. Make sure the media staging area is far enough away from the incident and from staff and students that no one is questioned who does not want to be. Remember, you will need the media to tell parents where to pick up their kids and at what times, so try to help them out a little bit also. Besides, if you do not give them information, they will go looking for it.

ACCOUNTING FOR STUDENTS

Another major task that is difficult to accomplish during a crisis situation at a school is being able to account for students. During the preparedness stage the school district should consider how it will instruct school officials to account for and release students during a crisis.

Parents struggled to find out where their children were after the events at Columbine. In fact, one parent stated, "I learned of my child's death by opening the paper the next morning, and on the front cover they had a picture of my son Danny laying shot on the ground." No parents should have to learn of their child's death in this manner. Schools should make every attempt possible to work with first responders to identify which students are being sent to which hospitals. Being able to keep track of this information will of course once again reflect on the level of communication that is taking place between school officials and first responders.

It does not have to be a tragedy on the scale of Columbine to have accountability problems crop up. Even in a more routine occurrence such as a bomb threat, accountability becomes difficult. With today's technology it does not take long for parents and the media to find out that a school has been evacuated because of a bomb threat. Within a matter of minutes parents will start showing up trying to get their children released from school so they do not have to wait outside while the school is searched. How should a school handle such a situation? During the preparedness stage is a good time to discuss this question.

To throw yet another wrinkle into the plan, many schools have not thought through exactly how these plans apply to students with special needs. It is important to think about which resources you will be able to devote to these students. How will you get these young people out of the building? What if the elevators stop working in your building? Do you have a plan for getting staff or students in wheelchairs out of the building? Schools also must consider those students on their campus who because of disabilities do not respond well to change or breaking their routines, such as students with autism. All of these are things your crisis planning committee must consider in preparing for an emergency.

EMERGENCY KITS

Finally, when considering preparedness one must consider the things a school would need to respond to an emergency. In many states schools are sent by their attorney general's office or their Department of Education a list of items they should have on hand during a crisis. These items are often stored in portable kits so that during an emergency they are easy to carry. Some of the universally accepted items that should go in these kits include the following:

1. Maps. Maps of the surrounding areas near the school should be included in the kit. These maps should identify roads leading in and out of the school campus. They will help responders understand the traffic patterns and intersections that will be affected during a crisis. In addition, relocation sites and routes of how to get to those relocation sites can be identified on these maps. Schools should keep several copies of these maps in the kit.

2. Floor Plans. When first responders arrive on your campus in response to an emergency, most likely they are not going to be very familiar with your school. Have several copies of the floor plan available to help first responders orient themselves to the layout of the school. Floor plans should identify important building features such as locations of the fire alarm turnoff, utilities shutoff, sprinkler system shutoff, cable television shutoff, first aid kits, and fire extinguishers. In addition, the floor plans should show the location of all telephones and telephone wall jacks,

computer locations, and all other devices that may be useful for communication during a critical incident.

3. Blueprints. Architectural blueprints should be kept in the kits because this detailed information is important for SWAT teams, especially during a bomb threat. The facility personnel should have access to such blueprints.

4. Aerial Photographs. Aerial photos of the school and surrounding area can assist law enforcement officials and emergency responders involved in the critical incident.

5. Evacuation Plan with Routes and Safe Rally Points. Each school should have an evacuation plan with exit routes and safe rally points clearly marked. In addition, each school should have an alternate evacuation plan in case of unforeseen factors such as a chemical spill. Each evacuation route should have a safe rally point located away from the school.

   Procedures to cut off the following:

   • Fire Alarm. School shooters have been known to pull fire alarms to try to get students to leave the protection of their classrooms during a lockdown. Being able to shut down the fire alarm may assist law enforcement officer in finding an intruder on campus. As you are probably aware, fire alarms are often loud and cover up the noises that the intruder may be making.

   • Utilities. In order to prevent an intruder from having access to explosive chemicals such as gas in science labs, schools may find it necessary to shut down certain utilities. We also know that gas lines and water lines tend to break sometimes, so having procedures readily available on how to shut these utilities off can be extremely helpful.

   • Sprinkler System. Fire and law enforcement officials may determine during a crisis that the sprinkler system is deterring the progress of the law enforcement officials to stop an intruder on campus. In these cases law enforcement and fire officials will try to determine which threat presents the most danger to the school population.

   • Cable Television. During past active shooter and hostage situations, the perpetrators have used cable news outlets to gain information about what law enforcement is doing outside the school building.

6. Directional Signs. Having signs created before an incident will decrease the responsibility of responders on the day of the incident. The more signs a school posts during the emergency, the fewer questions that school officials and emergency responders will have to answer. Some signs a school should consider creating before an emergency include ones that say Incident Command Post, Staging Area, Pick Up, Drop Off, Media, and Medical Services, to name a few. The school should also have some markers and papers available in the kit so it can make additional signs if needed.

7. Keys and/or Codes. A master key or master code and other important keys to the school building(s) will be necessary for an effective response by law enforcement and first responders. These keys should be easily

identifiable by tags. The keys for the school could be placed in a separate locked container within the kits as an additional security measure. Fire department officials recommend keeping the master key in a Knox box outside the school. A Knox box is a nondestructible box mounted near the building entrance. The fire department controls the master key to the box, giving them immediate access during an emergency.

8. Faculty and Staff Roster. A faculty and staff roster should list those with first aid and emergency services training and their cell phone numbers. In addition, the roster should identify those individuals with special needs.

9. Bus Roster and Route. Knowing where buses are supposed to be during an emergency can be invaluable information.

10. Student Release Forms. Accounting for students during an emergency can be a difficult task. The student release form gives staff an easy way to track those students who have been signed out by a parent or guardian.

Contact List. The contact list should include the following:

- Law enforcement
- Emergency responders
- Local hospitals
- Counselors in secular and spiritual fields
- School phone numbers
- Volunteers
- Parents
- Media contacts (yes, it seems crazy, but you might actually want to contact the media during an emergency to get your message out)

Additionally, the Department of Homeland Security advises schools to have a shelter-in-place supply kit. The items in these kits would be used when a school is asked to shelter-in-place for emergencies such as a chemical spill or severe weather. Shelter-in-place supplies include the following:

- Precut plastic sheeting and duct tape to cover windows, doors, air vents, or other openings. Wet cloth towels can also be used if plastic is not available.
- Battery-powered radio.
- Flashlight (with extra batteries).
- Telephone or communication device.
- Hygiene items if restroom facilities are not available (e.g., plastic bucket with a tight lid, garbage bags).
- First aid kit.
- Water and snacks.

- Games and books.
- Any specialized student health care items, including medications and equipment.[1]

All of these are items that should be included in the school's kit, but what about each teacher? What should teachers have in their classrooms to be prepared for an emergency? The answer may vary greatly depending on the area of the country in which you live. For example, a teacher living in earthquake country should have more supplies on hand than a teacher in an area that face threats that are much more predictable. A few items that are universally recommended include the following:

- First aid kit
- Bottled water
- The school emergency plan
- A source of quick sugar for a diabetic students, such as cake icing
- Red and green cards to communicate with law enforcement during a lockdown and with administrators during a fire drill

During a lockdown the red and green cards are used to communicate the status of the classroom. The teacher displays a card in the external classroom window and one in a window to the hallway or slides one under the hallway door. During a lockdown a green card means that we do not need emergency medical aid in this classroom right now. A red card during a lockdown means that we do need emergency medical help in this classroom right away. If a teacher does not display a card in the classroom window or slide a card under the door, law enforcement will assume the intruder may be in that classroom. It is important to note that not every state or jurisdiction has adopted this procedure. Some in the law enforcement community argue that this system draws unnecessary attention to occupied classrooms. Although this is a good argument, it is my feeling that information provided to law enforcement and first responders through the card system is invaluable.

The creation of the red and green card system came after the tragedy at Columbine. As mentioned in a previous chapter, one of the victims in that case was a teacher named David Sanders. David was shot very early on in the incident and dragged into a science lab, where he waited almost four hours for treatment. This was despite the students making their very best efforts to get Mr. Sanders help. Mr. Sanders's official cause of death was later stated to be bleeding to death. Many contend that if a better communication system had been available, maybe Mr. Sanders's life could have been saved. In the aftermath of this horrible situation, the red and green card system was created. It was the hope of those behind the system to eliminate another staff member or student bleeding to death.

During a fire drill the red and green cards can also be used to communicate, but in this case it is normally teachers communicating to other school staff members. During a fire drill the green card held up by a teacher upon evacuating the school building means that all of my students are accounted for. The red card conversely means that the teacher is missing a student and he or she could possibly still be in the building. This is a quick method that administrators can use to know if they need to tell rescuers to go and look for a child in the school building.

CONCLUDING THOUGHT

When thinking through how I can help prepare my school for the day that I hope will never come, it is important to take a couple of key steps, including having a district-level plan; having a school-level plan; creating good communication between all partners involved in the crisis planning process; developing student accountability plans; maintaining a school crisis kit; and ensuring teachers have the resources they will need in their classroom to respond to a crisis. Being prepared for a crisis takes time and resources, but all of the efforts will be well worth it if a crisis hits your school.

Chapter 16

Responding to a Crisis

William L. Lassiter

So what happens if you actually have to use your crisis plan? If a school has done the proper preparation, the staff should feel confident in the way they will respond. That is not to say that everything will go as you hope that it will. The very definition of a crisis means that some form of chaos is going to be involved.

The first step in responding to a crisis effectively is to determine whether there is a real emergency occurring and what kind of emergency it is. In a school environment it may be difficult to determine the true nature of an event, so school officials will need to rely on all of their resources during an emergency to make this determination.

In this chapter you will learn about the four most common responses to emergency situations that can occur in schools: evacuation, reverse evacuation, shelter-in-place, and lockdown. This chapter cannot answer every question a school official may have about emergency response, but it does build a firm foundation from which schools can build their plans for responding to common emergencies.

EVACUATION

Most people are familiar with evacuation procedures because we have all done them. The most common drill conducted by schools and businesses is the evacuation drill, more commonly know as the fire drill. The purpose of an evacuation is to remove students and staff from harm by having them exit the building. Evacuation can be used to respond to fires, bomb threats, explosions, or gas leaks. A proper evacuation will get students and staff far enough away from the building that they are no longer in harm's way. The Bureau of Alcohol,

Tobacco and Firearms recommends that staff and students are at least 1,000 feet away from the school building during a bomb threat.

Upon learning of a hazard such as a fire that may threaten the lives of staff and students, a staff member should either use the fire alarm system or a two-way communications device to alert the rest of the school to the emergency. Upon hearing the fire alarm, staff should instruct students to evacuate the classroom and building in accordance with the posted evacuation procedure. If the primary evacuation route is blocked, a secondary evacuation route should be used. Every class-room should have these routes posted, and it is recommended that they be posted in the same spot in each classroom. Upon exiting the building, staff should assemble their students in a designated spot out-side the building. They will need to account for all their students and communicate with administration if a student is missing.

Reverse Evacuation

A reverse evacuation is the process for moving students and staff indoors quickly. Some reasons for reverse evacuation include gunshots, drive-by shooting, notification by law enforcement that an armed indi-vidual may be in the area, and so forth.

The plan for reverse evacuation should include the following:

- Notification to staff and students that a reverse evacuation has been ordered with instructions to have all staff and students move into the building.
- Upon getting as many staff, students, and visitors into the school as possi-ble, the school should be locked.
- All visitors will need to report to the front office for further instructions.

Once a reverse evacuation has been conducted, administrators may decide to move to a shelter-in-place or a lockdown, depending on the type of incident occurring.

SHELTER-IN-PLACE

Shelter-in-place is the third common response to an emergency situa-tion. During a shelter-in–place, students are often moved to a secure location in the school building and held there until the threat is over. Shelter-in-places can be used to respond to severe weather, earthquakes, chemical spills, or biological attacks. They involve the following actions:

- Close the school.
- Follow the school's crisis plan.
- Conduct a reverse evacuation to bring staff and students inside.
- Ask all visitors to stay for their safety and security.

- Announce that the school is going to a shelter-in-place.
- Have all staff and students moved to the designated shelter-in-place room. The room should have access to bathrooms, phone lines, and disaster supplies.
- Close and lock all windows and doors.
- If there is danger of an explosion, make sure all blinds are closed.
- Turn off the heating, air conditioning, and ventilation system.
- Consider allowing students to use cell phones to inform their parents that they are all right and will be staying at school until the threat is over. If you decide to allow students to use their cell phones, they should be monitored and asked to keep conversations short to not tie up cell tower traffic.
- Account for all students.
- Upon receiving the "all clear," students should be asked to exit the building while the heating, air conditioning, and ventilation system are turned back on.

Often during a shelter-in-place situation, the procedures schools need to undertake change because of the type of emergency, so schools should follow any additional instructions given by emergency responders.

LOCKDOWN

Lockdowns are used to protect students and staff members from intruders on a school campus. The theory behind a lockdown is that by putting a barrier between the intruders and their possible targets, you decrease the likelihood of students and staff members getting hurt. At first glance this may not seem the most effective solution, but the reality is that in many of the school shootings where it has been used the loss of life has been mitigated by this procedure.

Why does it work? Upon looking at the past history of active shooters, researchers have noticed common traits. An active shooter would be defined as someone who is indiscriminately firing a weapon, someone who is not necessarily aiming for a particular individual but rather hurting whomever he or she gets to first. The mentality of these active shooters is "I want to hurt as many people as I possible can in the shortest amount of time that I can do it." With this understanding in mind, it should be much clearer why lockdown works. Many times teachers ask me, and rightfully so, "How is my little door going to stop a gunman armed with an assault rifle or a shotgun?" My answer is, "If individuals really want to get into your classroom, you are right: a door is not going to stop them; but most likely they are not targeting your classroom over any other part of the school building. So why would they waste time and resources trying to break into your classroom when the room right down the hall might be unlocked with just as many targets in it?" With this being said, where do must active shooters go when they target a school campus? They go to any areas where large amounts of student congregate, such as libraries, cafeterias, gyms, and auditoriums, or they wait until a class change and target students and staff in the hallway. So is lockdown foolproof? Absolutely not. But is it the best solution to a bad situation? Yes.

Lockdown works by having staff alert the administration or someone near a communications device that they have spotted an intruder. Upon receiving that notification, the administration or whoever has access to the communications system in the school will issue the schoolwide lockdown. As mentioned in the chapter on preparedness, I recommend that you do not use any type of code to issue the lockdown, but rather use plain English. In other words, the lockdown would sound something like this: "This is a lockdown alert; all staff and students need to enter the closest classroom and lock their doors." This leaves no ambiguity about what you want people to do. Upon hearing this alert, staff should do the following:

- Clear the hallways of students
- Lock classroom doors
- Turn off lights
- Move students to a corner where they will not be easily seen from a window
- Account for students
- Use the red and green card system if applicable in your jurisdiction
- Remain in lockdown until another announcement is made to give the "all clear"

Upon learning of an intruder on campus, administration will want to do the following:

- Request that the staff member who saw the intruder call 911
- Call the school resource officer or school security to alert them of the situation
- Issue the schoolwide lockdown alert
- Lock the front office
- Turn off all bell systems that alert students and staff to the beginning and end of classes (having the bell sound may confuse people into thinking the lockdown is over)
- Retrieve the school's crisis kit, so that law enforcement will have all those items they may need upon arriving on campus
- Assist law enforcement when they arrive on the campus (remember, law enforcement will be the incident commanders for this situation, so rely on them to make decisions about what the school should do next)

Administrators should delegate tasks so that as many of these functions that can be done at the same time are done at the same time.

SPECIAL SCENARIOS

What about mobile classrooms, or modular classrooms? Teachers assigned to these units should lower their student profile to lessen their chances of being hit by a stray bullet. Mobile units often do not have walls that are thick enough to stop bullets, so by lowering your own and your students' profile you lower the likelihood of injury. The best way to lower one's profile is by lying on the floor. I often get the question: Should I move my students to a more secure location in the school building? I reply that that is not recommended. You are safer behind a locked door and not drawing attention to the fact that you exist than running across the school campus with a bunch of students yelling and screaming.

During a lockdown, it is very likely that at least one class will be outside. What would be the most effective response for these teachers and their students? First, it is important to point out that these teachers will need some type of communications device to alert them to the pending emergency. Without an alert system they could accidentally direct their students to walk right into harm's way. Next, they should try to determine the nature of the threat. If they are unsure of the nature of the threat, they should move their students to an established safe rally point. Safe rally points are predetermined points that will provide students and staff with natural protection. For example, a safe rally point may be behind a row of trees or a building. Teachers should also move their students to safe rally points if it is determined that the threat is between their class and the school.

The only circumstance in which it might make sense to try to return to the school is if the perpetrator of the crime is coming toward the teacher and students and is not in between the school and the class. In this rare case, it might make more sense to seek shelter in the school. However, in most active shooter incidents teachers will not know where the gunmen is, so it is safest for teachers and their students to move away from the danger instead of toward it. Once at the safe rally point, teachers should wait for law enforcement to arrive to give them further instructions. If the school has properly designated its safe rally points, the administration will be able to tell law enforcement where to check and see if any staff or students are at those points.

Finally, the last scenario and the one that no one wants to think about: what do you do if an intruder gains access to a classroom and begins indiscriminately shooting students and staff? The truth is that there is no good answer to this situation, but the best advice I can give is to tell the students to run. If you have ever heard the tapes of the 911 calls during the incident at Columbine, you most likely remember the librarian yelling at the kids to get under the tables. She thought she was giving the kids the best advice possible, but when the gunmen entered the library, they began to shoot the students on the floor. The students had no chance of surviving. They would have been better off if they had gotten up and started running, which is what happened in the cafeteria, where the bloodshed was much less. Moving targets are much harder to hit, and running also creates a sense of chaos for the gunmen. Will people get hurt using this strategy? Yes, but the loss of life could be far less than letting the gunmen walk around the room and shoot people lying on the ground.

In the last few years several companies have sprung up that aim to teach students and staff how to fight back against a gunman in a classroom. I am often asked if these classes are a good idea, and in my opinion they are not. I believe that if you train your staff to respond in an appropriate way, the chances of this type of situation occurring are very low. Besides that, these classes teach students to fight back by throwing books and other objects at the gunmen. I can envision a kid bringing a gun to school and someone, recalling this training, deciding to throw a book at the armed student, thus escalating the situation. I would much rather have students run to get an adult than try to take matters into their own hands.

There are variations of lockdown that are used by schools for all types of different situations. Some schools go to lockdown during a drug or weapon search to ensure that no students can go to their locker to remove contraband before they are searched. Schools often use a hybrid of a lockdown and a shelter-in-place if there is a threat in the community that may or may not be coming toward the school. For example, if someone robs the bank down the street, the school may choose to go to a variant of the normal lockdown procedure. These variants can include locking just the external doors of the school and allowing operations to continue as normal inside the school building. The other form this can take is having teachers lock down their rooms but continuing class as normal. If a school is unsure about the nature of the threat, I recommend that it go to the full-scale lockdown first and make a determination later if some lower level of lockdown is what is really called for in the situation.

CONCLUDING THOUGHT

The four most common responses to school emergencies have been presented in this chapter. Once again, it is important to point out that individual schools will need to determine variations of these plans that will work best for their environments.

Conclusion: Pulling It All Together

William L. Lassiter
and Danya C. Perry

The last thing that we want to do is have you, the reader of this book, walk away feeling overwhelmed, or believing that the problem is too great to overcome. So, in this conclusion, we want to tell you one last story about how we (in the following story, this means Lassiter and Perry) assisted a school in pulling all the elements described in this book together.

The phone call came into our office from a deeply troubled district administrator who was seeking help for one of his newly minted principals. The district administrator told us that the principal might be cautious about reaching out for help but that he was in desperate need of it. The district administrator set up a morning meeting between us and the school administrator. When we arrived at the school, we were quickly ushered into the principal's office, where we met with the principal and the school's safe school planning team.

The principal began to describe the situation that was occurring on the campus. He said,

"The main problem is that we have a group of students who are making threats to conduct a Columbine-type assault on our school building. The last two days these young men—according to our secretary they sounded like young men—have called in similar threats to blow up the school and shoot students. We have of course evacuated the building each time we received these threats to protect the lives of our students and staff."

Lassiter asked, "Well, do you have any knowledge of why the students might be making these threats and who the students are?"

The principal stated, "Yes, we have a pretty good idea of who they might be, but we have no clue why they are doing it."

Perry asked, "Well, let's start with the 'who' first, and then we might be able to move to the why later."

The principal stated, "Well, it appears to be this group of 'freaks'— that is what the students call them."

Lassiter questioned, "Freaks? What do you mean by that?"

"Well, you know, it is some of those gothic kids, you know, just like the type that attacked Columbine."

Lassiter asked, "Besides the fact that these students fit the so-called profile or the stereotype of what a school shooter should look like, do we have any evidence that these are the boys causing the problem?"

The principal stated, "Well, we have heard plenty of rumors that they are the boys." He added, "It all started on September 11, when the gothic students mocked a group of students gathered around the flagpole to pray for the victims of the terrorist attacks that happened last year. You know, that school shooter up there in Kentucky targeted students praying around a flagpole also." We both nodded in a knowing fashion. "Well, the word started to spread like wildfire around the campus that the Goths were going to blow up the school. Of course, the word also started to spread around the community."

Lassiter asked, "Did they get in trouble?"

The principal said, "Yeah, we pulled all the boys together that we thought might have played a role in it down to the gymnasium, where I and the school resource officer gave them a good talking to."

Lassiter asked, "How many boys did you pull together down there?"

"All of them that we thought might have played a part in it."

"So all of them that people stated played a role in it?"

The principal said, "No, I mean all of those gothic kids."

We both responded, "Huh?" Then Lassiter asked, "Well, how did that go for you?"

The principal said, "Not too well. It seems to have actually brought those gothic kids closer together."

After this initial meeting, we knew we had our work cut out for us. One of the first things we wanted to do was meet with the students to find out what *they* thought was going on at the school. We facilitated a study circle in which a group of students were allowed to express their impressions of what was happening. We asked the principal to send us the leaders of the gothic students and the students the principal thought had been the most angered by the Goths' disrespectful display. The first thing we noticed as students entered the study circle session was that the "Goth" students sat on one side and the remaining youth sat on the other.

We began the study circle by breaking the ice and telling the story about how we met. Perry began: "We may not look like we have anything in common—a black man who grew up in a poor neighbor-hood and a white man who grew up in the middle-class suburbs. At first glance that was what we thought also. But it turns out we have a lot in common, and we have a lot about us that is different. Those differences are what make our friendship interesting. So to start out today, let's talk about some of the things you might have in common with the people sitting around you in the circle. Then we can make our way to talking about some of our differences."

Next, we allowed the youth to speak their minds. We were pleasantly surprised that the concerns were not irreparable. Students felt scared because of the actions by the "Goth" students and the "Goth" students felt ostracized and singled out. Some of the thought-provoking questions that were asked included the following:

- Do you believe a conducive learning environment is attainable at your school?
- What is your role in making the school safer?
- Do students perpetuate the problem? Educators?

It was interesting to see how the so-called Goths and Preps quickly started to realize they had more in common than they thought. After discussing the issues for a while, we discovered the root of the problem for the gothic kids began when a local church in the community hosted a contest. The contest was called "Save a Soul Week." The contest worked like this. The student who brought the greatest number of friends to church on a particular Sunday would win a 27-inch color television. So all the kids targeted the Goths to get their souls saved, because they clearly looked like they needed to be saved (according to one of the students). The student said, "Look at all the black they are wearing and those demonic t-shirts." Lassiter remembered thinking, "A Metallica t-shirt is demonic; hey, I used to wear those."

One of the Goths said, "I must have been asked 50 times a week of that 'save a soul' thing if I considered having my soul saved. I felt like I was being harassed! I go to church every week, but these guys were judging me just because I wear a certain t-shirt."

It was interesting to see the other students' reactions to these comments. It was like they had never considered that maybe multiple people were targeting these same students. They started to see how such a little thing grew into something much larger. We showed the youth violence continuum to the students and then discussed how their behaviors grew from something that was well intentioned into a big issue.

By the end of the session the group decided to take a united stand and create a student-led organization called "Students Stepping Out of Circles (SSOC)." SSOC organized activities around the issues of youth violence. One of the first things the group did was facilitate study circles in every homeroom a week later. After completing these study circles, which by all accounts went a long way toward breaking the tension among students, the administration that was skeptical about our presence at first was starting to embrace our involvement.

With our guidance and the principal's support, SSOC continued with this effort by conducting an assessment of the school's culture. SSOC members developed a survey, disseminated it to their peers and teachers, and took it home to parents. Upon analyzing the results, the SSOC members were surprised that almost three-quarters of their classmates stated they had been bullied at school in the last month, and almost a quarter said they had been physically attacked at school. These were just two of the more shocking findings to come out of the student-initiated survey. We asked the SSOC members, "Well, now that you have the results, what are you going to do with the information?"

After deliberating about it for a while, the students said, "We need to share this information with everyone so we can make a change on our school campus." They subsequently met with the principal to discuss their plan. Administrators decided to support the students and have them move forward with a very unique awareness campaign. Since their group was called SSOC, they decided to go out and purchase some socks and write statistics on them. These socks were then hung around the school bearing the results of the survey conducted by the students. We can tell you, it was hard to ignore socks hanging on the walls.

The next day, as students started to enter the building, they saw the socks hanging around the halls, and of course they were curious why they were there. As students approached the socks, they started to read the statistics. According to members of SSOC and the staff at the school, the socks were all the buzz on the school campus the next day. This activity alone was the flagship of the SSOC movement. One could see the empowerment on the students' faces when visiting with them the next time. They were ready to do more.

The students were not the only ones; the staff and community members were also ready to do more. So we created a comprehensive safe school plan with the school. The school addressed bullying through a whole-school staff development hosted by Lassiter for parents and community members. Lassiter even got a chance to address the church that hosted the Save a Soul Week; he talked about bullying and how they could play a role in reducing it. The school developed a threat assessment team so that it could assess and handle the next threat made on the school campus in a productive way instead of allowing it to grow into a bigger issue. We even reexamined its crisis plan, addressing everything from put-downs to lockdowns. Did it take time and resources? Of course, but in the end, the school was a more conducive and safer learning environment.

When the SSOC students reassessed their school at the end of the school year, the number of students who had been bullied in the last month had dropped by over 50 percent since their first survey. Even more compelling was that 93 percent of students said they now felt safe on the school campus, which was up from 60 percent from the first survey. That made all the planning and extra work worth it, and the reality is that you can do it at your school also. Start by addressing the put-downs, the trash talk, and the culture of disrespect, and you too may realize the difference that a little early prevention can make in the end.

Notes

INTRODUCTION

1. Bill Miller and Francis Hopkins, "After-School Fight Leaves 1 Dead, 2 Hurt: Bystanders Are Shot at Park near Millbrook," *News & Observer*, April 27, 1993, News section.

2. Matthew Eisley, "Echo of Shots Lingers at School," *News & Observer*, April 28, 1993, News section.

3. Dudley Price, "Millbrook Mourns Slain Teen," *News & Observer*, April 30, 1993, News section.

4. Rachel Dinkes, Emily Forrest Cataldi, Grace Kena, and Katrina Baum, *Indicators of School Crime and Safety: 2006*, 2006. NCES 2007–003/NCJ 214262). U.S. Departments of Education and Justice. Washington, DC: U.S. Government Printing Office.

5. National Center for Education Statistics, *Crime, Violence, Discipline and Safety in U.S. Public Schools: Findings from the School Survey on Crime and Safety: 2003–04*, (NCES 2007–302rev). U.S. Department of Education, National Center for Education Statistics. Washington, DC: U.S. Government Printing Office.

6. Centers for Disease Control, *2005 Youth Risk Behavior Survey Results*, 2006. National Center for Chronic Disease Prevention and Health Promotion, Division of Adolescent and School Health.

CHAPTER 1

1. Paul C. Violas, Steven Tozer, and Guy B. Senese, *School and Society: Historical and Contemporary Perspectives*, 4th ed. (Boston: McGraw-Hill Humanities/Social Sciences/Languages, 2001), 121.

2. Department of Juvenile Justice and Delinquency Prevention–Center for the Prevention of School Violence, "What is School Violence?" Department of Juvenile Justice and Delinquency Prevention–Center for the Prevention of School Violence, http://www.ncdjjdp.org/cpsv/library/question_month.html.

3. K. Dwyer, D. Osher, and C. Warger, *Early Warning, Timely Response: A Guide to Safe Schools* (Washington, DC: U.S. Department of Education, Office of Special Education and Rehabilitation Services, Office of Special Education Programs, 1998).

4. Joseph D. Dear, *Creating Caring Relationships to Foster Academic Excellence: Recommendations for Reducing Violence in California Schools* (Sacramento: California Commission on Teacher Credentialing, 1995).

5. National Youth Violence Prevention Resource Center, "School Violence Fact Sheet," National Youth Violence Prevention Resource Center, http://www.safeyouth.org/scripts/facts/docs/school.pdf.

6. Gloria Zradicka, "Persistently Dangerous School Criteria," Education Commission of the States, http://www.ecs.org/clearinghouse/47/00/4700.htm.

7. Irvin Schonfeld, "Chapter 9: School Violence," in *Handbook of Workplace Violence* (Thousand Oaks, CA: Sage Publications, 2006), 169–210.

CHAPTER 2

1. "Epidemic," Merriam-Webster Online, http://www.merriam-webster.com.

2. Dinkes, R., Cataldi, E.F., and Lin-Kelly, W. (2007). *Indicators of School Crime and Safety: 2007* (NCES 2008–021/NCJ 219553). National Center for Education Statistics, Institute of Education Sciences, U.S. Department of Education, and Bureau of Justice Statistics, Office of Justice Programs, U.S. Department of Justice. Washington, DC.

3. National School Safety Center, "School Associated Violent Deaths," National School Safety Center, http://www.schoolsafety.us/pubfiles/savd.pdf.

4. Rachel Dinkes, Emily Forrest Cataldi, Grace Kena, and Katrina Baum, *Indicators of School Crime and Safety: 2006.* National Center for Education Statistics, Institute of Education Sciences, U.S. Department of Education, and Bureau of Justice Statistics, Office of Justice Programs, U.S. Department of Justice. Washington, DC.

5. Ibid.

6. Rachel Dinkes, Emily Forrest Cataldi, and Wendy Lin-Kelly, *Indicators of School Crime and Safety: 2007,* 2007. National Center for Education Statistics, Institute of Education Sciences, U.S. Department of Education, and Bureau of Justice Statistics, Office of Justice Programs, U.S. Department of Justice. Washington, DC.

7. Paul Guerino et al., *Crime, Violence, Discipline and Safety in U.S. Public Schools: Findings from the School Survey on Crime and Safety: 2003–04* (Washington, D.C.: National Center for Education Statistics, 2006).

8. Dinkes, Cataldi, and Lin-Kelly, *Indicators.*

9. Karen Gray-Adams, *Report on the Implementation of the Gun-Free Schools Act in the States and Outlying Areas* (Washington, DC: U.S. Department of Education, Office of Safe and Drug-Free Schools, 2007).

10. Centers for Disease Control and Prevention, Surveillance Summaries, Morbidity Mortality Weekly Report, *Youth Risk Behavior Surveillance—United States, 2007* (Atlanta, GA: U.S. Department of Health and Human Services, 2008, Vol. 57, No. SS-4).

11. Craig A. Anderson et al., "The Influence of Media Violence on Youth," *Association for Psychological Sciences* 4, no. 3 (2003): 81–110.

12. Craig A. Anderson and Brad J. Bushman, "Effects of Violent Video Games on Aggressive Behavior, Aggressive Cognition, Aggressive Affect, Physiological Arousal, and Prosocial Behavior: A Meta-Analytic Review of the Scientific Literature," *Psychological Science* 12, no. 5 (2002), http://www3.interscience.wiley.com/journal/118998785/abstract?CRETRY=1&SRETRY=0.

13. Gray-Adams, *Report on the Implementation of the Gun-Free Schools Act.*

14. U.S. Department of Education, NCES Digest of Education Statistics 2003, at Table 147 Percent of high school seniors reporting drug use, by type of drug and frequency of use: Selected years, 1975 to 2004.

15. Advancement Project and the Civil Rights Project at Harvard University, *Opportunities Suspended: The Devastating Consequences of Zero Tolerance and School Discipline Policies* (Cambridge, MA: The Civil Rights Project at Harvard University, 2000). http://www.eric.ed.gov/ERICDocs/data/ericdocs2sql/content_storage_01/0000019b/80/17/21/dd.pdf

16. D. Kirby, "Understanding What Works and What Doesn't in Reducing Adolescent Risk-Taking," *Family Planning Perspectives* 33, no. 6 (2001): 276–81.

17. Janis Whitlock, *Fostering School Connectedness*, a collaboration of Cornell University, University of Rochester, and the New York State Center for School Safety (Ithaca, NY: ACT for Youth, Cornell University, 2003).

18. Kirby, "Understanding What Works."

19. Timothy Thornton et al., *Best Practices of Youth Violence Prevention: A Sourcebook for Community Action*, rev. ed. (Atlanta, GA: Centers for Disease Control and Prevention, National Center for Injury Prevention and Control, 2002).

20. Kathleen Cotton and Karen R. Wikelund, "Parent Involvement in Education," Northwest Regional Educational Laboratory, 2001, http://www.nwrel.org/scpd/sirs/3/cu6.html.

21. Jeffrey Fagan and Franklin E. Zimring, eds., *The Changing Borders of Juvenile Justice* (Chicago: University of Chicago Press, 2000).

22. Center for the Prevention and Study of Violence, "Judicial Waivers: Youth in Adult Courts," FS-008, 1999, http://www.colorado.edu/cspv/publications/factsheets/cspv/FS-008.pdf.

23. Office of Juvenile Justice and Delinquency Prevention, "Juvenile Justice Reform Initiatives in the States 1994–1996," http://ojjdp.ncjrs.org/pubs/reform/contents.html.

24. Center for the Prevention and Study of Violence, "Judicial Waivers."

CHAPTER 3

1. Sandra Rief, *How to Reach and Teach Children with ADD/ADHD: Practical Techniques, Strategies, and Interventions* (San Francisco: Jossey-Bass, 2005), 55–59.

2. Ray W. Christner, Arthur Freeman, and Rosemary Mennuti, eds., *Cognitive Behavioral Interventions in Educational Settings: A Handbook for Practice* (New York: Taylor & Francis Group, 2006), 163–71.

3. Bessel A. van der Kolk, J. Christopher Perry, and Judith Lewis Herman, "Childhood Origins of Self-Destructive Behavior," *American Journal of Psychiatry* 148 (1991): 1665–71.

4. Mayo Foundation for Medical Education and Research, "Antisocial Personality Disorder," 2008, http://www.mayoclinic.com/health/antisocial-personality-disorder/DS00829.

5. Alan McEvoy and Robert Welker, "Antisocial Behavior, Academic Failure, and School Climate: A Critical Review," *Journal of Emotional and Behavioral Disorders* 8 (2000): 130–40.

6. Communities That Care, "Availability of Drugs," 2007, http://casat.unr.edu/bestpractices/bprf.htm.

7. Communities That Care, "Availability of Firearms: Delinquency and Violence," 2007, http://casat.unr.edu/bestpractices/bprf.htm.

8. The National Commission on Teaching and America's Future, "Unraveling the 'Teacher Shortage' Problem: Teacher Retention Is Key," 2002, http://www.ncsu.edu/mentorjunction/text_files/teacher_retentionsymposium.pdf.

CHAPTER 4

1. U.S. Department of Education, *Early Warning Timely Response: A Guide to Safe Schools*, http://cecp.air.org/guide/guide.pdf.

2. Ibid.

3. Ibid.

4. Bryan Vossekuil et al., *The Final Report and Findings of the Safe School Initiative: Implication for the Prevention of School Attacks in the United States* (Washington, DC: U.S. Secret Service and U.S. Department of Education, 2002), http://www.ustreas.gov/usss/ntac/ssi_final_report.pdf.

5. Ibid.

6. Ibid.

7. Ibid.

CHAPTER 5

1. R. Edmonds, *Effective Schools for the Urban Poor*, 1979, http://www.ed.utah.edu/ELP/CourseMaterials/Cori6010F06/effec.pdf.

2. R. Jessor, "Successful Adolescent Development among Youth in High-Risk Settings," *American Psychologist* 48 (1993): 117–26.

3. J. Garbarino, *Adolescent Development: An Ecological Perspective* (Columbus, OH: Charles E. Merrill, 1985), 78–83.

4. Office of Juvenile Justice and Delinquency Prevention, "Predictors of Youth Violence," 2000, http://www.ncjrs.gov/html/ojjdp/jjbul2000_04_5/contents.html.

5. J. D. Hawkins, D. P. Farrington, and R. F. Catalano, "Reducing Violence through the Schools," in *Violence in American Schools: A New Perspective*, edited by D. S. Elliott, B. A. Hamburg, and K. R. Williams (New York: Cambridge University Press, 1998), 188–216.

6. D. S. Elliott and S. Menard, "Delinquent Friends and Delinquent Behavior: Temporal and Developmental Patterns," in *Delinquency and Crime: Current Theories*, edited by J. D. Hawkins (New York: Cambridge University Press, 1996), 28–67.

7. J. D. Coie et al., "Childhood Peer Rejection and Aggression as Predictors of Stable Patterns of Adolescent Disorder," *Development and Psychopathology* 7 (1995): 697–713.

8. C. L. Bagwell et al., "Peer Clique Participation and Social Status in Preadolescence," *Merrill-Palmer Quarterly* 46 (2000): 280–305.

9. J. D. Hawkins and J. G. Weis, "The Social Development Model: An Integrated Approach to Delinquency Prevention," *Journal of Primary Prevention* 6 (1985): 73–97.

10. J. Epstein, *School, Family, and Community Partnerships: Preparing Educators and Improving Schools* (Boulder, CO: Westview Press, 1983), 101–19.

11. Statistics Canada, "Education Matters," 1993, http://www.statcan.ca.

12. R. B. Ekstrom et al., "Who Drops Out of High School and Why? Findings from a National Study," *Teachers College Record* 87 (1986): 356–73.

13. H. Stattin and D. Magnusson, "The Role of Early Aggressive Behavior in the Frequency, Seriousness, and Types of Later Crime," *Journal of Consulting and Clinical Psychology* 57 (1989): 710–18.

14. M. C. Wang, G. D. Haertel, and J. H. Walberg, "Toward a Knowledge Base for School Learning," *Review of Educational Research* 63 (1993): 249–94.

15. R. Loeber and D. P. Farrington, *Serious and Violent Juvenile Offenders: Risk Factors and Successful Interventions* (Thousand Oaks, CA: Sage Publications, 1998), 13–22.

16. A. McCray and L. Neal, "Movement Matters: The Need for Culturally Responsive Teaching," *Journal of the New England League of Middle Schools* (Spring 2003): 28–33.

17. Edmonds, *Effective Schools.*

18. J. Belsky, "Child Maltreatment: An Ecological Perspective," *American Psychologist* 35 (1980): 320–25.

19. R. W. Roeser, J. S. Eccles, and A. J. Sameroff, "Academic and Emotional Functioning in Early Adolescence: Longitudinal Relations, Patterns, and Prediction by Experience in Middle School," *Development and Psychopathology* 10 (1998): 321–52.

20. R. E. Slavin, *Cooperative Learning: Theory, Research, and Practice* (Upper Saddle River, NJ: Prentice Hall, 1989), 14–21.

CHAPTER 6

1. U.S. Secret Service and U.S. Department of Education, *The Final Report and Findings of the Safe School Initiative: Implication for the Prevention of School Attacks in the United States.* Washington, DC, 2002, http://www.ustreas.gov/usss/ntac/ssi_final_report.pdf.

2. James Alan Fox et al., *Bullying Prevention Is Crime Prevention*, Washington, DC, 2003, http://www.opi.state.mt.us/pdf/SafeSchools/Bullying.pdf.

3. J. D. Hawkins et al., "A Review of Predictors of Youth Violence," in *Serious and Violent Juvenile Offenders: Risk Factors and Successful Interventions*, edited by R. Loeber and D. P. Farrington (London: Sage Publications, 1999), 106–46.

4. H. Stattin and D. Magnusson, "The Role of Early Aggressive Behavior in the Frequency, Seriousness, and Types of Later Crime," *Journal of Consulting and Clinical Psychology* 57 (1989): 710–18.

5. The National Center on Addiction and Substance Abuse, *Criminal Neglect: Substance Abuse, Juvenile Justice and the Children Left Behind*, 2004, http://www.casacolumbia.org/absolutenm/articlefiles/379-Criminal%20Neglect.pdf.

6. Department of Health and Human Services, Centers for Disease Control and Prevention, "Violence Prevention and United States Students," 2007, http://www.cdc.gov/HealthyYouth/yrbs/pdf/yrbs07_us_violence.pdf.

7. Kaiser Family Foundation, and Children Now, "Talking with Kids about Tough Issues: A National Survey of Parents and Kids," 2001, http://www.kff.org/mediapartnerships/loader.cfm?url=/commonspot/security/getfile.cfm&PageID=13791.

8. D. Olweus, *Bullying at School: What We Know and What We Can Do* (Cambridge, MA: Blackwell, 1993), 34.

9. Ibid., 34–43.

10. T. R. Nansel et al., "Bullying Behaviors among US Youth: Prevalence and Association with Psychosocial Adjustment," *Journal of the American Medical Association* 285, no. 16 (2001): 2094–2100.

11. J. H. Hoover, R. Oliver, and R. J. Hazler, "Bullying: Perceptions of Adolescent Victims in the Midwestern USA," *School Psychology International* 13 (1992): 5–16.

12. Olweus, *Bullying at School.*

13. Ibid.

14. Gary Becker, "Crime and Punishment: An Economic Approach," *Journal of Political Economy* 76 (1968): 169–217.

15. Nansel et al., "Bullying Behaviors."

16. D. Olweus, *Aggression in the Schools: Bullies and Whipping Boys* (Washington, DC: Hemisphere, Wiley, 1978).

17. John Scott, *Understanding Contemporary Society: Theories of the Present,* edited by G. Browning, A. Halcli, and F. Webster, 2000, http://privatewww.essex.ac.uk/~scottj/socscot7.htm.

18. Olweus, *Bullying at School.*

CHAPTER 7

1. M. W. Klein, "The Value of Comparisons in Street Gang Research," *Journal of Contemporary Criminal Justice* 21 (2005): 135–52.

2. L. Savelli, *Gangs across America and Their Symbols* (Michigan Center, MI: Looseleaf Law Publications, 2004), 3–10.

3. Ibid.

4. James C. Howell, *National Youth Gang Trends,* 2003, www.iir.com/nygc.

5. Gottfredson Associates, Inc., "Gang Problems and Gang Programs in a National Sample of Schools," 1999, http://www.gottfredson.com/gang.htm.

6. R. E. Tremblay et al., *From Childhood Physical Aggression to Adolescent Maladjustment: The Montreal Prevention Experiment* (Thousand Oaks, CA: Sage Publications, 1996), 268–98.

CHAPTER 8

1. R. Bodine, D. Crawford, and F. Schrumpf, *Creating the Peaceable School: A Comprehensive Program for Teaching Conflict Resolution* (Champaign, IL: Research Press, 1994).

2. H. Bisno, *Managing Conflict* (Beverly Hills, CA: Sage Publications, 1988); and M. A. Rahim, *Managing Conflict: An Interdisciplinary Approach* (New York: Praeger, 1989).

3. K. Girard and S. Koch, *Conflict Resolution in the Schools* (San Francisco: Jossey-Bass, 1996).

4. B. Cartledge and J. F. Milburn, *Teaching Social Skills to Children: Innovative Approaches* (Needham Heights, MA: Allyn and Bacon, 1986).

5. Ibid.

6. D. D. Buchman and J. B. Funk, "Video and Computer Games in the '90s: Children's Time Commitment and Game Preference," *Children Today* 24 (1996): 12–16.

7. R. Shores et al., "Classroom Influences on Aggressive and Disruptive Students with Emotional and Behavioral Disorders," *Focus on Exceptional Children* 26, no. 2 (1993): 140.

8. D. Kim, D. Soloman, and W. Roberts, "Classroom Practices Enhance Students' Sense of Community" (paper presented at the annual meeting of American Educational Research Association, San Francisco, 1995).

9. T. Allen, "Creating Community in Your Classroom," *Education Digest* 65, no. 7 (2000): 23–27.

10. J. T. Knippen and T. B. Green, "How the Manager Can Use Active Listening," *Public Personnel Management* 23, no. 2 (1994): 357–59.

11. J. Rademacher, K. Callahan, and V. Pederson-Seelye, "How Do Your Classroom Rules Measure Up?" *Intervention in School and Clinic* 33 (1998): 284–89.

CHAPTER 9

1. C. Powell, *My American Journey* (New York: Random House, 1996), 12–17.

2. National Mentoring Partnership, "What Is Mentoring?" 2008, http://www.mentoring.org/mentors/about_mentoring

3. G. M. Dondero, "Mentors: Beacons of Hope," *Adolescence* 32 (1997): 881–86.

4. M. T. McLearn et al., *Mentoring Matters: A National Study of Adults Mentoring Young People* (Philadelphia: Public/Private Ventures, 1998).

5. Ibid.

6. J. Grossman, N. Resch, and J. Tierney, *Making a Difference: An Impact Study of Big Brothers/Big Sisters* (Philadelphia: Public/Private Ventures, 1995).

7. L. LoSciuto et al., "An Outcome Evaluation of Across Ages: An Intergenerational Mentoring Approach to Drug Prevention," *Journal of Adolescent Research* 11 (1996): 116–29.

8. National Mentoring Partnerships, "Support for Mentors," 2008, http://www.mentoring.org.

9. J. Terry, "A Community/School Mentoring Program for Elementary Students," *Professional School Counseling* 2 (1999): 237–40.

CHAPTER 10

1. S. E. Smith, "Parent-Initiated Contracts: An Intervention for School-Related Behaviors," *Elementary School Guidance and Counseling* 28, no. 3(1994): 182–88.

2. I. Warner, "Parents in Touch: District Leadership for Parent Involvement," *Phi Delta Kappan* 178 (1991): 372–75.

3. J. Johnson and A. Duffett, *Where We Are Now: 12 Things You Need to Know about Public Opinion and Public Schools* (New York: Public Agenda, 2003).

4. S. Tangri and O. Moles, *Parents and the Community: An Educators' Handbook* (New York: Longman, 1987).

5. R. M. Becher, *Parent Involvement: A Review of Research and Principles of Successful Practice* (Urbana, IL: ERIC Clearinghouse on Elementary and Early Childhood Education, ED 247–032, 1984).

6. L. Moll et al., "Funds of Knowledge for Teaching: Using a Qualitative Approach to Connect Homes and Classrooms," *Theory into Practice* 31 (2001): 132–41.

CHAPTER 11

1. R. B. Warren and D. I. Warren, *The Neighborhood Organizer's Handbook* (Notre Dame, IN: University of Notre Dame Press, 1977), 167–96.

2. B. T. Washington, *Up from Slavery* (Radford, VA: Wilder Publications, 2008), 49–58.

3. B. Jones, "Defining Your Neighborhood," in *Neighborhood Planning: A Guide for Citizens and Planners* (Chicago: Planners Press, 1979), 8–11.

4. M. Homan, *Promoting Community Change: Making It Happen in the Real World* (Pacific Grove, CA: Brooks/Cole, 1994), 37–41.

5. R. E. Petty, D. T. Wegener, and L. R. Fabrigar, "Attitudes and Attitude Change," *Annual Review of Psychology* 48 (1997): 609–47.

CHAPTER 12

1. Bradford Chaney and Laurie Lewis, *Public School Principals Report on Their School Facilities: Fall 2005* (Washington, DC: U.S. Department of Education, National Center for Education Statistics, 2007).

2. U.S. Department of Education, National Center for Education Statistics, *Condition of America's Public School Facilities: 1999*, http://nces.ed.gov/surveys/frss/publications/2000032/index.asp?sectionID=7.

3. George Kelling and Catherine Coles, *Fixing Broken Windows: Restoring Order and Reducing Crime in Our Communities* (New York: Free Press, 1996); James Q. Wilson and George L. Kelling, "Broken Windows: The Police and Neighborhood Safety," 1982, http://www.theatlantic.com/doc/198203/broken-windows.

CHAPTER 13

1. Dewey Cornell et al., "Guidelines for Student Threat Assessment: Field-Test Findings," *School Psychology Review* 33, no. 4 (2004): 527–46.

2. Shane R. Jimerson, Stephen E. Brock, and Katherine C. Cowan, *Threat Assessment: An Essential Component of a Comprehensive Safe School Program*, National Association of School Psychologists, 2005, http://www.nasponline.org/resources/principals/nassp_threat.pdf.

3. Mary Ellen O'Toole, *The School Shooter: A Threat Assessment Perspective* (Quantico, VA: Critical Incident Response Group [CIRG], National Center for the Analysis of Violent Crime [NCAVC], FBI Academy), 2004, http://www.fbi.gov/publications/school/school2.pdf.

4. Robert Fein et al., *Threat Assessment in Schools: A Guide to Managing Threatening Situations and to Creating Safe School Climates* (Washington, DC: U.S.

Department of Education, Office of Elementary and Secondary Education, Safe and Drug-Free Schools Program and U.S. Secret Service, National Threat Assessment Center, U.S. Secret Service/ Department of Education Report), 2002, http://www.ustreas.gov/usss/ntac/ssi_guide.pdf.

5. O'Toole, *School Shooter*.

6. Fein et al., *Threat Assessment in Schools*.

7. Ibid.

8. Ibid.

9. Ibid.; and http://www.ustreas.gov/usss/ntac/ssi_guide.pdf, 50.

10. http://www.ustreas.gov/usss/ntac/ssi_guide.pdf, 55–57.

11. Cornell et al., "Guidelines."

12. O'Toole, *School Shooter*.

13. Ibid.

14. Ibid.

CHAPTER 14

1. M. J. Ellsworth, *The Bath School Disaster*, 1928, http://daggy.name/tbsd/tbsd-t.htm#ChapterOne.

2. *60 Minutes II*, "What Really Happened at Columbine?" MMI Viacom Internet Services Inc., CBS News, 2001, http://www.cbsnews.com/stories/2001/04/17/60II/main286144.shtml.

3. *60 Minutes II*, "What Really Happened?"

4. Ibid.

5. New Hampshire Department of Safety, http://www.nh.gov/safety/divisions/bem/documents/NIMSQA1305.pdf.

6. New Hampshire Department of Safety, "NIMS Compliance." http://www.nh.gov/safety/divisions/fstems/nims.

7. Ibid.

8. David Cowan and John Kuenster, *To Sleep with the Angels: The Story of a Fire* (Chicago: Reed Business Information, Inc., 1996).

9. Hal Bruno, "Old Lessons Continue to Go Unheeded," *Firehouse*, http://cms.firehouse.com/print/Politics-and-Law/Old-Lessons-Continue-To-Go-Unheeded/43$399.

10. "2006 Top Newsmakers: Orange High School Shooting," http://www.wral.com/news/local/story/1118005.

CHAPTER 15

1. American Red Cross, "Fact Sheet on Shelter-in-Place," 2003, http://www.nationalterroralert.com/readyguide/shelterinplace.pdf.

Bibliography

Advancement Project and the Civil Rights Project at Harvard University. *Opportunities Suspended: The Devastating Consequences of Zero Tolerance and School Discipline Policies.* The Civil Rights Project at Harvard University, 2000. http://www.eric.ed.gov/ERICDocs/data/ericdocs2sql/content_storage_ 01/0000019b/80/17/21/dd.pdf.

Allen, T. "Creating Community in Your Classroom." *Education Digest* 65, no. 7 (2000): 23–27.American Red Cross. "Fact Sheet on Shelter-in-Place." 2003. http://www.nationalterroralert.com/readyguide/shelterinplace.pdf.

Anderson, Craig A., and Brad J. Bushman. "Effects of Violent Video Games on Aggressive Behavior, Aggressive Cognition, Aggressive Affect, Physiological Arousal, and Prosocial Behavior: A Meta-Analytic Review of the Scientific Literature." *Psychological Science* 12, no. 5 (2002). http://www3.interscience. wiley.com/journal/118998785/abstract?CRETRY=1&SRETRY=0.

Anderson, Craig A., et al. "The Influence of Media Violence on Youth." *Association for Psychological Sciences* 4, no. 3 (2003): 81–110.

Bagwell, C. L., et al. "Peer Clique Participation and Social Status in Preadolescence." *Merrill-Palmer Quarterly* 46 (2000): 280–305.

Becher, R. M. *Parent Involvement: A Review of Research and Principles of Successful Practice.* Urbana, IL: ERIC Clearinghouse on Elementary and Early Childhood Education, ED 247-032, 1984.

Becker, Gary. "Crime and Punishment: An Economic Approach." *Journal of Political Economy* 76 (1968): 169–217.

Belsky, J. "Child Maltreatment: An Ecological Perspective." *American Psychologist* 35 (1980): 320–25.

Bisno, H. *Managing Conflict.* Beverly Hills, CA: Sage Publications, 1988.

Bodine, R., D. Crawford, and F. Schrumpf. *Creating the Peaceable School: A Comprehensive Program for Teaching Conflict Resolution.* Champaign, IL: Research Press, 1994.

Bruno, Hal. "Old Lessons Continue to Go Unheeded." *Firehouse.* http://cms. firehouse.com/print/Politics-and-Law/Old-Lessons-Continue-To-Go-Unheeded/43$399.

Buchman, D. D., and J. B. Funk. "Video and Computer Games in the '90s: Children's Time Commitment and Game Preference." *Children Today* 24 (1996): 12–16.

Cartledge, B., and J. F. Milburn. *Teaching Social Skills to Children: Innovative Approaches*. Needham Heights, MA: Allyn and Bacon, 1986.

Center for the Prevention and Study of Violence. "Judicial Waivers: Youth in Adult Courts" (1999): FS-008. http://www.colorado.edu/cspv/publications/factsheets/cspv/FS-008.pdf.

Centers for Disease Control and Prevention. *Morbidity Mortality Weekly Report: Youth Risk Behavior Surveillance-United States, 2007*. Atlanta, GA: U.S. Department of Health and Human Services (2008). Vol. 57, No. SS-4.

Chaney, Bradford, and Laurie Lewis. *Public School Principals Report on Their School Facilities: Fall 2005*. Washington, DC: U.S. Department of Education, National Center for Education Statistics, 2007.

Christner, Ray W., Arthur Freeman, and Rosemary Mennuti, eds. *Cognitive Behavioral Interventions in Educational Settings: A Handbook for Practice*. New York: Taylor & Francis Group, 2006.

Coie, J. D., et al. "Childhood Peer Rejection and Aggression as Predictors of Stable Patterns of Adolescent disorder." *Development and Psychopathology* 7 (1995): 697–713.

Communities That Care. "Availability of Drugs." South Deerfield, MA: Channing Bete Company, 2007. http://casat.unr.edu/bestpractices/bprf.htm.

———. "Availability of Firearms: Delinquency and Violence." South Deerfield, MA: Channing Bete Company, 2007. http://casat.unr.edu/bestpractices/bprf.htm.

Cornell, Dewey, et al. "Guidelines for Student Threat Assessment: Field-Test Findings." *School Psychology Review* 33, no. 4 (2004): 527–46.

Cotton, Kathleen, and Karen R. Wikelund. "Parent Involvement in Education." Portland, OR: Northwest Regional Educational Laboratory, 2001. http://www.nwrel.org/scpd/sirs/3/cu6.html.

Cowan, David, and John Kuenster. *To Sleep with the Angels: The Story of a Fire*. Location Published: Ivan R. Dee, Inc. 1996.

Dear, Joseph D. *Creating Caring Relationships to Foster Academic Excellence: Recommendations for Reducing Violence in California Schools*. Sacramento: California Commission on Teacher Credentialing, 1995.

Department of Health and Human Services, Centers for Disease Control and Prevention. "Violence Prevention and United States Students." Atlanta, GA: Centers for Disease Control and Prevention, 2007. http://www.cdc.gov/HealthyYouth/yrbs/pdf/yrbs07_us_violence.pdf.

Department of Juvenile Justice and Delinquency Prevention, Center for the Prevention of School Violence. "What Is School Violence?" Raleigh, NC: Department of Juvenile Justice and Delinquency Prevention, Center for the Prevention of School Violence, 2002. http://www.ncdjjdp.org/cpsv/library/question_month.html.

Dondero, G. M. "Mentors: Beacons of Hope." *Adolescence* 32 (1997): 881–86.

Donoghue, P. J., and M. E. Siegel. *Are You Really Listening? Keys to Successful Communication*. Notre Dame, IN: Ave Maria Press, 2005, 164–78.

Dwyer, K., D. Osher, and C. Warger. *Early Warning, Timely Response: A Guide to Safe Schools*. Washington, DC: U.S. Department of Education, 1998.

Edmonds, R. "Effective Schools for the Urban Poor." *Educational Leadership*, 1979: 15–24. http://www.ed.utah.edu/ELP/CourseMaterials/Cori6010F06/effec.pdf.

Ekstrom, R. B., et al. "Who Drops Out of High School and Why? Findings from a National Study." *Teachers College Record* 87 (1986): 356–73.

Elliott, D. S., and S. Menard. "Delinquent Friends and Delinquent Behavior: Temporal and Developmental Patterns." In *Delinquency and Crime: Current Theories*, edited by J. D. Hawkins. New York: Cambridge University Press, 1996, 28–67.

Ellsworth, M. J. *The Bath School Disaster*. 1928. http://daggy.name/tbsd/tbsd-t.htm#ChapterOne.

Epstein, J. *School, Family, and Community Partnerships: Preparing Educators and Improving Schools*. Boulder, CO: Westview Press, 1983.

Fagan, Jeffrey, and Franklin E. Zimring, eds. *The Changing Borders of Juvenile Justice*. Chicago: University of Chicago Press, 2000.

Fehrmann, P. G., T. Z. Keith, and T. M. Reiners. "Home Influence on School Learning: Direct and Indirect Effects of Parental Involvement on High School Grades." *Journal of Educational Research* 80 (1987): 330–36.

Fein, Robert, et al. *Threat Assessment in Schools: A Guide to Managing Threatening Situations and to Creating Safe School Climates*. Washington, DC: U.S. Department of Education, Office of Elementary and Secondary Education, Safe and Drug-Free Schools Program and U.S. Secret Service, National Threat Assessment Center, U.S. Secret Service/ Department of Education Report, 2002. http://www.ustreas.gov/usss/ntac/ssi_guide.pdf.

Fox, James Alan, et al. *Bullying Prevention Is Crime Prevention*. Washington, DC: Fight Crime, Invest in Kids, 2003. http://www.opi.state.mt.us/pdf/SafeSchools/Bullying.pdf.

Garbarino, J. *Adolescent Development: An Ecological Perspective*. Columbus, OH: Charles E. Merrill, 1985.

Ginsburg, Kenneth. *A Parent's Guide to Building Resilience in Children and Teens*. Elk Grove, IL: American Academy of Pediatrics, 2006.

Girard, K., and S. Koch. *Conflict Resolution in the Schools*. San Francisco: Jossey-Bass, 1996.

Gottfredson, Gary, and Denise C. Gottfredson. "Gang Problems and Gang Programs in a National Sample of Schools." Ellicott City, MD: Gottfredson Associates, 1999. http://www.gottfredson.com/gang.htm.

Gray-Adams, Karen. *Report on the Implementation of the Gun-Free Schools Act in the States and Outlying Areas*. Washington, DC: U.S. Department of Education, Office of Safe and Drug-Free Schools, 2007.

Grossman, J., N. Resch, and J. Tierney. *Making a Difference: An Impact Study of Big Brothers/Big Sisters*. Philadelphia: Public/Private Ventures, 1995.

Guerino, Paul, et al. *Crime, Violence, Discipline, and Safety in U.S. Public Schools: Findings from the School Survey on Crime and Safety: 2003–04*. Washington, DC: National Center for Education Statistics, 2006.

Hawkins, J. D., D. P. Farrington, and R. F. Catalano. "Reducing Violence through the Schools." In *Violence in American Schools: A New Perspective*, edited by D. S. Elliott, B. A. Hamburg, and K. R. Williams. New York: Cambridge University Press, 1998, 188–216.

Hawkins, J. D., and J. G. Weis. "The Social Development Model: An Integrated Approach to Delinquency Prevention." *Journal of Primary Prevention* 6 (1985): 73–97.

Hawkins, J. D., et al. "A Review of Predictors of Youth Violence." In *Serious and Violent Juvenile Offenders: Risk Factors and Successful Interventions*, edited by R. Loeber and D. P. Farrington. London: Sage Publications, 1999, 106–46.

Homan, M. *Promoting Community Change: Making It Happen in the Real World.* Pacific Grove, CA: Brooks/Cole, 1994.

Hoover, J. H., R. Oliver, and R. J. Hazler. "Bullying: Perceptions of Adolescent Victims in the Midwestern USA." *School Psychology International* 13 (1992): 5–16.

Howell, James C. *National Youth Gang Trends.* Tallahassee, FL: National Youth Gang Center, 2003.

Jessor, R. "Successful Adolescent Development among Youth in High-Risk Settings." *American Psychologist* 48 (1993): 117–26.

Jimerson, Shane R., Stephen E. Brock, and Katherine C. Cowan. *Threat Assessment: An Essential Component of a Comprehensive Safe School Program.* Bethesda, MD: National Association of School Psychologists, 2005. http://www.nasponline.org/resources/principals/nassp_threat.pdf.

Johnson, E. H. *Handbook on Crime and Delinquency Prevention.* New York: Greenwood Press, 1987, 1–12.

Johnson, J., and A. Duffett. *Where We Are Now: 12 Things You Need to Know about Public Opinion and Public Schools. A Digest of a Decade of Survey Research.* New York: Public Agenda, 2003.

Jones, B. "Defining Your Neighborhood." In *Neighborhood Planning: A Guide for Citizens and Planners.* Chicago, IL: Planners Press, 1979, 8–11.

Kaiser Family Foundation and Children Now. "Talking with Kids about Tough Issues: A National Survey of Parents and Kids." 2001. http://www.kff.org/mediapartnerships/loader.cfm?url=/commonspot/security/getfile.cfm&PageID=13791.

Kelling, George, and Catherine Coles. *Fixing Broken Windows: Restoring Order and Reducing Crime in Our Communities.* New York: The Free Press, 1996.

Kim, D., D. Soloman, and W. Roberts. "Classroom Practices Enhance Students' Sense of Community." Paper presented at the annual meeting of American Educational Research Association, San Francisco, 1995.

Kirby, D. "Understanding What Works and What Doesn't in Reducing Adolescent Risk-Taking." *Family Planning Perspectives* 33, no. 6 (2001): 276–81.

Klein, M. W. "Street Gangs: A Cross-National Perspective." In *Gangs in America III*, edited by C. R. Huff. Thousand Oaks, CA: Sage Publications, 2002, 237–254.

———. "The Value of Comparisons in Street Gang Research." *Journal of Contemporary Criminal Justice* 21 (2005): 135–52.

Knippen, J. T., and T. B. Green. "How the Manager Can Use Active Listening." *Public Personnel Management* 23, no. 2 (1994): 357–59.

Loeber, R., and D. P. Farrington. *Serious and Violent Juvenile Offenders: Risk Factors and Successful Interventions.* Thousand Oaks, CA: Sage Publications, 1998.

LoSciuto, L., et al. "An Outcome Evaluation of Across Ages: An Intergenerational Mentoring Approach to Drug Prevention." *Journal of Adolescent Research* 11 (1996): 116–29.

Mayo Foundation for Medical Education and Research. "Antisocial Personality Disorder." 2008. http://www.mayoclinic.com/health/antisocial-personality-disorder/DS00829.

McCray, A., and L. Neal. "Movement Matters: The Need for Culturally Responsive Teaching." *Journal of the New England League of Middle Schools* Spring (2003): 28–33.

McEvoy, Alan, and Robert Welker. "Antisocial Behavior, Academic Failure, and School Climate: A Critical Review." *Journal of Emotional and Behavioral Disorders* 8 (2000): 130–40.

McLearn, M. T., et al. *Mentoring Matters: A National Study of Adults Mentoring Young People.* Philadelphia: Public/Private Ventures, 1998.

Moll, L., et al. "Funds of Knowledge for Teaching: Using a Qualitative Approach to Connect Homes and Classrooms." *Theory into Practice* 31 (2001): 132–41.

Moore, C. W. *The Mediation Process.* San Francisco: Jossey-Bass, 1986, 24.

Nansel, T. R., et al. "Bullying Behaviors among US Youth: Prevalence and Association with Psychosocial Adjustment." *Journal of the American Medical Association* 285, no. 16 (2001): 2094–100.

National Center for Education Statistics. "Survey on School Crime and Safety." Washington, DC: U.S. Department of Education, 2004.

National Center on Addiction and Substance Abuse. *Criminal Neglect: Substance Abuse, Juvenile Justice and the Children Left Behind.* New York: Casa Columbia, 2004. http://www.casacolumbia.org/absoluterm/articlefiles/379-Criminal%20Neglect.pdf.

National Clearinghouse for Educational Facilities at the National Institute of Building Sciences. "Low-Cost Security Measures for School Facilities." 2008. http://www.edfacilities.org/pubs/low_cost_measures.pdf.

National Commission on Teaching and America's Future. *Unraveling the "Teacher Shortage" Problem: Teacher Retention Is Key.* 2002. http://www.ncsu.edu/mentorjunction/text_files/teacher_retentionsymposium.pdf.

National Mentoring Partnership. "Support for Mentors." 2008. http://www.mentoring.org.

———. "What Is Mentoring?" 2008. http://www.mentoring.org/mentors/about_mentoring.

National School Safety Center. "School Associated Violent Deaths." Westlake Village, CA: National School Safety Center, 2008.

National Youth Violence Prevention Resource Center. "School Violence Fact Sheet." Rockville, MD: National Youth Violence Prevention Resource Center, 2002. http://www.safeyouth.org/scripts/facts/docs/school.pdf.

New Hampshire Department of Safety. http://www.nh.gov/safety/divisions/bem/documents/NIMSQA1305.pdf.

Office of Juvenile Justice and Delinquency Prevention. "Juvenile Justice Reform Initiatives in the States 1994–1996." http://ojjdp.ncjrs.org/pubs/reform/contents.html.

———."Predictors of Youth Violence." 2000. http://www.ncjrs.gov/html/ojjdp/jjbul2000_04_5/contents.html.

Olweus, D. *Aggression in the Schools: Bullies and Whipping Boys*. Washington, DC: Hemisphere, Wiley, 1978.

――――. *Bullying at School: What We Know and What We Can Do*. Cambridge, MA: Blackwell Publishers, 1993.

O'Toole, Mary Ellen. *The School Shooter: A Threat Assessment Perspective*. Quantico, VA: Critical Incident Response Group (CIRG), National Center for the Analysis of Violent Crime (NCAVC), FBI Academy, 2000. http://www.fbi. gov/publications/school/school2.pdf.

Petty, R. E., D. T. Wegener, and L. R. Fabrigar. "Attitudes and Attitude Change." *Annual Review of Psychology* 48 (1997): 609–47.

Powell, C. *My American Journey*. New York: Random House, 1996.

Rademacher, J., K. Callahan, and V. Pederson-Seelye. "How Do Your Classroom Rules Measure Up?" *Intervention in School and Clinic* 33 (1998): 284–89.

Rahim, M. A. *Managing Conflict: An Interdisciplinary Approach*. New York: Praeger, 1989.

Rief, Sandra. *How to Reach and Teach Children with ADD/ADHD: Practical Techniques, Strategies, and Interventions*. San Francisco: Jossey-Bass, 2005.

Roeser, R. W., J. S. Eccles, and A. J. Sameroff. "Academic and Emotional Functioning in Early Adolescence: Longitudinal Relations, Patterns, and Prediction by Experience in Middle School." *Development and Psychopathology* 10 (1998): 321–52.

Savelli, L. *Gangs across America and Their Symbols*. Michigan Center, MI: Looseleaf Law Publications, 2004.

Schonfeld, Irvin. "Chapter 9 School Violence." In *Handbook of Workplace Violence*. Thousand Oaks, CA: Sage Publications, 2006, 169–210.

Scott, John. "Rational Choice Theory." In *Understanding Contemporary Society: Theories of the Present*, edited by G. Browning, A. Halcli, and F. Webster. Thousand Oaks, CA: Sage Publications, 2000. http://privatewww.essex. ac.uk/~scottj/socscot7.htm.

Shores, R., et al. "Classroom Influences on Aggressive and Disruptive Students with Emotional and Behavioral Disorders." *Focus on Exceptional Children* 26, no. 2 (1993): 140.

60 Minutes II. "What Really Happened at Columbine?" MMI Viacom Internet Services Inc., CBS News, 2001. http://www.cbsnews.com/stories/2001/04/17/60II/main286144.shtml.

Slavin, R. E. *Cooperative Learning: Theory, Research, and Practice*. Upper Saddle River, NJ: Prentice Hall, 1989.

Smith, S. E. "Parent-Initiated Contracts: An Intervention for School-Related Behaviors." *Elementary School Guidance and Counseling* 28, no. 3(1994): 182–88.

Statistics Canada. "Education Matters." 1993. http://www.hrsdc.gc.ca/eng/cs/sp/hrsd/prc/publications/research/1995-000015/page06.shtml.

Stattin, H., and D. Magnusson. "The Role of Early Aggressive Behavior in the Frequency, Seriousness, and Types of Later Crime." *Journal of Consulting and Clinical Psychology* 57 (1989): 710–18.

Tangri, S., and O. Moles. *Parents and the Community: An Educators' Handbook*. New York/London: Longman Press, 1987.

Terry, J. "A Community/School Mentoring Program for Elementary Students." *Professional School Counseling* 2 (1999): 237–40.

Thornton, T., et al. *Best Practices of Youth Violence Prevention: A Sourcebook for Community Action* (Revised). Atlanta, GA: Centers for Disease Control and Prevention, National Center for Injury Prevention and Control, 2002.

Tremblay, R. E., et al. *From Childhood Physical Aggression to Adolescent Maladjustment: The Montreal Prevention Experiment.* Thousand Oaks, CA: Sage Publications, 1996.

"2006 Top Newsmakers: Orange High School Shooting." Posted: Dec. 26, 2006, Updated: Dec. 27, 2006. http://www.wral.com/news/local/story/1118005.

U.S. Department of Education, National Center for Education Statistics. *Condition of America's Public School Facilities: 1999.* http://nces.ed.gov/surveys/frss/publications/2000032/index.asp?sectionID=7.

Van der Kolk, Bessel A., J. Christopher Perry, and Judith Lewis Herman. "Childhood Origins of Self-Destructive Behavior." *American Journal of Psychiatry* 148 (1991): 1665–71.

Violas, Paul C., Steven Tozer, and Guy B. Senese. *School and Society: Historical and Contemporary Perspectives*, 4th ed. Washington, DC: McGraw-Hill Humanities/Social Sciences/Languages, 2001, 121.

Vossekuil, Bryan, et al. "The Final Report and Findings of the Safe School Initiative: Implication for the Prevention of School Attacks in the United States." Washington, DC: U.S. Secret Service and U.S. Department of Education, 2002. http://www.ustreas.gov/usss/ntac/ssi_final_report.pdf.

Wang, M. C., G. D. Haertel, and J. H. Walberg. "Toward a Knowledge Base for School Learning." *Review of Educational Research* 63 (1993): 249–94.

Warner, I. "Parents in Touch: District Leadership for Parent Involvement." *Phi Delta Kappan* 178 (1991): 372–75.

Warren, R. B., and D. I. Warren. *The Neighborhood Organizer's Handbook.* Notre Dame, IN: University of Notre Dame Press, 1977.

Washington, B. T. *Up from Slavery.* Radford, VA: Wilder Publications, 2008.

Whitlock, Janis. *Fostering School Connectedness.* Ithaca, NY: ACT for Youth, Cornell University, 2003.

Wilson, James Q., and George L. Kelling. Broken Windows: The Police and Neighborhood Safety. 1982. http://www.theatlantic.com/doc/198203/broken-windows.

Zradicka, Gloria. "Persistently Dangerous School Criteria." Denver, CO: Education Commission of the States, 2003. http://www.ecs.org/clearinghouse/47/00/4700.htm.

Index

About the Author

WILLIAM L. LASSITER began working for the Department of Juvenile Justice and Delinquency Prevention–Center for the Prevention of School Violence in 1997 as a researcher. By 2003 he had become the manager of the center, where he has coordinated a number of initiatives. These include: coauthoring the script for *Critical Incident Response: Recommendations for Schools, Law Enforcement, and Emergency Responders for Putting Together the Tools They Need to Respond to a Crisis*, and the accompanying video *A Critical Incident: What to Do in the First 20 Minutes*; the "What We Want to Be Is Bully-Free" campaign; and the National Evaluation of School Resource Officers. Lassiter received the 2007 Hamilton Fish Institute's National Award of Service for his outstanding work in the area of school violence prevention.

DANYA C. PERRY has served as an education consultant for the past 10 years, assisting many organizations in their mission to ensure academic proficiency, provide a conducive learning environment, and mobilize the community for youth. He currently works for Communities in Schools of North Carolina as a field services specialist. In this position, he has spearheaded statewide initiatives aimed at school violence prevention, focused specifically on gangs and gang-related activity. Perry has also worked for the nationally recognized Center for the Prevention of School Violence since 1997.